Record Keeping in Psychotherapy and Counseling

Protecting Confidentiality and the Professional Relationship

Ellen T. Luepker, M.S.W., B.C.D

with assistance from

Lee Norton, Ph.D., M.S.W.

watercolor illustrations by

R. Scott Chase

Brunner-Routledge
New York and Hove

Published in 2003 by
Brunner-Routledge
29 West 35th Street
New York, NY 10001
www.brunner-routledge.com

Published in Great Britain by
Brunner-Routledge
27 Church Road
Hove, East Sussex
BN3 2FA
www.brunner-routledge.co.uk

Brunner-Routledge is an imprint of the Taylor & Francis Group.
Printed in the United States of America on acid-free paper.

10 9 8 7 6 5 4 3 2 1

Library of Congress Cataloging-in-Publication Data

Luepker, Ellen.
  Record keeping in psychotherapy and counseling : protecting confidentiality and the professional relationship / Ellen Luepker with Lee Norton.
      p. cm.
  Includes bibliographical references and index.
    ISBN 1–58391–306–8 (pbk.)
  1. Psychiatric records.   I. Norton, Lee, Ph.D., L.C.S.W.   II. Title.
    RC455.2.M38 L84 2002
    651.5'04261—dc21

                                                        2002009825

Contents

Acknowledgments

Many persons contributed generously to the creation of this book. First, count-less members of the Clinical Social Work Federation (CSWF) inspired and encouraged me during my tenure as chair of the CSWF Committee on Law. The members of that committee contributed much knowledge and time: Dr. Janet Warren, Dr. Lee Norton, Jeanne Melton, Maria Tupper, Mary Beth Smith, Lane Veltkamp, Dr. Howard Snooks, Julie Jenks Zorach, Barbara Nordhaus, Gail Levinson, Virginia McIntosh, Laurie Conaty, Janet Vogelsang, Dr. Diane Rotnem, and Linda Weiskoff. My appreciation goes also to several colleagues for providing impetus and support for a workshop we held on record keeping, which formed the initial outline for this text: Ken Adams, Esq., Roy Freed, Esq., Lynne Lockie, Dr. Roger Miller, Dr. David Phillips, Betty Jean Synar, Imgaard Wessell, Dr. Carolyn Saari, Dr. Denny McGihon, Dr. Golnar Simpson, Laura Groshong, and Dr. Nancy Hammond. Finally, my thanks to CSWF past presidents for their supportive leadership: Dr. Adrienne Lampert, Dr. Chad Breckenridge, Dr. Elizabeth Phillips, Dr. Golnar Simpson, and Keith Meyers.

I am indebted to Dr. Lee Norton for standing by me during all phases of this project, helping write the book proposal, reviewing my drafts of chap-ters, contributing her knowledge of the legal system and teaching methods, and suggesting ways to express the information more clearly. My thanks also to Lee's family and others in her life who were supportive of her while she was helping me.

Many other mental health professionals and lawyers also were kind to review drafts of chapters or provide information: Elizabeth Horton, Patricia Conrad, Robert Donolley, Dr. Nancy Kobrin, Kathleen Muller, Tom McSteen, Esq., James Abourezk, Esq., Gary Schoener, Dr. Rex McGhee, Dr. Charles

Figley, Anne Freed, Dr. Clara Michael, and Barry Boss, Esq.

Helen Michael, my research assistant, shared her keen insights, optimism, efficient literature searches, and edits of chapters. This kept me going in the final stages.

R. Scott Chase provided spirited watercolor illustrations that helped the book come alive.

Others helped editorially, including the fine staff at Brunner-Routledge: Dr. George Zimmar, Shannon Vargo, and Kenneth J. Silver. In addition, Catherine E. Taylor and Dr. Henry Blackburn generously gave me their time and invaluable editorial consultation.

Finally, I am grateful to Louise Ingham Thompson, my mother, for being a strong role model for tackling difficult issues and to my father, Dr. Prescott Thompson, for being my longest-term professional mentor. Also to my sons, Dr. Ian Luepker and Carl Leupker, for sustaining me with their faith. My husband, Dr. Russell Luepker, made this book possible through encouraging me to trust in myself.

Introduction

The purpose of this book is to meet the urgent need for knowledge about record keeping in clinical practice, supervision, and training.

The inspiration for this book came from my father, Dr. Prescott Thompson, a retired psychiatrist and analyst. He has been a faithful and kind teacher who endowed me with a commitment to a high standard of care for patients. My father left his general medical practice in California to become a psychiatrist in Kansas because he wanted to understand what his patients were "really needing." It seemed to him that his patients' physical pain often emerged from emotional suffering. Throughout his career he collaborated with colleagues and worked with countless patients who provided him pieces of this psychological puzzle. He discovered a meaningful professional relationship makes sense of suffering.

My father's commitment to developing healing relationships with his patients became an enduring interest of mine. From adolescence on, I watched him and his colleagues wrestle with issues that lie at the heart of restoring patient health. In a dinner-table conversation one evening, he spoke about how he and his colleagues felt confidentiality was the key to protecting the doctor–patient relationship. One of his colleagues noted that psychiatry seemed to be at a crossroads. My father and his colleagues were in the midst of an "historical dilemma" as they attempted to find ways to respectfully respond to a court's need for their patient's information. The group was stalwart: They knew they must protect the patient's confidentiality at all costs. I remember the fear I felt at the thought that my father could go to jail for refusing to surrender patient records to a judge.

Little did I know that the thread of patient confidentiality would be woven into the fabric of my 30 years as a psychotherapist and that I would someday play a part in attempting to educate courts about the critical need for confidentiality of psychotherapy records. When I served as chairperson of the Committee on Law for the Clinical Social Work Federation, I had responsibility for developing an *amicus* brief in the *Jaffee v. Redmond* case, which dealt with the same issue I had learned about over dinner years before. I was thrilled when the U.S. Supreme Court understood our message about the critical need for confidentiality in psychotherapy and when it upheld psychotherapy patients' right to privileged communication in federal courts (*Jaffee v. Redmond*, 1996).

My father helped me in other ways that became some of the most important messages in this book. I learned that the quality of doctor–patient relationships rested not only in patient confidentiality, but in patients' trust in their practitioners, and I saw that the vehicle of trust is reliability. When I was in college and worked at a psychiatric hospital for children, I would sometimes take my guitar to play songs with the patients. One morning, when my father was giving me a ride to the hospital, I realized I had forgotten my guitar. My father gently asked, "Did you promise you would bring it today?" When I nodded, he quietly told me how important it is to follow through on any promises we make to patients. Without complaining about how it might make him late to his office, he slowly turned the car around, and returned to the house so I could retrieve the guitar. That incident, and the lesson I learned

from it, became etched into the values of my practice. Fidelity to one's promises is the sister of confidentiality. Many years later, after the Walk-In Counseling Center asked me to provide treatment services to clients who had suffered from clergy and health care practitioners' sexual boundary violations, I learned that broken promises are as harmful as the original injuries with which patients come to practitioners.

As a practicing clinician, I eventually became involved in forensic work. Here again I turned to my father for guidance. The first time I testified in court he explained the process and taught me skills to remain objective and maintain credibility. Later, Dr. Janet Warren and I developed a volunteer consultation service for members of the Clinical Social Work Federation. Much of what I have offered practitioners was based on my father's wisdom.

Let me fast-forward from the personal experiences that contributed to the development of this book to some of the other important factors that complete the circle. In my role as chairperson of the Committee on Clinical Social Work and the Law over the past decade, hundreds of psychotherapists called me with urgent questions and concerns about records. Clinicians wanted to know whether they should keep records and, if so, what they should include; how long they should keep records; how to respond to subpoenas and other third party requests for records. Practitioners were especially concerned about confidentiality. Many believed that documentation of their patients' sensitive disclosures was dangerous to their clients. In their conscientious desire to protect their clients' privacy, many competent, experienced therapists and clinical supervisors dismissed the importance of records as a way to ensure accountability and quality of care.

Practitioners also called me about responsibilities for records in anticipation of their retirement or in the event they should unexpectedly become incapacitated. Spouses of deceased private practitioners, too, worried when their spouses had not left directions and they consequently did not know how to respond to ongoing requests for records. Unfortunately, there has been little professional attention to the need to develop plans for records in preparation for interruption or closure of practices.

A majority of the records I have reviewed in malpractice cases have been sparse, illegible, or nonexistent. Sadly, in some instances, the reputations and careers of competent clinicians and supervisors who provided good care have suffered needlessly, simply because they had not adequately documented their professional services.

All mental health professional organizations recognize the critical need for records and for protecting the privacy of those records. Many states have made record keeping a statutory requirement for mental health practitioners. But state statutory guidelines vary widely. For example, by as late as 1997, only four social work boards (Florida, Minnesota, New York, and Texas) included rules governing record keeping; the majority of state boards did not. Sadly, gaps in states' regulatory guidance still persist. Unfortunately, none of these sources provides a specific format nor discusses a theoretical basis for generating client records.

Furthermore, competent record-keeping skills are hard to come by. Graduate school curricula and clinical supervision rarely address the subject. Practitioners are left to muddle through. They may adopt record-keeping systems used by their internships or places of employment (Kagle, 1991), but do not understand the rationale for these procedures. Lack of solid record-keeping skills leaves clinicians unable to balance the critical need for accountability and quality of care against the need for confidentiality.

In 1997, after Dr. Elizabeth Phillips asked me to chair an ad hoc committee on record keeping for the Clinical Social Work Federation and to present a workshop on record keeping to its board of directors, board members requested I write a text on record keeping. Based upon my knowledge of members' concerns and questions, I agreed there was a compelling need for such a book, but did not want to tackle it alone. I therefore asked one of my committee members, Dr. Lee Norton, for assistance. Lee is gifted in stating complex concepts succinctly. In her work helping attorneys to develop mitigating factors to argue against the death penalty, she has reviewed thousands of medical records. She shares my idealism about using records as therapeutic tools. She agreed to provide me with the moral support and feedback to drafts of my chapters that I knew I would need to complete this project.

The information and opinions I have presented here are based upon my professional experience as a licensed psychologist and licensed independent clinical social worker, including the following: (a) clinical practice with children, adults, and families in various mental health settings; (b) clinical practice and research with patients and families who have experienced sexual and other professional boundary violations in treatment; (c) teaching and clinical supervision of new professionals and graduate students in psychology and clinical social work; (d) training of mental health practitioners in the United States and other countries on ethics issues; and (e) consultation on professional standards to regulatory boards and attorneys. I have also relied upon Dr. Norton's suggestions for ways I could present the concepts in this book more clearly and upon her extensive professional experience in the legal system, where she has trained practitioners to be witnesses and has trained attorneys to work with mental health experts.

After agreeing to write a book on record keeping, I reviewed the literature to see if there were other texts on record keeping and was surprised to find so few (Moline, Williams, & Austin, 1998; Zuckerman, 1997; Mitchell, 2001; Kagle, 1991). The texts I found did not cover many of the clinical issues that I discovered are of central concern to psychotherapists, such as how to use records as therapeutic tools; how to handle fears about the legal system's requests for records and testimony; how to develop plans to implement the federal privacy rule; how to systematically craft supervisory records; how to teach record keeping to students, interns, and new professionals; and how to prepare plans for records in the event of interruptions in or closure of practice. I knew my text would inevitably overlap with other texts on record keeping, but I wanted to fill a need by emphasizing these critical clinical concerns.

I intend this book to be a supportive reference, offering a general orientation and practical suggestions. However, it is not legal advice nor clinical consultation. Practitioners should consult their regulatory boards, lawyers, and clinical colleagues whenever they have questions in specific cases. They should rely on their own attorneys and professional associations to keep abreast of their respective jurisdictions' laws and the evolving modifications in federal rules that govern record keeping and protect the privacy and security of patient-identifiable information. While this book includes examples of forms for illustrative purposes, it does not contain a comprehensive collection of forms.

I have organized the book into 11 chapters. Most of the chapters begin with a summary of relevant ethical and legal issues. Case examples illustrate concepts in each chapter. Appendices provide excerpts from ethics codes and samples of forms. Chapter 1 discusses the purposes of clinical records. Chapter 2 identifies why and how to document the process of informed consent. Chapter 3 presents answers to psychotherapists' most frequent questions about characteristics and contents of good records. Chapter 4 summarizes ethical and legal requirements for protecting confidentiality and exceptions to confidentiality. Chapter 5 follows with practical tips for policies and procedures that can protect confidentiality and security of records. Chapter 6 discusses the factors to consider in deciding how long to keep records and offers a sample record retention policy and procedure. Chapter 7 discusses how therapists can creatively use records with their patients as therapeutic tools in treatment. Chapter 8 emphasizes the need for keeping supervisory records. Chapter 9 emphasizes the need to generate record-keeping skills in students and new clinicians and offers practical tips for teaching record keeping. Chapter 10 presents an orientation to the legal system, including advice for handling subpoenas, using professional judgment to determine whether and how to release records, and methods for testifying in depositions and trials. Chapter 11 suggests a way to craft plans for records in preparation for interruptions in or closure of a psychotherapy practice.

The primary audience for this text includes all professionals who practice, supervise, and teach psychotherapy or counseling. The concepts in this book are generic. They are designed to be helpful to psychotherapists or mental health counselors of all professions, regardless of clinical orientations, in the fields of clinical social work, psychiatry, clinical and counseling psychology, marriage and family therapy, nursing, counseling, and pastoral counseling.

Both beginning and experienced practitioners can benefit from the content of this book. New psychotherapists can absorb a logical system of thinking about and documenting treatment. More experienced therapists will gather new ideas that can easily be incorporated into their current clinical practices.

The text can be useful in any graduate school curriculum that trains psychotherapists. Students will gain a helpful framework for thinking about and generating client records. Similarly, instructors and intern supervisors can rely upon the text in teaching record keeping and in evaluating student performance.

The text can be a resource in clinical supervision of new professionals and in consultation as well. Professionals in other fields will find it worthwhile also. Attorneys and judges can learn about aspects of record keeping in psychotherapy, including mental health professionals' ethical duties to protect patients' confidentiality and the roles psychotherapists may or may not be able to play in legal settings.

A final compassionate word for my readers. I have never met a practitioner who keeps "perfect" psychotherapy records. It's still worthwhile to strive to do the best we can. I have approached this project with humility, mindful of the draining demands in daily psychotherapy practice. I am also aware that what transpires between words during psychotherapy sessions is often as important or more important than the words. It is therefore virtually impossible to document the "whole truth" of what transpires in psychotherapy sessions. In writing this book, I have looked for ways to provide information that will make record keeping easier, not more of a burden. I would ask my readers to consider not so much what they have done wrong in the past, but what they can take from this book to make record keeping easier and better today and in the future, to benefit themselves as well as their patients.

Purposes of Clinical Records

All mental health organizations have codes of ethics that highlight the paramount importance of protecting patient confidentiality and maintaining the highest professional standards to protect patient welfare. Sadly, very few mental health organizations or state laws define and describe the characteristics involved in competent record keeping. This leaves practitioners to use what little they learned in graduate schools or internships, or to devise their own policies in a virtual vacuum. However, several recent developments are challenging graduate schools, clinical supervisors, and therapists to focus on documentation. First, the federal privacy rule now requires practitioners who generate identifiable health care information electronically to develop written information that explains to their patients how they use treatment records and how they protect the privacy of those records (United States Department of Health and Human Services, 2001a). Second, increasing numbers of malpractice complaints are forcing clinicians and supervisors to create more careful documentation. Third, higher rates of litigation in our society mean that more practitioners are receiving subpoenas for patients' records and are struggling to find ways to respond and still protect their patients' privacy. Fourth, more therapists are anticipating retirement and must make advance plans for their patients' records.

The need for knowledge and methods in record keeping has never been more urgent. The goal of this book is to provide specific methods that can help therapists write, maintain, and use records to preserve their patients' confidentiality, the professional relationship, and to promote healing.

Systematic clinical records are essential for the following reasons:

1. Records facilitate communication between therapists and clients: Records help clients understand their problems, make meaningful decisions about

their treatment, develop insight, and become partners in their own healing. Records help to create trust in professional relationships. The process of informing patients about why and how practitioners maintain and protect their records demonstrates commitment to patient welfare. Permitting patients to review their own records can help create an atmosphere of safety and mutual respect.

2. Records form the basis of sound diagnoses and appropriate treatment plans: Reviewing records over time allows therapists to identify significant patterns and modify diagnostic hypotheses and treatment plans. Keeping records also allows practitioners access to more dates and information than they can reliably maintain in memory.

3. Records provide for continuity of care: Clear, concise records allow other practitioners to follow and understand what has occurred in therapy and the rationale for interventions. New practitioners can pick up where previous therapists left off or explain to patients why they are recommending a different course of action. Without good records, patients' need for continuity of care suffers.

4. Records are necessary for clinical supervision: Records are indispensable tools for evaluating and remediating knowledge and skills. Reviewing records allows supervisors to see how well supervisees or trainees are developing clinical hypotheses and treatment plans and to help them document their findings and interventions appropriately. Through discussions of records, trainees gain greater objectivity, which ensures better treatment for patients.

5. Records satisfy the requirements of contractual obligations with third party payers: In many instances, mental health services cannot be reimbursed without documentation of diagnoses, treatment plans, and client progress. A clear record of events also facilitates writing appropriate reports about patients.

6. Records are practitioners' and clinical supervisors' best (and often only) protection against allegations of unethical and harmful treatment: We live in a highly litigious society, sometimes euphemistically referred to as the Age of Accountability. Detailed records are the best protection against specious claims. Contemporaneous documentation of events, agreements, and professional decisions can provide proof of good-faith efforts.

For these reasons and more, it is essential that practitioners become proactive about keeping coherent, concise, accurate, and timely patient records, and that they assiduously protect the confidentiality of those records.

Documenting Informed Consent

Imagine a 49-year-old woman who lives with her husband and three teenage children in a small upper-midwest city. Her marriage has been bad for many years and is getting worse. She cannot sleep, concentrate, or focus. She cries easily, feels helpless, and wants to die. She is also having nightmares again about her father's brutal beatings when she was a child. She does not know she is suffering from symptoms of posttraumatic stress disorder. But, she recognizes her symptoms of depression because she was hospitalized for depression several years ago. She consults her family physician, who prescribes some kind of psychotropic medication, but it causes dizziness, making it impossible to drive to work. She therefore stops taking the medication but doesn't go back to her physician to tell him about the side effects. She doesn't know that if she did consult him again, her doctor could refer her to a psychiatrist to explore other options. She feels desperate. She knows she needs help. Where can she find a therapist who will not immediately tell her to get a divorce? She wants to see if she can salvage her marriage.

One afternoon while driving to her daughter's volleyball game, she hears a psychologist on the car radio telling about her counseling approach with clients who sound like they have similar problems. She likes the therapist's voice. She intuitively feels this therapist might be able to help her also. The next day she makes an appointment. She tells her new therapist details about all of her problems, including nightmares of her child abuse, unhappiness in her marriage, symptoms of depression, and medication side effects. The therapist says she is "against using medications" and recommends against them. The therapist does not provide the patient with any objective information on the benefits and risks of different courses of treatment. Since the client has no previous experience with psychotherapy, she does not know she is entitled to this information.

The woman wants her husband to be able to tell "his side of the marriage problems" so agrees with her therapist's recommendation that the therapist speak alone with her husband. After meeting with the client's husband, the therapist tells the woman that her husband is "evil" and "dangerous" and that the client should "definitely get a divorce as soon as possible." The woman by now has developed a bond with her new therapist. She trusts her and experiences her as warm, caring, and charismatic. She feels desperate for attention and for love. The therapist, again, does not discuss treatment options or the pros and cons of a particular course of action with the patient.

To make a long story short, the woman takes her therapist's advice and gets a divorce. She never receives the information she requires to understand posttraumatic stress disorder and depression. She never learns about appropriate options for treatment, including the need to develop her own inner resources for finding solutions to her problems. She wonders to this day whether she could have salvaged her marriage.

What is wrong with this picture?

Since 1980, I have received many referrals of patients who have described detrimental experiences in a variety of psychotherapy settings. Most patients said they did not receive sufficient information about their conditions and methods of psychotherapy—including roles of the patient and therapist, options for treatment, and exceptions to confidentiality—and so could not make rational, informed decisions about treatment. In a survey study of dissatisfied patients, I asked what they thought would most improve the quality of therapy. With few exceptions, the respondents cited the need for "consumer education" to help them understand what is appropriate and effective treatment (Luepker, 1999).

One of the biggest changes in psychotherapy practice over the past several years has been the evolution of the doctrine of informed consent. This means that competent adult patients (or their legal representatives) have the right to receive information from health care professionals about their conditions, the risks and benefits of proposed treatments and of adjunct treatments, such as medications, or other treatment techniques, and the risks and benefits of no treatment. The emphasis on patient education over the past decade appears to have positively affected patients' and mental health practitioners' understanding of what patients need to know about psychotherapy. It has helped patients make meaningful decisions about their treatment. While the degree and quality of patient education vary depending on geographic location, I have observed that patients are taking a more active role in gathering information about treatment. This has led to a "demystification" of psychotherapy and an evolving collaborative model.

While research literature shows that many different types of psychotherapy are beneficial, it is critical in any treatment modality to document that clients have received and understood essential information and have been able to make meaningful decisions about their treatment. Documentation of the process of informed consent demonstrates that therapists are fulfilling their duties. Documentation gives greater protection to therapists as well as to patients. Documentation of informed consent adds credibility.

This chapter will provide an overview of the informed consent process and options for how practitioners can document it. It will address the following: (a) legal and ethical bases for informed consent, (b) key questions that psychotherapists should answer and document when providing clients with opportunities for informed consent, (c) practical strategies for documenting informed consent in patients' records at each stage of treatment, and (d) a case example that illustrates documentation of informed consent. This chapter does not offer clinical or legal advice in a given situation. Practitioners must obtain information about the laws and ethics codes of their states and professional organizations and obtain clinical or legal consultation to answer questions about specific case situations.

SOCIETAL, LEGAL, AND ETHICAL BASES
FOR INFORMED CONSENT

Western society has long valued medical patients' right to accurate and thorough information about medical treatment options and the relative risks and benefits of those options. This societal value has led to an increasing emphasis in medicine and social sciences on the importance of the right to self-determination. After World War II, the Nuremberg Codes and Principles prevented experimentation on human subjects without informed consent (Piper, 1994). Later, in 1957, in the Salgo case in the United States, a physician was held liable for not giving his patient sufficient information to make it possible for the patient to make an intelligent decision regarding treatment (Sanford, Hartnett, & Jolly, 1999).

State laws vary regarding how much information practitioners must give their patients regarding diagnosis and treatment. Courts have debated this question. They have given psychotherapists some latitude in making decisions regarding how to carry out this doctrine to prevent harm to the individual and to society. Courts have decided that physicians should exercise thoughtful discretion in disclosing potentially disturbing information to the patient (Piper, 1994).

The federal privacy rule (HIPAA), adopted April 14, 2001, and amended August 14, 2002, requires practitioners who generate patient-identifiable information electronically (whether stored in a computer, on paper, or shared orally) to provide patients with a written notice of privacy practices and to make a good faith effort to receive written acknowledgment of receipt of this notice. Practitioners who are "covered" under the rule must implement these informed consent procedures by April 14, 2003. For example, practitioners must inform patients in writing about how their identifiable health information may be used, disclosed, and stored. The rule also requires that practitioners inform patients of their rights to have access to their records and to request amendments to their records. Psychotherapists must also inform patients in writing about their options to file a grievance if they are concerned about violations of the rule's provisions (U.S. Department of Health and Human Services, 2001a; Federal Register, 2002). See chapter 4 for further discussion of the federal privacy rule and chapter 5 for further discussion of policies and procedures that may assist practitioners to implement the rule.

All of the mental health organizations include requirements for informed consent in their ethics codes. They uniformly mandate that practitioners provide sufficient information to psychotherapy patients (or to those who are responsible for patients' treatment) in order for patients or their representatives to be able to make meaningful decisions regarding treatment. While it is implicit in all ethics codes that informed consent should be in writing, the

American Association of Marriage and Family Therapy makes the need for documentation of informed consent explicit (AAMFT, 2001). See appendix A for ethics codes' informed consent requirements.

KEY QUESTIONS TO CONSIDER IN DOCUMENTING INFORMED CONSENT

Psychotherapy patients have taught me that they have several questions that are integral in developing a successful therapeutic working alliance and achieving the best possible therapeutic outcomes. Here are typical questions patients have. Practitioners should document that they have provided answers to these questions and that their patients have understood and been able to meaningfully consent.

- Are the practitioners' credentials, training, and experience relevant to the kinds of problems I need help for?
- Does my therapist keep my communications in psychotherapy confidential?
- What are exceptions to protecting my confidentiality?
- What procedures do my therapist and office staff follow to protect my confidentiality?
- What are my therapist's fees?
- How and when will my payments be due?
- Does my therapist agree to payment arrangements, such as sliding fee scale or pay-over-time?
- If I fail to make payments, what are the consequences? For example, does my therapist use the services of a collection agency?
- If I am planning to use my insurance coverage or other third party reimbursement, does my third party payer require information about me? If so, is this disclosure of information acceptable, and if not, are there alternatives?
- When I signed my insurance contract did I give my insurance company the right to review my entire records? If I did allow for disclosure, am I comfortable with that degree of disclosure? Do I give permission to my therapist to fulfill my third party payer's demand for information? If not, are there alternatives or remedies?
- What is my diagnosis and what does it mean?
- How did my therapist come to that conclusion about my diagnosis?
- What does my therapist recommend would be helpful to me? Does my therapist recommend treatment or no treatment? If treatment, what kind of treatment and what will be involved?
- What are the expected outcomes of the recommended treatment?

- What are the risks in the proposed treatment?
- Are there alternative treatments? If so, what are they and what are the possible risks and benefits?
- What could happen if I had no treatment?
- What are the recommended frequency and expected duration of the proposed treatment? Why?
- How will I and my therapist know when I am ready to finish therapy?
- When I no longer need therapy, will I have the option to return to my therapist as needed?
- Who will provide care to me in case of emergencies if my therapist is unavailable?
- If I don't like what is happening in treatment, what do I do?

DOCUMENTATION THAT SHOWS INFORMED CONSENT

The process of providing and documenting informed consent takes place at all stages of the professional relationship: before, during, and at completion of the initial evaluation; and at relevant junctures during treatment. Three types of information that practitioners should document are: (a) what information the clinician discussed with the client, (b) whether in the clinician's judgment the patient (or patient's representative) is competent to understand and make a meaningful decision regarding treatment, and (c) the client's decision. The following discussion illustrates the informed consent process at various stages of treatment and information required to document this process.

Preliminary Verbal and Written Information

It is helpful to send potential patients written information about what to expect in psychotherapy and to ask them to read this prior to their first session and sign that they have done so. This procedure provides an initial overview and allows patients time to formulate questions they can discuss in the initial session. If done, clients should sign or therapists should document that clients have received and read the information.

Preliminary information that documents informed consent should include a written description of the therapist's practice protocols, such as (a) the patient's rights to confidentiality, (b) exceptions to confidentiality, (c) security procedures to protect patient-identifiable information, (d) where and how to make a complaint about treatment, and (e) a summary of billing procedures. (For an example of information that can be mailed to new clients prior to their initial appointment, see appendix B, "Sample Client Information Form.")

Initial Interview

The first session should begin by reviewing in detail a "client information" pamphlet or brochure, even when clients state verbally or show by their signatures that they have read and understood it. If the client did not bring the information, did not read it, is illiterate or non-English-speaking and thus unable to read it, the session should be devoted to guiding the client through each section. Therapists should be sure to emphasize and elicit responses regarding the following:

- relevant information regarding the practitioner's professional training, experience, philosophy of psychopathology, and treatment plans;
- confidentiality parameters and exceptions to confidentiality;
- amount of practitioner's fees;
- who is responsible for payment of psychotherapy services;
- payment policy for missed appointments;
- if third party payer, what disclosure of confidential information will be required for reimbursement;
- consent for disclosure to third party payer;
- consent for necessary collaboration with other treating professionals and what this might entail;
- what types of questions the therapist will be asking in the initial evaluation and why.

On Completion of Initial Evaluation

By the completion of the initial evaluation, the clinician should be satisfied that the patient fully understands the clinician's opinions and policies regarding (a) diagnosis and treatment recommendations, (b) the risks and benefits of various treatments or no treatment, (c) the limitations of psychotherapy, (d) the frequency and estimated number of sessions required to achieve the client's goals, (e) responsibility for payment and missed sessions, and (f) how available the therapist is to the client and procedures for "emergency" situations.

Again, practitioners should document whether, in their professional opinion, the client was able to give consent to treatment, grounds for this judgment, and whether the client consented to treatment. When therapists craft a written treatment plan with their clients, signed by both client and therapist (see Appendix C for a sample treatment plan form), practitioners can document mutual agreement on diagnoses and treatment plan.

During Treatment

Psychotherapy is not a static process; it ebbs and flows depending on a number of variables. As patients and clinicians work together, new information and issues emerge that may alter the clinicians' working hypotheses about diagnoses and treatment. Similarly, patients may come to view their situation in a different light. Changing impressions—on the part of patients and clinicians—should be discussed frequently and treatment goals and interventions altered as necessary, always through a collaborative process. Practitioners may also receive third party requests for information about clients, or require additional information, such as through testing or medical or other consultations, which they should discuss with clients to obtain informed consent. Practitioners should document all such discussions. The sample revised treatment plan form in appendix D can be used throughout treatment for documenting progress, new problems, and procedures that practitioners have discussed with their patients.

If a patient makes no progress during treatment, or becomes worse, the situation should be acknowledged and discussed promptly. All available options, including obtaining consultation, terminating therapy, or referring the patient to another practitioner, should be explored openly and directly. These discussions, and any resultant decisions, including whether treatment has ended by mutual agreement or not, should be documented. For an example of a form that can be used with clients to demonstrate discussion (or the inability to have discussion) about the ending of treatment, see appendix E, "Closing Summary."

Methods for Documenting Informed Consent

Methods for documentation of informed consent vary, but a narrative form is clearest. Signed treatment plans are also effective strategies to document clients' consent to treatment. Some practitioners use "informed consent checklists" that clients can sign and date to help practitioners stay focused on what information they need to discuss with their clients and what consent they must obtain. Practitioners should choose a method for documentation of informed consent that works best for them and that clearly conveys (a) whether clients are competent to give consent to treatment and on what grounds clinicians have based this conclusion, and (b) all discussions with clients about informed consent.

CASE EXAMPLE

The following case example illustrates informed consent discussions in the initial stage of the patient's evaluation and individual treatment process and how the practitioner documents these discussions.

Preliminary Stage

A psychiatrist referred an overwhelmed 40-year-old Caucasian, English-speaking woman, Jane Smith, to a psychotherapist for treatment of a major depressive disorder and posttraumatic stress disorder. The woman was hospitalized at the time, and her treatment included psychotropic medications and other services to help stabilize and protect her from harming herself. The psychiatrist recommended that the patient begin working with the therapist before discharge from the inpatient unit. The goal was to help the patient make the transition from the hospital to outpatient treatment.

The patient agreed with her psychiatrist's referral to outpatient treatment and called the therapist. Over the phone, the therapist provided preliminary information about his practice and asked if he could mail the potential patient a packet, including a client information form (see appendix B) and a questionnaire for the patient to read, fill out, and bring to the first session to discuss with the therapist.

The therapist was careful to find out whether it was all right with the patient for him to mail an informational brochure to her home address and documented the patient's consent: "11/1/01: Patient gave verbal consent for me to mail the packet of intake information to her home address. She stated she will read it and complete the forms and bring them with her to her initial evaluation appointment on 11/11/01 at 1:00 p.m."

Initial Evaluation

In the patient's initial appointment, the patient produced the intake information and stated that she had read it. The therapist observed that the patient was physically and mentally shaken, overwhelmed, and sad. She was, nevertheless, oriented to time, person, place, and situation, was coherent, and her attention and comprehension seemed adequate. He observed and documented that she was able to engage in a discussion about her condition and to understand the information he provided. Accordingly, he wrote: "Patient stated she read and understands the "client information" I mailed her. She also completed the questionnaire and face sheet."

After the therapist asked the client what she knew about the therapist and reasons for being referred, the patient told him her understanding. She then asked the therapist about his professional experience with clients who had similar problems. He shared information about his professional credentials and experience relevant to the kinds of problems for which she needed help. He documented: "Patient had adequate information regarding her psychiatrist's referral and I answered her questions regarding my professional background and experience with patients who suffer from similar problems."

The therapist also shared payment requirements, inquired about her wish to use third party reimbursement, and told her what information about her condition the insurance company would require in order to pay for the therapist's services. The therapist obtained her written consent, which he placed in her record, to share necessary information with the insurance company. The therapist documented: "We discussed fee arrangements. Client agreed to make her copayment at the time of each session. She requested that my billing office bill her insurance company for reimbursement of her sessions. She understands and signed permission for me to provide her insurance company with diagnosis and treatment plan, dates of sessions, and understands that if the company requires further information, that I will first inform her before sending anything more."

The therapist discussed parameters of confidentiality, including exceptions to confidentiality. He explained what disclosures of her confidential information would be necessary for providing effective treatment, such as routine communication and collaboration with her psychiatrist for the purposes of clarifying her diagnosis and treatment planning, and with the clinical psychologist who would be providing psychological testing. He obtained the patient's written consent for all routine collaborations with other professionals necessary for her treatment and placed the signed consent in her file. He documented: "I discussed parameters of confidentiality, exceptions to confidentiality, and routine disclosures required for treatment with patient. She stated she understood and agreed."

The therapist then gave the patient an overview of the types of questions he would be asking in the initial evaluation, such as what problems she was having, history of problems, what she hoped could be different in her life, her childhood background, etc., and obtained her verbal consent to proceed with the evaluation.

At the end of the initial evaluation, the therapist reflected to the client what he had learned from the preliminary information. He stated that he thought the client was in a very fragile emotional state and that she suffered from numerous problems, including moderate to severe depression, anxiety, overwhelming intrusive memories of physical and sexual trauma in earlier adulthood that had been triggered by a recent crisis, and suicidal thoughts. The therapist also expressed his concern that the client had very weak control over her suicidal impulses and that she was unstable, in that she had trouble focusing, concentrating, sleeping, and eating. He told the client that he thought her most pressing problem was symptoms related to posttraumatic stress disorder and explained that the first step was to help the client reestablish physical equilibrium and a sense of internal and external safety.

He discussed the treatment options he recommended for her and shared information about how these techniques were helpful to other clients with similar conditions. The treatment techniques he proposed and documented having discussed with her included the following: (a) first he would help her to become stable, e.g., to feel safe from suicidal impulses and to begin to sleep and eat well and focus; (b) later, once she was stable, he would help her learn about various exercises she could use to help herself, such as "grounding" or "anchoring" herself in the present in order to control her flashbacks, writing a narrative of her traumatic events and how these had affected her, keeping a "flashback journal" to write down and externalize her memories, learning relaxation visualizations to begin teaching herself how to calm herself and focus on the here and now, and drawing images of herself before, during, and after her traumatic experiences. He also documented that he had explained the extreme importance of support from others in the successful treatment of posttraumatic stress disorder. He documented that he asked her to begin writing down a list of people whom she could trust to call upon when she needed help.

The therapist ended the initial session by explaining to the client that a number of treatments for posttraumatic stress disorder were now being used with extremely good results and that the client's symptoms were likely to subside. He noted that the risks of treatment for posttraumatic stress disorder included feeling worse as the patient shared the traumatic events with the therapist. The therapist assured the client that they would continually work together on her problems at her own pace and would use all tools available to help the client feel better. He documented that he advised the client that she needed to indicate whether she felt ready or not to begin any particular treatment strategy so that she could go at her own pace.

He noted in the record: "See signed treatment plan, attached, that patient has agreed upon in her initial evaluation today." (See appendix C for a sample treatment plan form.)

During Treatment

After the patient was no longer suffering from impulses to kill herself, the therapist discussed options for treatment that he felt the patient might now be ready for. The patient agreed that she felt safer and could now consider options the therapist had previously discussed. She stated she was ready to write a narrative about her traumatic events. The therapist and patient revised the treatment plan to reflect the improvement the patient had made and the new goals. The therapist wrote in the progress note: "See revised treatment plan that reflects progress: Patient is no longer thinking of killing herself and she has achieved a sense of safety sufficient to begin one of the proposed treatment options, which is to write a narrative of the traumatic events. Benefits (to externalize trauma) and risks (discomfort from unwelcome memories) discussed with patient."

SUMMARY

This chapter has elaborated the concept of informed consent to include the therapeutic value of including the client in the process of record keeping and the importance of demystifying psychotherapy. Effective psychotherapy is a collaborative effort in which therapists share relevant clinical information, explain and illustrate possible benefits and risks of therapy to clients, and maintain an atmosphere of joint problem solving and skill building throughout therapeutic relationships. This chapter presented information to be documented before and during treatment to indicate (a) whether the patient was able to make meaningful decisions regarding the treatment; and (b) whether the therapist obtained the patient's informed consent for treatment.

Characteristics and Contents of Good Records

Good record keeping is essential to good psychotherapy. But psychotherapists often lack knowledge about record keeping. The most frequent questions or concerns practitioners have asked me include:

- After writing up the initial evaluations, I don't keep records other than scribbling down notes for myself during each session—what should I be doing?
- If I am writing periodic summaries for my client's managed care company, do I also need to keep notes on every session?
- Is it all right to take notes during a session or should I wait until after the session?
- What should I keep out of the therapy record?
- How long do progress notes for therapy sessions need to be?
- What needs to be in an authorization form for release of client information?
- I have been seeing so many clients that I have not had time to write my progress notes after every session, but now I'm having trouble catching up on so many past sessions! How can I manage this problem?

Because of the paucity of authoritative guidelines and literature on good record keeping, practitioners have trouble finding answers to their questions about record keeping. The purpose of this chapter is to answer the most frequent questions practitioners have asked me and provide a model of record keeping that promotes the integrity of the psychotherapist's clinical practice. Having information and a system for record keeping can make it easier to create more consistent and comprehensive clinical records and prevent pitfalls.

The first section discusses the characteristics of good records. The subsequent section spells out key questions that need to be answered in good records. The third section presents essential contents of good records, and the following section describes what should not be included records. The final section discusses options for methods of record keeping.

CHARACTERISTICS

Our records must convey, in humane, legible, and plain language, accurate and contemporaneous answers to "who, why, what, when, and how?" A good record is a clear "picture" or "mirror" of a client. It contains a series of sketches that depict moments in time as well as historical processes, such as clients' history, needs, and the work they engage in during treatment to solve their problems. When we write records, we should be mindful that our clients, their family members, and others could read the records and form impressions about the client's experiences and about the quality of the therapy. Therefore, our "pictures" must contain the hues and shades that define the uniqueness and complexity of the client. Anyone reading our records should be able to accurately identify the tools and techniques we used to evaluate, diagnose, and treat a patient, as well as unmistakable evidence that we made consistent, good-faith efforts to provide the best care possible and avoid causing harm.

Legible (to Self and Others)

Professionally written records are legible. Legible records are essential for continuity of care and for the humane and responsible treatment of clients. Amazingly, this simple concept is lost on a staggering number of practitioners. For example, many talented therapists have conscientiously told me they believe they can best protect their patients by making their records illegible to anyone but themselves. But when records are illegible, the following questions remain: Even if legal rules or ethics codes did not require that we keep legible records, what would happen if we died tomorrow? How could our colleagues accurately understand our diagnosis and treatment plan and effectively attend to our patients' needs? If a patient's relatives had legitimate access and wanted to see a deceased relative's records after his suicide, would they be able to determine from the therapy records that we had treated their loved one competently and compassionately and took every precaution to prevent the death?

Germane

Good records include only information that is germane to diagnosis, treatment, progress (or lack thereof), and outcomes. One of the most critical areas to include is any risk factors present in the client's condition or environment, for example, suicidal ideation, noncompliance with medication, or risk-taking behavior. Document each of these carefully, followed by recommendations to the client and any preventive actions taken.

Reliable

Notes should be empirical. They should identify the source of the information. If the information is subjective, it should be preceded by, "The client stated," or "The client said his employer stated . . ." If the information is objective, it should be preceded by, "The patient twitched, cried, expressed anger, etc." If the therapist makes an interpretation or conclusion, it should be preceded by, "It appeared that . . ." or "It seemed that the client . . . ," followed by facts upon which we developed those hypotheses.

Never include conclusions that cannot be supported theoretically or empirically or that are prejudicial, such as "client seems to be a victim of sexual abuse" or "the client's mother was un-nurturing."

Logical

Treatment plans follow logically from the diagnoses. Progress notes should show treatment geared toward resolving the stated problems. When I have reviewed records in malpractice cases, psychotherapists have appeared to do the wrong thing when their treatment approach did not follow logically from their diagnoses. In one case, for example, a therapist limited her treatment plan for a man who suffered a moderate major depressive disorder to "exploration of his early childhood experience." The treatment plan did not mention attention to other issues that are central to the treatment of major depressive disorder, such as his suicide risk, alcohol use, vegetative symptoms, or lack of control over environmental stressors.

Prompt

Record progress notes promptly, preferably immediately after each session. While most practitioners jot down notes during sessions, these sporadic words are too fragmented to convey a comprehensible summary of a session. Therefore, it is essential to take a few moments immediately after sessions to write down just two or three sentences to summarize the essence of the sessions. Also, progress notes that practitioners generate after seeing six clients in a row or that they write days or even weeks after a session with a client are less reliable and are subject to error due to intervening events. The "50-minute hour" emerged from the need to take time between sessions to record salient information.

Chronological

Keeping records chronologically and not using a new sheet of paper for each session allows others to tell that the records are complete and have not been tampered with.

KEY QUESTIONS TO ANSWER IN A GOOD RECORD

Clinical records should paint a clear picture of the patient, what the therapist did, and why. In order to do this, the following questions should be addressed in clinical records:

- Who is requesting psychotherapy and for what purpose?
- What is my role?
- How would I describe the client? (Use empirical data.)
- What are the client's specific presenting problems? (According to both the patient and collateral sources if available.)
- What circumstances or events made the client seek psychotherapy now?
- What does this client say, in the client's own words, that he or she wishes could be different in his or her life? What are the patient's goals?
- What is the history of the client's problems?
- What prior efforts has the client made—successful and unsuccessful—to solve his or her problems?
- What is the patient's life history, including: development, school, family and other relationships, work, financial issues, sexuality, alcohol use, non-prescription drug use, and current living arrangements?
- What is the patient's medical and psychiatric history, including any former diagnoses? (This may involve getting previous records or talking to professionals who previously treated the client.)

- What further information will I require in order to understand the client's history of problems?
- Do I have the necessary consent to provide, receive, or exchange the information needed for treatment planning and clinical care?
- What safety issues, if any, for my client and for others must I consider?
- How will I minimize potential risks to the patient's safety or to the safety of others?
- What treatment plan has the best chance of helping to solve this patient's specific problems and why?
- Do I require consultation or collaboration with others in order to make a diagnosis and treatment plan?
- What specific procedures would best facilitate the proposed treatment plan and what information makes me think so?
- Have I given my patient information, which he or she can understand, regarding the diagnosis and proposed treatment with me, including possible risks and benefits of treatment options and no treatment?
- Have I discussed with my patient our respective rights and responsibilities?
- Have I informed my client of limitations to privacy and confidentiality?
- Has my patient (parents or legal guardians) consented to treatment?
- When and for how long are my sessions with the client?
- Is my client achieving the goals he or she set forth?
- If progress is unsatisfactory or if the client is getting worse, have I made appropriate efforts to improve the treatment plan, such as consulting with another professional, referring the client to another professional, or recommending the termination of psychotherapy?
- Have I appropriately utilized resources to rule out the medical causes of my clients' problems, such as psychiatrists, neuropsychologists, neurologists, or others?
- How will I and my patient know when he or she is ready to terminate therapy?
- When termination occurs, have I summarized the problems, treatment intervention, and progress, and is the reason for and nature of termination clear to me and my client?
- What, if any, follow-up procedures should I recommend?
- Have I discussed follow-up procedures with my client at termination?

ESSENTIAL CONTENTS OF A GOOD RECORD

The following is a format that lists the essential contents of a good record. I have found it easy to use in my own practice and in my supervisees' practices.

It has helped me and my supervisees fulfill the various purposes of record keeping. The first part of this section describes the basic structure of the record, including the phases of evaluation, treatment, and termination. The second part lists other essential contents to remember along the way.

Face Sheet

Placing a face sheet at the front of a chart allows immediate access to the information we frequently use (see appendix F for a sample face sheet). It also promotes continuity of care when working with other practitioners. Face sheets should include, at minimum, the following information:

- date of first appointment,
- client's name,
- date of birth,
- address,
- home and work numbers and which number is permissible to call as needed,
- emergency contacts,
- source of referral,
- legal guardianship information as appropriate,
- name and address of the person or party responsible for payment of services,
- name and address of third party payers,
- third party payer subscriber and group numbers.

Evaluation

The evaluation is essential because it provides the basis for provisional diagnoses and decisions regarding services clients may need. Treatment strategies should continuously refer back to the initial data and be modified later based upon additional assessment information. The initial evaluation also provides data that can be used to assess the client's progress or complete a treatment summary. Here are eight topics that should be included in the documentation of an initial evaluation:

IDENTIFYING INFORMATION

We start with identifying information which outlines the contour of our clients. As we explore further, we begin to see their complexity, richness, and uniqueness. The identifying information should include the following:

- client's name,
- gender,
- age,
- marital status,
- racial and cultural background,
- living arrangements,
- any children and their ages,
- status and type of employment,
- source of referral,
- reason(s) for referral.

The identifying information section can be brief. Here is an example:

> *Identifying Information:* Nancy Jones, 48-year-old divorced Caucasian woman, employed as a hospital nurse, has physical and legal custody of her two daughters, ages 14 and 16, with whom she is living in her own home. She was referred by her psychiatrist, Dr. Adams, for psychotherapy to deal with stressors associated with her job.

PRESENTING PROBLEMS

A presenting problem is the reason a client seeks help. Start the session with simple questions about problems that have prompted the client to seek help and how the client sees the problems. The specific problems provide focus and direction for the rest of the interview.

Therapist: What is it that brought you here today?

Patient: I'm upset.
    I'm having problems with my supervisor.
    I cry all the time.
    My son and I are fighting all the time.

HISTORY OF PROBLEM

"There is no meaning without context" (Mishler, 1979). The client's history is one of the most critical aspects of the evaluation. It brings into focus the long journey that brought the client to us. Some of the questions that best elicit the client's history are the following:

- What made the client decide to come for help?
- Onset of problems: When did the problems start?
- Context of onset of problems: What was happening in the client's life when the problems began?

- Who did what to whom during the course of the problems?
- What has the client tried in attempting to solve the problems?
- What strategies have been helpful or not helpful?
- What has made certain strategies helpful or not helpful?
- What would the client hope to change in his or her life?
- What type of help does the client want?

SIGNIFICANT CHILDHOOD AND OTHER LIFE HISTORY

This section forms the backdrop for our client's picture. It informs us about our client's life experiences and patterns of behavior. It helps us formulate hypotheses about potential transference or other issues that we will experience with our clients and be required to manage. And it helps us know what kind of prognosis we might reasonably expect. In this section we include historical information such as the following:

- birth experience and circumstances surrounding birth,
- description of parents and siblings and home conditions,
- family relationships and themes in family life,
- school performance and experience with school,
- childhood and adult friendships,
- employment and work functioning.

It may be useful to use genograms or other visual tools to help us understand the context and meaning to our patients of their childhood and other historical experiences and events.

MEDICAL HISTORY

When there are physical symptoms that impair our patients' ability to function, including the inability to sleep or eat properly, it may be impossible for them to make use of psychotherapy. Also, what appear to be psychological problems may really be physiological. It is necessary, therefore, to gather information regarding our clients' past and present physical health. It helps us know what medical needs they may have, what other professionals may already be involved in their care, what risk factors may apply, and what referrals and multidisciplinary collaboration may be necessary.

SUBSTANCE USE

When patients are abusing substances such as alcohol or nonprescription drugs, they must first attend to these problems before they can make use of psychotherapy. Thus exploration and documentation of substance use is an essential component of a good evaluation.

INTERVIEW OBSERVATIONS AND MENTAL STATUS

In this section of our evaluation summary, we attempt to describe our clients in such a way that they can be readily visualized, either by ourselves or another professional who may need to provide service to them. The information in this section helps us further clarify what clinical intervention is necessary. Descriptions of our clients in this section include but aren't limited to the following:

- physical characteristics: body build, hair color, type of clothing, grooming, facial expression;
- appropriateness of appearance to the situation;
- mental status: affect, speech, mood, thought content, judgment, insight, memory, impulse control, attention, focus, concentration, and orientation to person, place, and time;
- observations at various junctures of the interview.

DIAGNOSIS AND TREATMENT PLAN

Diagnoses should be based on a comprehensive evaluation, including the above information, other diagnostic tools, and collateral consultation if necessary. Treatment plans, in turn, should be based on diagnoses. However, neither diagnoses nor treatment plans are static; they are subject to change based upon new information, the client's response to specific treatments or medications, or external events. Changes in diagnoses or treatment plans should be documented in detail and include the specific contemporaneous reasons for modifications. In this way, the clinician is consistently using a scientific model in which "working hypotheses" are tested and altered according to the client's current status and response to treatment and environmental factors. See appendix C for a sample treatment plan form and appendix D for a sample revised treatment plan form.

Ongoing Treatment Progress Notes

Progress notes document what occurs in therapy, especially whether clients are achieving the goals they identified in their treatment plans. Progress notes can be brief, often only a paragraph. But they should allow the reader (who could be anyone, including the client) to see the focus of the session. Each progress note should show that what transpired in the session was relevant to the client's problems. Here are examples of progress notes showing a therapist's continuing focus on the client's presenting problems and treatment plan:

10/30/00: After reviewing her goals in the treatment plan we established last week (see individual treatment plan), Jane stated she still feels afraid of telling husband she is upset that he continues to do volunteer work instead of getting a job. She stated she continues to feel like a victim in her marriage: She stated she pays all the bills while her husband does what he pleases. In response to my question of whether she has always felt afraid of confrontation, she described memories of her mother's anger at her when she was a young child, her fear of her mother's anger, and how her fear of her husband's anger is reminiscent of what she felt with her mother. We discussed techniques for recognizing past experiences and anchoring herself in the present in order to clarify her options as a step toward taking action to gain more control in her life.

11/ 7/00: Jane stated she wants to be able to confront her husband about her need for him to contribute money to the family expenses, but continues to feel afraid. She said she is having trouble focusing and thinking clearly, and that she "dissolves into tears" when she tries to talk with him. I discussed the possibility of depression and referred her to M. Smith, M.D., for a psychiatric evaluation and to discuss with him whether she may need an antidepressant.

1/13/01: Dr. Smith able to see Jane immediately. She stated that he prescribed Celexa, 20 mg daily. Stated she is already feeling calmer and feels able to think more clearly.

1/20/01: Jane reported she was able to talk frankly, without fear, with her husband. She told him she had been feeling distressed that he was spending his time volunteering rather than finding another job to reduce the debt he was incurring on her credit cards.

Termination or Closing Summary

The closing summary completes the picture, like the final chapter of a book. Like the landing of a plane, terminations can be bumpy, sometimes smooth (Kobrin, N., 2001, personal communication). It should summarize the problems, treatment interventions, progress or lack thereof, and how treatment ended. A termination note can be brief. It should include the following:

- problems for which client requested help,
- treatment given,
- progress if any,
- reason for termination,
- statement of whether the therapist and client mutually agreed that therapy

was completed or whether the client terminated therapy against the therapist's recommendation,

- status of termination: What recommendations have we given to our clients for addressing their ongoing problems? Have we advised our clients they may return as needed? Have we referred our clients elsewhere, and if so, to whom?

The closing summary should be written in narrative form in the patient's record. Practitioners can also document the termination of treatment on a form. (See appendix E for a sample closing summary form.) Here is an example of a practitioner's closing or termination summary. Her summary provides an overview of the client's problems, what transpired during treatment, and the client's status at the end of treatment.

> Ms. Brown and I agree that she has made progress in resolving her problems and I support her decision to end treatment with me today. In summary, Ms. Brown, 43 y.o., unmarried, employed as an engineer, was initially referred to me on 8/18/00 by Dr. Adams, her psychiatrist, who was treating her bipolar mood disorder. Ms. Brown's presenting problems included: history of relationship problems due to her mood swings and distress at not having enough time with significant other; concerns that significant other lacked interest in her; inability to decide whether she should try to improve the relationship or end it. Her mood instability improved with Lithium and she felt ready to begin psychotherapy. Her goals were to clarify her feelings and consider her options in regard to her relationship with her significant other. *Progress:* She was seen in weekly individual sessions from 8/18/00 through 10/1/00; weekly joint counseling sessions with her significant other from 10/1/00 to 2/1/01; and monthly joint sessions with her significant other from 2/1/01 to 5/1/01. Initial phase of treatment provided education about the effects of her bipolar mood disorder and the need for a mood stabilizer; how her condition had affected her relationships with family and significant other; what she liked and what she wanted to be different in her relationship with her significant other. Joint counseling helped her review the relationship strengths and problems to clarify respective needs and to negotiate these. Within four months of joint sessions, Ms. Brown made progress in learning to speak about her needs and to articulate these to her partner. She identified appropriate communication tools for "fighting fairly" and practiced these with her significant other with excellent results. Ms. Brown has clarified that she wants to remain in the relationship and is feeling more hopeful and stable in her relationship. She understands she may return to this office for further help as needed in the future.

Other Essentials to Include

Now that we have discussed the "skeleton" or outline of our records, here are other essential contents we must keep in mind during documentation of evaluation and treatment. These essentials include the following.

CLIENT'S NAME ON EACH PAGE

Practitioners can make occasional filing errors. By having our client's name on each page, we prevent trouble in our own practices. In the event that other persons need to have access to our records, they, too, can avoid confusion in records when the patient is identified on each page.

DATE OF SERVICE, THERAPIST'S SIGNATURE, AND THERAPIST'S DEGREE ON EACH ENTRY

Dates help us keep track. When did the traumatic event happen in my patient's life? When did my patient and I discuss that upsetting event in therapy? When did I make that referral to the psychiatrist? When did I make that report to child protective services? In order for our records to be honest, credible, and appropriate, dates of treatment need to be consistent, although separate from, dates of service that appear in billing records. Finally, by signing each entry with our name and degree, it is clear to anyone that we provided the service.

BILLING RECORDS WITH MATCHING DATES, TYPE OF SERVICE, LENGTH OF SESSIONS, AND TYPE OF PAYMENTS

Clinical records should include a separate section devoted to billing. This documents when we rendered the sessions, the length and type of service we provided, the cost of services, and in what form the services were paid, e.g., cash, check, or credit card. Clear, consistent billing practices enhance the therapeutic relationship by having the client consistently invest in his or her own treatment, and protect the practitioner by documenting financial transactions.

All financial arrangements, including flexible or special arrangements, should be carefully noted. For example, therapists may make arrangements to reduce their fees or, in the case of indigent clients, provide services free of charge.

Consistent, predictable billing procedures help us maintain a structure for our clients and ourselves. When clients can take responsibility for keeping current with their payments, for example, or when they adhere to a consistent payment plan over time, they can feel more comfortable as a participant in the therapeutic relationship. The billing record promotes an atmosphere of partnership in the fiscal domain of therapy.

CONSENT FORMS

Consent forms are the foundation of clinical treatment. They serve several important purposes. First, no clinical work can commence without permission from the client. This implies that the client be thoroughly informed about all aspects of psychotherapy and, more important, take responsibility for the serious process in which they intend to engage. Second, consent forms protect the practitioner by documenting an agreement, or contract, between the client and the practitioner. Third, consent forms enhance the client's emotional and mental motivation for effective treatment.

Consent forms should be thorough but easy to understand and should be discussed with the client before being signed. There are four general types of consent forms:

Consent to Provide Treatment: Unless there are extraordinary circumstances, consent to proceed with an evaluation or with treatment is necessary before practitioners can begin providing services. (See chapter on informed consent section "Preliminary Verbal and Written Information.") Psychotherapists also need to continue obtaining consent to treatment, during evaluations when discussing diagnostic impressions and treatment recommendations, and during treatment when new diagnoses and revised treatment plans emerge. Clinicians should note in their records when these discussions occurred and the general context of the discussions. In addition to verbal agreement, it is best for the client to sign and date a form consenting to treatment. This form or forms may be placed behind the face sheet or in another easy-to-find place in the file. (A time-saving and therapeutically useful method to document informed consent is to create and co-sign the treatment plan with the client. Appendices C and D include sample treatment plan forms that can be developed and signed by both practitioner and patient to demonstrate clients' participation and consent to treatment. Interns and other practitioners in supervision can also use these forms to indicate clients' understanding and consent to supervisors' review of their cases and records.)

Consent for Billing: Patients' consent for billing should be documented. Therapists should identify in writing, prior to beginning treatment, who is responsible for payment of services, whether the client requests bills be sent to a third party, and if so, what information will need to be sent for processing claims, and to whom third party reimbursement will be made. Appendix F includes examples of statements that clients can sign to indicate their understanding and consent to billing policies and procedures.

Consent for Treatment of a Minor Child: With very few exceptions therapists cannot treat minors without written consent from the child's legal guardian. Failure to assiduously adhere to this rule can lead to serious legal action against therapists for asking the wrong parent for consent to treat a minor child. For example, a desperate therapist called me to say he had contact only with a child's mother, who was divorced from the child's father. The mother had initiated treatment for her daughter and had been bringing the child to treatment. The therapist had carefully obtained the mother's consent to treat her minor child. Unfortunately, the therapist realized later that he had failed to ask the mother whether she had legal custody of the child. He discovered she did not have legal physical custody, and therefore had no authority to give the therapist permission to treat her minor child. The therapist did not discover the problem until the child's father, who did have legal custody, learned of his daughter's treatment and became angry at the therapist.

In addition to obtaining consent for treatment from the legally authorized parent, I have found it is also important to discuss with parents the delicate issues of confidentiality when treating minor children. For example, it is critical that parents or legal guardians understand how important it is to balance parents' or guardians' need for essential information against the children's need for confidentiality. Even when such a discussion is not legally binding, I ask parents or guardians to sign a form indicating that they understand the need for this delicate balance. (See appendix G for example of a consent form for treatment of a minor child.)

Consent for Disclosures to Third Parties: Practitioners need to obtain valid signed authorization for releases of confidential information to third parties that are outside of the routine provision of care. (See chapter 4 for a discussion of ethical requirements and chapter 5 for a discussion of policies and procedures.) Practitioners can usually obtain guidelines for contents of authorization forms from their own professional regulatory boards or professional associations. Practitioners who are covered under the federal privacy rule can find authorization requirements in the amendments to the rule (Federal Register, 2002). (For a sample authorization of release of information form see appendix I.) Information necessary in an authorization form for release of identifiable information generally includes:

- client's full name and address, with an identifier (e.g., birth date or social security number to prevent mistaken identity);
- name and address of person or organization to receive the information;
- specific information requested;
- purposes for releasing the confidential information (for example, "to clarify diagnosis and treatment planning");
- date or event when authorization expires (in some states it is one year, in others, six months);
- client's right to revoke consent at any time, except to the extent action in reliance on the consent has already happened;
- client's or guardian's signature and date;
- witness's signature and date;
- any consequences for refusing to sign;
- notarization if necessary.

It is useful to maintain a record of disclosure to third parties. (See appendix H for sample "Record of Non-routine Disclosures" form.)

REFERRALS

We have a professional duty to recognize the limitations of our abilities. If we cannot complete a thorough assessment, formulate a diagnosis, or provide the kind of treatment a client needs, we should refer the client to another professional. The date of the referral, reasons for the referral, and the name of the person to whom the client was referred should be recorded in the client's file.

For example:

12/1/01: I referred Tom Jones to Dr. Smith, psychiatrist at Caring Clinic, for psychiatric evaluation of his symptoms of depression and whether antidepressant medication would be helpful.

8/4/02: I referred Bill Doe to his primary care physician, Dr. Jones, for medical evaluation of the "strange sensations" he reported having in his head.

Preventive Action Taken

At all phases of evaluation or treatment, when patients become dangerous to themselves or to others, it is essential that practitioners document the preventive action they have taken to protect their clients or others. Examples of preventive actions could include discussions with patients, consultations with other professionals, referrals, and legally mandated reporting. Risks for which practitioners take preventive action include: suicide ideation and planning; patients' wish to act upon sexual or violent feelings or intent toward therapists; suspected abuse of children; suspected abuse of vulnerable adults; or foreseeable intent to kill an identified person. Other risks in therapy that may also require some type of preventive action include therapists' strong feelings of attraction, anger, or anxiety and therapists' physical or mental conditions that impair their ability to practice safely. While it is usually inappropriate for therapists to document their personal problems in a patient's record, it is important to record the preventive steps they took to promote client welfare, such as professional consultation or termination of treatment due to the therapist's personal circumstances.

Suicide Risk: The importance of documenting suicide risk cannot be overstated. It protects patients as well as therapists. Consider the following case example of a competent therapist who became vulnerable to erroneous charges of negligence only because she did not document her conscientious efforts to prevent her patient's suicide.

A deceased patient's wife claimed, in her personal injury case, that the psychotherapist had not taken appropriate action to prevent her husband's suicide. The therapist stated that she had, in fact, taken the following appropriate preventive action. First, she had discussed thoroughly with her patient his thoughts of suicide and his ideas about how he would kill himself. The client had assured her in a verbal contract that he was not going to kill himself. Second, knowing that her client was still at risk, given his age (30) and gender (male) and his history of previous suicide attempts, the therapist consulted the client's psychiatrist about his suicide ideation and suicide plan. Third, the therapist referred the client to the psychiatrist for an immediate evaluation. Unfortunately, the therapist had not documented her discussions with her patient about his symptoms of depression and suicide thoughts and plan, her consultation with his psychiatrist, nor her referral of her patient to a psychiatrist for an emergency evaluation. The jury could not tell, therefore, whether she had or had not done what she claimed. Her failure to record any preventive actions gave the erroneous appearance that she had irresponsibly contributed to her client's death, which undermined her defense in the legal case.

When patients are suicidal, practitioners should document the following:

- Current psychological symptoms, such as emotional pain, vegetative symptoms, external stressors, agitation, irritability, rages, violence, hopelessness, self-acceptance, impulsivity, symptoms of depression

- Recent evidence of passive or active suicide ideation and planning: whether client stated she was thinking of killing herself and had a plan; whether there were other behaviors suggestive of risk, such as writing a suicide note, recently making a will or funeral arrangements, etc.
- Assessment of other risk factors: race, gender, age, psychiatric history, alcohol use, history of previous suicide attempts, history of another family member's suicide, social isolation, accessibility of a weapon

Here is an example of a psychotherapist's documentation of a patient's suicide risk and the preventive actions he took to suicide:

Fred has been suffering from moderate major depressive disorder for six months, has been on an antidepressant for three months, under the care of Dr. Smith. While his symptoms of depression improved after taking the antidepressant, he stated he has recently been feeling hopeless, is having difficulty concentrating, focusing, sleeping, and cannot eat. It has been six months since his wife died and he states he is "obsessing" about his wife's death "more than ever." Two days ago, he began thinking actively about dying and in answer to my question, told me he had the following specific plan to kill himself: he would drive himself over the bridge near his cabin. Other risk factors for suicide include: sister killed herself when she was 15; he has no children left at home (they are in college in other states); he recently was laid off from his job; he recently resumed drinking alcohol after two years of sobriety.

Discussed all of the above with the patient and called Dr. Smith's office to request emergency consultation. Patient stated: (a) he would not act upon his suicidal thoughts because of his strong Catholic faith; (b) he felt able to call me if he felt like he might act on his wish to kill himself; (c) he agreed to stop drinking, contact his AA sponsor, and attend an AA meeting tonight; (d) he promised to keep the appointment with Dr. Smith tomorrow morning; (e) he will attend his company's meeting with human resources in two days in order to learn about alternative work options; (f) will return to see me at our appointment next week on February 10, 9:00 a.m.

Duty to Warn: When clients make a serious, convincing, and specific threat of harm against a specific, clearly identified victim, practitioners must make reasonable efforts to prevent harm and document that they have done so. Interventions might include the following: trying to diffuse the anger, trying to dissuade the client from violent solutions, asking the client permission to discuss the situation with significant others, attempting to get the client to give up weapons or put away weapons, or enlisting family members' help to seek solutions. When clinical interventions fail to prevent risk of harm to an intended victim, practitioners must communicate the threat to the potential victim or, if unable to make contact with the potential victim, to the law enforcement agency closest to the potential victim or to the client making the threat. The duty becomes even stronger when practitioners have knowledge of the client's past violent behavior or past careless behaviors (e.g., reckless drunken driving which appeared suicidal or homicidal) and current symptoms of depression. Practitioners must prepare themselves for such contingencies by informing themselves about their own states' legal regulations governing "duty to warn or protect" situations. They can obtain information about their specific duties by asking their regulatory boards for information or by consulting their attorney.

Answers to the following questions must be documented in the record:

- What was the specific threat and toward whom, in the client's own words? For example, "I am so angry at my ex-wife that I am going to kill her when she returns to her home tonight from work" or "I have been learning how to build a bomb from instructions on the internet . . . and got what I needed to build a bomb . . . and am building the bomb now in my basement . . . so I can blow up my school and get back at the kids that have been calling me names."
- Was the threat imminent? For example, "I am going to drive over to my ex-wife's house right now and kill her" or "I am going to blow up my school tomorrow morning." Or not imminent? For example, "One of these days I am going to kill my ex-wife . . . mark my words" or "if the kids don't stop bullying me, after I finish building the bomb, I will blow up the school."
- What consultation did I obtain in order to clarify the risk and options I should take (if the threat is not imminent and there is time to get consultation)? For example, "I obtained consultation from Dr. Smith, Joe's psychiatrist, who agreed it is necessary to call Joe's ex-wife at her work and warn her of Joe's threat so she can take steps to protect herself. He suggested I give Joe's ex-wife the names of resources, such as the name and telephone number of a shelter for battered women."
- Whom did I contact to warn? (Names of intended victim, or law enforcement agency, addresses, and telephone numbers.)
- What did I state to the intended victim or law enforcement agency? For example, "I am calling you because your ex-husband, Joe, just

left my office, was very angry at you, said he was planning to kill you tonight after you returned to your home after work. I tried very hard to diffuse his anger and dissuade him, but he left very angry and while I cannot predict dangerousness for certain, I believe he is capable of carrying out his threat. The reason I am calling is that I have a legal duty to warn you in order to do my best to protect you from harm." Therapist waits for response from ex-wife, who sounds scared and is taking the threat seriously. "You might already have an idea how you can protect yourself from harm, but I wanted to give you the name of a shelter where women can go to be safe when they are in danger. Do you have a pencil to write it down?"

- What did the intended victim or law enforcement official state in response? For example, "Sergeant Nelson of the 3rd precinct stated he would immediately 'dispatch an officer to the ex-wife's home so that an officer would be there if Joe arrives.'"
- What was the outcome of the threat?

Duty to Report Suspected Child, Vulnerable Adult, or Other Abuse: Practitioners must follow their state regulatory board requirements for reporting suspected abuse and document all reports they make to protective agencies. They should inquire how soon their states require that they submit mandated reports of suspected abuse. Documentation of suspected abuse reports follows the same format for documentation in any duty-to-report case. The following needs to be included: client's identifying information (name, address, phone number); practitioner's name and title and address; what the client stated; what preventive action the practitioner took; what consultation the practitioner obtained; name and telephone number of the organization and person the practitioner called to report the suspected abuse; response of that person; and follow-up plans. For example:

11/2/01: In her individual session today Mary stated that she was unable to control her anger with her 8-year-old daughter Nancy. In her words: "I started drinking again because I felt so depressed. This morning I was in a hurry to get to work. I was furious with my daughter Nancy because she could not decide what clothes to wear. I slapped her really hard on the face, leaving welts and bruises." After listening to Mary's account of her behavior with her daughter and her wish to be in control of her behavior, I recommended we work together to clarify ways she can control her anger. She agreed. I also explained again that I am legally mandated to report suspected child abuse to the child protective agency. Mary chose to make the report with me. I placed the call, spoke with Ms. Anderson, intake worker, of the White

County Child Protective Services at 9:00 a.m., to report that Mary was in my office and willing to make the report of suspected child abuse herself. Mary did report all of the above information to Ms. Anderson and answered her questions. Ms. Anderson then told me that the agency would take the report and determine what, if any, action to take. After making the report to CPS, I then helped Mary consider options for controlling her anger with her daughter. Impression: Mary's starting again to drink alcohol reduced her capacity to maintain control over her impulsive behavior and anger. She wants to change, appears motivated and capable of identifying and taking necessary steps to control her behavior. After discussing specific options, Mary agreed to follow this plan: (a) She will stop drinking; (b) she will resume AA meetings near her job each week on Friday noon; (c) she will apologize to her daughter for slapping her; (d) she will tell her daughter she is getting help to control her behavior in the future; (e) she will talk with her daughter about ways to reduce stress in the morning, such as choosing and setting out school clothes the night before; (f) she will cooperate with CPS staff if they call and she will keep her appointment scheduled with me for next week to have my support and monitor her progress.

Duty to Report Threats Against the President of the United States: Reports of specific threats or plans to kill the president of the United States must be documented in the record, as well. The format for documentation of such reports to the federal agencies (FBI or Secret Service) is similar to documentation of other legally mandated reports: identifying information of client and practitioner; the threat the client stated; date and time of report; to whom the report was made; response of the individual receiving the report; follow-up actions.

CONTROVERSIAL CLINICAL DECISIONS

Although the need to make controversial clinical decisions might arise rarely, such decisions are necessary to document. This is because one approach may not fit every clinical situation. There are instances when practitioners' rigidity could be detrimental to their patients. While ethics codes explicitly proscribe only a few behaviors (such as sexual contact with clients and treating clients when seriously impaired), in most clinical decisions, therapists must weigh relative benefits and risks to clients (Schoener, 2001a, and Gartrell, N., 1992). Examples include: whether to disclose personal information about oneself; whether to accept from or give gifts to patients; whether to schedule evening appointments or home visits; whether to accept invitations to clients' social events; whether to extend a treatment session beyond the scheduled ending time; whether to treat the spouse or friend of a client.

What matters most is whether therapists have conscientiously considered the various factors in arriving at such clinical decisions. Therefore, the factors they have weighed must be documented in the record. The following discussion shows how a therapist handled complicated decisions regarding management of her client's expression of romantic feelings toward her.

Dr. Melfi, the competent female psychotherapist in the Home Box Office cable television series *The Sopranos*, made a decision to end a treatment session with her male patient, Tony Soprano, at exactly the scheduled time even though her patient had just professed his love for her and attempted to kiss her at the end of the session. As her patient approached her, she remained motionless, but ultimately averted his kiss. She appeared to be keenly aware that patients kissing their therapists was inappropriate in therapy, and understood her professional responsibility to talk with her client about his strong feelings that he had just acted out. But she always adhered impeccably to ending each session promptly after 50 minutes. She stated to her patient that it was important that they speak about the strong feelings he had just expressed for her, but since it was the end of the hour, would he be able to return for another appointment later in the day? Conscientiously sticking to the scheduled time frame of her clinical appointments was normally helpful, but in this instance it was not. Because of his work schedule, the client was unable to return for another appointment. By ending the session exactly on time and not taking a few moments to discuss what had just happened, the therapist missed the opportunity to bring closure prior to ending the session.

Even when practitioners realize later that their decision was not ideal, they should document their decision and reasons for it. I don't know how the conscientious therapist in the above example documented her complicated session. In her progress note, it might have been appropriate to document her decision making in this way:

> At the end of the session, Mr. Soprano stated that he wished his wife would dress in a "sexy" way. He stated he was attracted to women who dressed in an "understated" way and who were "gentle and sweet," like me, he said. He then walked over to me and kissed me on the cheek before I could push him away. Because kissing is not appropriate in therapy, I told him that we needed to discuss what just happened. Because it was the end of the session, however, and it is my usual procedure to maintain consistency of scheduled time for appointments, I stated we needed to end the appointment and offered him an appointment for later in the day. He stated he was unable to return later today. *Impression:* The important issues he spoke about and acted upon did not have appropriate closure in this session. I will raise these issues with him in the next session. *Plan:* I will speak with him in our next session next week about (a) my reflections

on how we did not have time to speak about his feelings and actions in this week's session; (b) how his feelings of love toward me are a natural response to therapy, but that communication in therapy is limited to words; (c) in future sessions we need to consider ways he can bring up important feelings earlier in his sessions so we will have sufficient time to discuss them before the end of the session. In addition to talking with him next week, I have also requested clinical consultation to discuss the most helpful way to manage these transference feelings.

In another case, involving a similar clinical issue, an adult male client said he felt his former therapist had handled a difficult situation appropriately. He said his previous therapist had reminded him of his mother, whom he regarded as an "angel." She had helped him so much in therapy that he felt indebted to her. He noted he idealized her just as he had revered his mother. Before one of his sessions with his former therapist, he said he felt "impulsive" and "wanted to provoke" his therapist into "becoming angry" with him. He said he therefore walked into his therapy session and in answer to his therapist's question about what he was feeling, he announced: "I am in love with my therapist." His statement seemed to catch her off guard, and elicited exactly the response he said he had wanted to provoke: His therapist did become angry with him, and she quickly responded: "Well, if that is how you feel, we need to end therapy." As he recalled, his former therapist then seemed to realize the situation required another response: She switched gears and spoke with him in an accepting and educative way about how normal such feelings of love toward one's therapist are in therapy, but that these feelings can be discussed and not acted upon in therapy. The client told me how much he appreciated her acceptance, her limits on his impulsive behavior, and her not abandoning him.

Interestingly, in her progress note of that session, the therapist documented other issues she and the patient had discussed on that day, but not his kissing her nor how she had handled it. I cannot know why she did not record this clinically significant incident. However, practitioners often leave out important events in therapy records when they feel personally uncomfortable with the situation or when they haven't known how to handle it. Had she documented this complex interaction, here is how she might have done it:

> Patient began session by stating: "I am falling in love with my therapist." After I suggested we could end therapy if he felt that way, and he got up from his chair and said "okay" and prepared to leave, I realized it would be more helpful to discuss his feelings. I asked him to sit back down so we could discuss the feelings he had just shared with me. I talked with him about how common it is for patients to develop strong feelings toward their therapists that can feel like love, that these feelings are useful to

discuss in therapy and understand, but are not acted upon. Patient said he had told me he was falling in love with me because he had wanted me to "get angry" at him. He appeared calmer and relieved by our discussion of his feelings and how we would handle his feelings in therapy and he went on to discuss his efforts in the past week to have better communication with his wife. For example, he stated . . .

COORDINATION AND CONTINUITY OF CARE BETWEEN PROFESSIONALS CARING FOR THE CLIENT

There are many occasions when effective treatment requires coordination with other professionals. For example, (a) if patients have been treated previously, we must read their records and speak with their prior practitioners; (b) if minor children are showing safety problems in school, we should consult with their teachers; (c) if clients are depressed, suicidal, or have somatic complaints, we should refer them to psychiatrists or other appropriate medical personnel for evaluation and medication. The need for such collaboration can arise at different junctures during treatment. Unfortunately, the increasing pressure on psychotherapists to see more patients in the same amount of time and for less money deters them from obtaining collateral data. This diminishes continuity of care and increases the risk to patients and others. As a result, psychotherapy training programs often omit the importance of collaborating with appropriate practitioners and otherwise ensuring continuity of care. Nevertheless, this crucial aspect of competent treatment should be observed and documented.

WHAT NOT TO INCLUDE

As noted in the section on characteristics of good records, I stressed the importance of only including what is relevant and germane to clients' problems and treatment. It makes common sense therefore that anything that is irrelevant to the diagnosis and treatment plan should not be included in the record. Other examples of contents that should not be included in records are the following:

Countertransference Fantasies

Countertransference fantasies can be diagnostically useful. They are valuable tools that allow practitioners to see clients from a different perspective and monitor their responses. For example, patients with borderline personality disorder and history of victimization frequently elicit strong feelings in therapists, such as rescue fantasies, "splitting" from colleagues, or temptations to bend usual procedures, such as not billing for missed appointments (Gabbard & Wilkinson, 1994; Luepker, 1989). We are responsible for being aware of and properly managing such feelings in order to provide adequate treatment. Documentation of countertransference impressions in the official record, however, does not contribute to the purpose or quality of the record and therefore should be omitted.

A better strategy is to obtain consultation and document that we received consultation regarding our questions and hypotheses about the client's diagnosis and treatment. It is appropriate to note whom we consulted and what insights and strategies we developed. In the following example, the therapist was able to document consultation for problems she was having appropriately managing treatment with an impulsive patient, but without including her own countertransference reactions. Even though she discussed her countertransference problems, including difficulties setting limits for her patient, with the consultant, her documentation about the consultation appropriately remained focused on the patient's needs in treatment:

> *11/20/01.* Consulted Dr. Smith regarding Jane Doe's missed appointments and cries for help in frequent telephone calls between sessions. Dr. Smith confirmed the importance of establishing firm structure. Strategies we discussed: (a) remind patient she must give 24-hour notice of missed appointment; (b) remind her of office procedure to charge for missed appointments without 24-hour notification; (c) discuss importance of being able to provide adequate attention to her needs, thus she needs to bring issues to appointments, not call in between sessions; (d) clarify together, in writing, on individual treatment plan; her problems, specific goals, and procedures in treatment.

Improper Alterations of Records

Practitioners need to avoid the appearance that they are hiding something (Dwyer & Shih, 1998). Records are like a laboratory notebook: occasional errors are expected and should be simply corrected, not obliterated. When there is an error, therapists should draw one line through the error, write "error," and insert the correction above or on the side, and initial. Or, make a note with a date: "See attached list of errors and corrections to the record." If practitioners do scratch out information, it gives the impression they did something wrong that they are wanting to hide.

Details Regarding Clients' Privileged Communications With Attorneys

Clients require support in order to survive severe stresses of litigation and frequently use their treatment sessions to discuss their lawsuits, including discussions with their attorneys. However, clients' communication with their attorneys is privileged. When therapists document clients' conversations with their attorneys, other persons who are involved in clients' lawsuits become privy to such information and clients' privilege is lost. When patients' discussions with their attorneys become a relevant focus of treatment, practitioners can document the focus of sessions by citing the material in general ways, without revealing specific data that is privileged. For example: "Client discussed matters related to her upcoming court case. The process of litigation continues to be a serious stressor."

Therapists' Personal Notes

Notes that are meant only to be helpful to practitioners are not relevant in our clients' official record. When we take just a few moments after each session to summarize the essence of what transpired, these types of notes eventually become unnecessary. They should be shredded periodically so that they do not accidentally end up in the official record. (The federal privacy rule uses the term "psychotherapy notes" to describe notes that are separate from the record, useful only to the therapist.)

METHOD OF RECORD KEEPING: DOES IT MATTER?

In my opinion, it does not matter what methods practitioners choose to use, as long as the records clearly and appropriately portray why the client is seeking help, that the treatment is focused on the client's presenting problems, whether there is progress, and that appropriate professional action is taken. Practitioners use various methods, such as (a) the "SOAPIE" problem-oriented record-keeping method, which emphasizes the problems and how the treatment addresses the problem, and (b) the "Focus Charting" record-keeping method, which emphasizes the focus of treatment (Townsend, 1999). I prefer to simply use the outline I have presented above. It stays consistently focused on clients' problems, states sources of information, and remains focused on the clinical interventions used to address the problems.

Regardless of record-keeping methods practitioners may choose, records that are written in narrative form to describe patients and their treatment

are easier to understand. Checklists are an invaluable method for systematically gathering data that is often overlooked in semistructured open-ended
interviews. However, checklists are rarely sufficient unto themselves. They
are most useful when they are combined with a narrative format.

SUMMARY

We can fulfill the purposes of records when we describe our clients clearly
and succinctly, along with the nature of their problems, the treatment interventions we employed, the extent and quality of their progress, the status of
termination, and our further recommendations. It is essential that records
reflect practitioners' integrity, knowledge, and good-faith efforts to assist
patients in achieving their goals. To this end, practitioners must systematically document informed consent, difficult ethical questions, preventive action, and consultation; answer evaluation questions; develop diagnoses and
working hypotheses; generate treatment plans; maintain consistent progress
notes; document a closing summary; and keep an accurate billing history.

Confidentiality and
Its Exceptions

Imagine a young woman whose mother is a prominent politician. She is depressed and has trouble sleeping. Her rapid mood shifts make it hard for her to control her thinking. She spends too much money and is anxious about her credit card debt. She knows she needs help but is afraid to get it. Her mother is in the midst of a highly publicized race for Congress. She recalls the stories her parents told her about a Democratic senator from Missouri, Thomas Eagleton, who had to withdraw as George McGovern's vice-presidential running mate when people discovered he was being treated for manic-depressive illness. More recent press coverage makes her wonder if she has the same problems as Eagleton (Associated Press, 1997; *Time*, 1996). What if she gets therapy and someone with a political axe to grind finds out and uses it against her mother? She wants nothing to stand in the way of her mother's chances of winning that seat her mother has wanted for years. She decides to suffer alone, even if it means fighting off those disturbing thoughts of suicide.

Or imagine a 31-year-old man who was in the middle of therapy when his wife left him. His wife filed for divorce and attempted to sabotage his chances of visitation with their preschool children because he had a mental illness. Even though he was stable and his mental health problems were not affecting his ability to care for his children, he was afraid. Since his wife was making his mental problems an issue in court, he worried that her attorney could get access to his mental health records. He therefore began clamming up in his psychotherapy sessions—afraid to tell his therapist everything for fear his wife could use what he said to his therapist to keep him away from his children.

Confidentiality is the cornerstone of effective psychotherapy. Patients must have implicit trust that therapists will respect and protect exquisitely intimate information (*Jaffee v. Redmond*, 1996). As these examples show, when patients lack trust that their information will be held in confidence they avoid seeking treatment or withhold important information.

Clinicians know that compromising client confidentiality undermines therapy and can cause harm to patients. One of the most frequent consultation requests I have received relates to demands therapists receive from insurance companies and attorneys for confidential patient information. Therapists have also described the disruption and anxiety they have felt when process servers have entered their waiting rooms with subpoenas or court orders. Many therapists have become so alarmed and confused by these unexpected events that they temporarily lose their clinical judgment and struggle with how to respond in the best interest of their patients and themselves. They worry about being pulled into litigation that could have enduring personal and professional repercussions.

Until recently, practitioners primarily relied upon their professional associations' codes of ethics and a "patchwork" of state and federal privacy laws for protection and guidance regarding confidentiality (U.S. Department of Health and Human Services, 2000). However, two events changed the political chessboard of confidentiality issues. In 1994, Karen Beyer, a Chicago clinical social worker, refused to release her psychotherapy patient's records to a federal court without her patient's consent. Her refusal became the focus of the U.S. Supreme Court's landmark decision (*Jaffee vs. Redmond,* 1996) to uphold psychotherapy clients' right to decide whether they will release their records in federal court. The court's decision in favor of patients' right to confidentiality in federal courts greatly empowered clients as well as clinicians, and established case law regarding confidentiality in the field of psychotherapy. Four years after the *Jaffee v. Redmond* decision, the Health and Human Services Department published its privacy regulations to protect patient-identifiable health care information that is transmitted electronically (Federal Register, 2000, December 28 and Federal Register, 2002, August 14). While many mental health organizations do not believe the federal privacy rule goes far enough to adequately protect confidential patient information (American Psychiatric Association, 2001b), they support the rule as a step in the right direction. At minimum, when a state's privacy regulations are less stringent or are non-existent, the new privacy rule offers uniform national standards that will help therapists both protect patient confidentiality and support the public good.

The purpose of this chapter is twofold: first, to orient the reader to the parameters of confidentiality and its exceptions, and second, to describe the ethical and legal guidelines that protect confidentiality and delineate its exceptions. The first section provides definitions of confidentiality, privacy, and privileged communication. The next section gives an overview of the parameters of confidentiality, including the need for exceptions. The third section discusses examples of threats to confidentiality that commonly arise both outside and inside psychotherapy offices. The fourth section presents professional ethics codes' requirements and exceptions for safeguarding confidentiality. The fifth section presents state and federal regulations that protect confidentiality. The sixth section discusses state and federal exceptions to confidentiality. The final section mentions other factors therapists should consider in making decisions about how best to protect their patients' confidentiality.

My intent in this chapter is to provide an overview of ethical and legal requirements that practitioners need to know before they can develop their own policies and procedures for safeguarding their patients' confidential information. (See chapter 5 for recommended policies and procedures.) This chapter is not legal advice, nor is it an exhaustive discussion of each ethical and legal guideline. Practitioners should consult their attorneys on how to understand and apply different laws to given case situations.

DEFINITIONS OF TERMS

It is important for clinicians to know the differences between the terms privacy, confidentiality, and privileged communication, which are defined below.

Right to Privacy

Privacy is a noun which means "seclusion, solitude, retreat, isolation, separateness, aloofness, separation, concealment" (Webster's, 1996). In psychotherapy, privacy is the limitation of awareness of personal information to the patient and to those whom the patient selects (Clough, Rowan, & Nickelson, 1999). Patients' right to privacy means that patients have the right to keep personal information secluded or concealed from others.

Right to Confidentiality

The words *confidential* and *confidentiality* derive from the same root but are distinct from one another. For example, *confidential* is an adjective. It means "secret" or "of or showing trust" (*Webster's*, 1996). *Confidentiality* is a noun. It means "entrusted with private matters." Applied to psychotherapy, confidential describes information to which no one is privy except the patient and therapist and those who must have the information in order to provide the service the patient requires. Confidentiality refers to the trust the patient places in the therapist to protect against the unauthorized or unlawful disclosure of the patient's confidential information.

Right to Privileged Communication (or Testimonial Privilege)

Privileged communication (or *testimonial privilege*) is a legal term that applies only in legal proceedings and pertains to the right to decide whether confidential information will be revealed in court testimony. The privilege belongs to the person who provided the information. The listener cannot disclose the information unless the speaker gives permission. Privilege protects the privacy of communications, for example, between husband and wife, attorney and client, clergy and church member, physician and patient, and psychotherapist and patient, from being revealed in court.

PARAMETERS OF CONFIDENTIALITY

While therapists are obligated to stringently protect patient confidentiality, there are exceptions to the patients' rights. Exceptions to the rule often relate to continuity of care, such as the need to routinely provide or discuss patient information with consultants, supervisors, or other professionals who are treating a patient. Similarly, it may be necessary to disclose patient records to health care administrators, regulatory agencies, or accreditation organizations.

Practitioners also must balance the need for confidentiality against the need for public safety, for example, when patients' lives are in imminent danger or patients are at risk of harming others. In these cases therapists have a legal and ethical duty to disclose information in order to keep patients and others safe.

THREATS TO CONFIDENTIALITY

External Threats

CHANGES IN HEALTH CARE MANAGEMENT SYSTEMS

Patterns inherent in health care management are rapidly eroding patient confidentiality. For decades all forms of patient information were considered private and unavailable to anyone except the therapist and a handful of persons who were working with the therapist. Even patients rarely saw their own files. But Appelbaum (2000) found that patient confidentiality became virtually nonexistent because various sources, such as pharmacies and insurance companies, had free rein to conduct marketing and other studies that readily revealed confidential patient information.

Chief among the needs of practitioners are strategies for preventing insurance companies from unauthorized and unnecessary access to patient records. In my capacity as national chairperson of the Committee on Law (Clinical Social Work Federation), psychotherapists routinely called me with concerns about how to protect their clients' confidentiality in response to insurance companies' demands apparently unwarranted for case reviews. For example, in one instance a psychiatrist reported he was horrified to overhear an insurance company reviewer casually comment, "Oh, I know this person," and then proceed to leaf through her acquaintance's psychiatric hospital chart with no compunction about the lack of patient consent. Indeed, upon further examination it became evident that there was no legitimate purpose for the review: The patient was not even a subscriber of the reviewer's company.

TECHNOLOGICAL DEVELOPMENTS

Recent technological developments also have posed a threat to patient confidentiality. Previously, psychotherapists felt safer because communication was slower and usually required personal contact. Therapists conferred with one another in person or via the telephone. They requested or conveyed information through letters or reports when they believed the exchange of detailed information was necessary. The use of electronic communication has increased the transmission of information at the cost of depersonalizing communication with patients and compromising confidentiality.

For example, one psychiatrist confided to me her distress when she accidentally pressed the wrong key on her computer, thus revealing identifying information and confidential mental health records of other practitioners' patients whose files were kept in the same program. Incidents like this one suggest that mental health practitioners and support staff are exposed to serious breaches in confidentiality. When the psychiatrist reported to the records administrator what had happened and the implications for patient confidentiality in such a large hospital, the administrator discounted her concerns with a wave of the hand. Not only was the hospital unable to manage critical security risks, it was astonishingly unconcerned with the ramifications of its technological deficiencies.

Unfortunately, this was not an isolated incident. The February 10, 1999, issue of the *Ann Arbor News* reported that a Michigan-based health care system accidentally posted the medical records of thousands of patients over the Internet (Wahlberg, 1999). On November 8, 2001, the *Star Tribune* reported that a psychology graduate student mistakenly posted the names and psychological evaluations of 20 Minnesota children on the University of Montana website when she thought she was copying their confidential data onto a secure computer (Lerner, 2001). "Hackers" have also stolen records by downloading confidential information from professionals' modems.

But the technological problems don't stop there. Leakages and interceptions can occur in "telemedicine," which purportedly brings teaching and supervision to remote areas (Stanberry, 1998), Internet "chat" rooms that provide patients with opportunities to "reduce their isolation and learn from one another" and practitioners with the chance to discuss mental health topics, and in e-mail, which offers "speedier communication" between patients and their therapists or between therapists and other professionals.

Hughes (2001) has identified several hazards to maintaining confidentiality of patient-identifiable health care information when communicating through e-mail:

- Messages can easily be sent to the wrong person by accident.
- Messages can be read off unattended computer screens (by unauthorized persons).
- Messages can easily be printed, forwarded, and stored in an unlimited number of paper and computer files.
- Messages are considered discoverable information in legal contexts.
- Messages may be used or disclosed for unauthorized purposes.
- Confidential health care information may be accessed in discarded media.
- Messages may be exposed by computer hackers.
- Messages may be forged by impostors.
- Messages can be easily intercepted and altered without detection.

- One party to the communication may falsely claim that the exchange of messages never took place.
- Senders may assume that messages were delivered when they were not.
- Recipients may not pick up their messages within the time frame assumed by senders.
- Messages may contain attachments that the recipient's software cannot read.
- Messages in written form are always subject to misinterpretation.
- Employers may screen messages sent to employee accounts.

INCREASING LITIGATION

Many psychotherapists who have spent their entire careers without coming into contact with an attorney are for the first time finding themselves embroiled in litigation ranging from personal injury suits to fierce custody battles. In most instances, practitioners are understandably worried about the implications of litigation on the efficacy of therapy. Indeed, in most cases, the legal system only serves to retraumatize or exacerbate the very symptoms for which the patient sought treatment. Increasing litigation has forced therapists to learn an entirely new facet of practice—forensics—and to adequately advise their patients about the potential harm of releasing confidential records to the legal system. (See chapter 10, section on "Handling Attorneys' Requests, Subpoenas, Court Orders, and Search Warrants" for information and strategies psychotherapists can use to handle interactions with the legal system.)

Internal Threats to Confidentiality

Threats to patients' confidentiality arise not only from external circumstances, but also from internal human negligence. Danish authors (Hasman et al., 1997) observed that health care professionals commonly discussed patients by name in hospital elevators and other open areas. Administrators in a Wisconsin hospital discovered "nosy employees" were logging onto a hospital computer and reading their nurse colleagues' medical record (Grady, 1997). In Arizona, when a pharmacy did not erase its records before selling its computer, a woman who purchased the computer at an Internet auction found thousands of patients' identifying information, including social security numbers and lists of their medications (Markoff, 1997). Further ways confidentiality can be breached in other aspects of the clinical domain include:

- leaving open files or stacks of files and open calendars on top of desks in unlocked offices,

- failing to close computers properly,
- stacking files in unlocked waiting-room closets, reception areas, or even in closets in practitioners' homes,
- addressing patients by name in waiting rooms and other public areas.

PROFESSIONAL ETHICS CODES' REQUIREMENTS FOR PROTECTING CONFIDENTIALITY

All mental health professions' ethical codes unanimously emphasize the necessity of protecting patients' confidential disclosures and obtaining written consent from patients or legally authorized persons before confidential communication can be disclosed. The only exceptions are cases where there is a legal compulsion to breach confidentiality. Professional ethics codes also apply these requirements to practitioners who are engaged in clinical research, supervision, and teaching. Further, many mental health organizations have updated their codes of ethics to include security standards for electronically generated and copied confidential information. (For samples of the confidentiality requirements of various professional associations' codes of ethics, see appendix J.)

STATE AND FEDERAL LAWS THAT PROTECT CONFIDENTIALITY

In addition to following their ethics codes, practitioners should also consider the following legal guidelines, including the federal privacy rule and the proposed federal security standards, to develop their own practice policies and procedures. (See chapter 5 for recommended policies and procedures to protect confidentiality.)

State Laws

PRIVACY LAWS

The nature of privacy protection varies from state to state. According to the Georgetown University study on health care privacy, "state laws, with a few notable exceptions, do not extend comprehensive protections to people's medical records." Several states' rules do not, for example, ensure patients' legal rights to see copies of their health care records (Health Care Privacy Project, 2001). When state privacy laws are more stringent than the federal privacy rules (see discussion below), the federal rule permits state laws to preempt the federal rule (United States Department of Health and Human Services, 2001a).

REGULATORY BOARDS

Regulatory boards are committees of publicly appointed individuals that guide and oversee various professions. Regulatory boards enforce legislative statutes and promulgate rules regarding professional standards of practice. For instance, in Florida, the "491 Board" governs the conduct of clinical social workers, marriage and family therapists, and licensed mental health counselors, and the "490 Board" governs psychologists. Some of the routine tasks that regulatory boards typically perform include the following:

- ensuring that requirements for licensure are met by each applicant,
- disseminating information to professionals about statutes and rules,
- enforcing legislative statutes that define standards of the appropriate professional conduct,
- hearing and making decisions regarding complaints about alleged professional misconduct.

Regulatory boards hold confidentiality as a supreme element of professional conduct. Nevertheless, boards also recognize the inevitable need for exceptions to confidentiality. Typical exceptions to confidentiality rules include but are not limited to the following:

- suspected child or elder abuse;
- sexual or physical abuse of vulnerable patients;
- sexual misconduct involving a mental health professional (this may include abusive use of authority, such as a supervisor sexually harassing a therapist or other employee);
- situations in which review of records is necessary to determine the presence or extent of professional misconduct, such as in regulatory board disciplinary actions and civil or criminal cases arising from allegations of misconduct.

State statutes and regulatory board requirements vary greatly. Some statutes are vague or lenient. For example, only 17 states have statutes that compel psychotherapists to report allegations of or suspected sexual maltreatment of patients by health care professionals. That is, if a therapist learns that another health care practitioner is having sexual relations or engaging in inappropriate sexual behavior with a patient, in only 17 states is he or she required to report this to the regulatory board. Similarly, child sexual abuse is defined differently across states. In Florida, sexual relations between two citizens where one is a child under the age of 16 and the other is more than 5 years older than the child is considered statutory rape. In Alaska, however, the legally defined "age of consent" is 13 years. Practitioners therefore need to learn what their reporting duties are to report suspected child abuse in their own states, including requirements for timing of reports and consequences for failure to report. The National Association of Social Workers, for example, has published a useful review of mandatory child abuse reporting requirements for social workers (McLeod & Polowy, 2000). However, it is always wise to telephone the relevant agency, such as child protective services, to inquire about one's reporting duty in a given case.

Regulatory boards also vary within individual states. For example, in Minnesota only two boards—psychology and social work—appear to enforce the Tarasoff rule regarding the "duty to warn or protect" a potential victim from harm. This means that if a client tells a therapist he intends to kill his wife, the therapist may not be required by law to break confidentiality in order to report the threat to the potential victim or law enforcement officials (Schoener, 2001b). When practitioners have questions about regulatory board requirements, they should consult their regulatory boards, professional associations, or attorneys.

PRIVILEGED COMMUNICATION LAWS

All 50 states have privileged communication statutes. The Illinois statute that grants privileged communication to psychotherapy clients of clinical social workers was tested in the U.S. Supreme Court after an Illinois federal appeals court disagreed with a lower court's ruling that Marylu Redmond, a psychotherapy patient of Karen Beyer, a Chicago clinical social worker, could withhold her psychotherapy records from federal court. In an unprecedented display of multidisciplinary solidarity, the major mental health professional associations cooperated and communicated as they developed their respective *amicus* briefs for the U.S. Supreme Court *Jaffee v. Redmond* case—and succeeded. In its landmark 1996 decision, the U.S. Supreme Court upheld the principle of privileged communication for psychotherapy patients in federal courts.

Federal Laws

THE CONSTITUTION

Privacy has been an enduring fundamental right throughout the history of the United States, but it has never been an absolute right. "Many of the most basic protections in the Constitution of the United States are imbued with an attempt to protect individual privacy while balancing it against the larger social purposes of the nation" (Federal Register, 2000). Many scholars believe that the spirit of the Fourth Amendment to the U.S. Constitution ("the right of the people to be secure in their persons, houses, papers and effects, against unreasonable searches and seizures, shall not be violated") extends logically to the right to privacy of health care information (Carter, 1999).

PRIVACY ACT OF 1974

In 1965, the House of Representatives established a Special Subcommittee on the Invasion of Privacy; and in 1973, the Department of Health, Education, and Welfare (now the Department of Health and Human Services) issued the Code of Fair Information Practice Principles, which formed the basis for the Privacy Act of 1974 that regulates information maintained by governmental agencies. According to the Privacy Act of 1974, the "right to privacy is a personal and fundamental right protected by the Constitution of the United States." This act regulates the government's use of personal information by limiting the disclosures of personally identifiable information, allowing consumers access to information about themselves, requiring federal agencies to specify the purpose for collecting personal information, and providing civil and criminal penalties for misuse of information (Privacy Act, 1974).

SOCIAL SECURITY ACT

The Advisory Committee on Consumer Protection and Quality in the Health Care Industry, a presidential advisory commission, acknowledged the lack of patient privacy and, in November 1997, recommended a Consumer Bill of Rights and Responsibilities. That same year, Congress required Medicare+Choice organizations to establish safeguards for individually identifiable patient information (Social Security Act, 1997).

EUROPEAN UNION DATA PRIVACY DIRECTIVE

Meanwhile, in 1995, elsewhere on our small planet, the European Union (EU) adopted a Data Privacy Directive, requiring its member states to have consistent privacy laws by October 1998. The EU urged countries in the rest of the world to adopt similar privacy laws (Stanberry, 1998).

HEALTH INSURANCE PORTABILITY AND ACCOUNTABILITY ACT OF 1996 (HIPAA)

Escalating concerns in the United States over the need for privacy legislation covering electronically generated medical information, as well as the

EU directive, caused Congress to enact the Health Insurance Portability and Accountability Act of 1996 (HIPAA). HIPAA mandated that if Congress failed to enact legislation to protect privacy of medical records by August 1999, the secretary of Health and Human Services (HHS) must promulgate regulations. Debates focused on the inherent conflict between the individual's right to privacy and the need for access to patients' health information for reasons of public health, research, insurance coverage, and health care management. Congress was indeed unable to resolve questions over how to protect the security and privacy of medical records. Therefore, the secretary of HHS, Donna Shalala, assumed responsibility for promulgating new rules. The privacy rule became final on April 14, 2001 and amended on August 14, 2001. Most health plans and health care providers covered by the new rule must comply with the new requirements by April 2003 (Currier & Sotto, 2001; United States Department of Health and Human Services, 2001a; Federal Register, 2002).

Proposed Federal Patient-Identifiable Health Information Security Standards. At the time this book is being written, it appears the proposed federal security standards will apply only to patient-identifiable information that is transmitted electronically. Any reports that are originally created by a computer system will be covered by the security standards, even when they are ultimately stored in a paper file. The standards will mandate that the same level of safeguards used to protect paper-based records must be applied for electronic health information. The security standards will apparently require careful planning in several areas: data backup, user authentication, message integrity, emergency mode operation, and disaster recovery. Practitioners can obtain further information about the development of the federal security standards on the U.S. Department of Health and Human Services website or by consulting their professional associations and attorneys.

Federal Privacy Rule. The federal privacy rules purpose is to ensure consistent levels of protection for confidentiality of patient-identifiable health care information across the United States. Its intent is to protect health care information that is generated electronically, whether stored electronically, orally, or on paper (Currier & Sotto, 2001). The rule emphasizes that health care practitioners and organizations ("covered entities") control the use and disclosure of patient-identifiable information, obtain authorization, and only disclose the "minimum necessary" to fulfill the intended purpose when sending protected health information to payers and to other outside parties requesting the information. The rule also requires practitioners to inform patients of their rights to have access to their own records and to request amendments to their records. Practitioners must provide patients with written notice of their privacy practices, make a good faith effort to receive written acknowledgment of receipt of this notice, and inform patients of their rights to file a complaint if there are violations of the privacy practices. The federal privacy rule also requires "covered entities" to have written "business associate" contracts and to designate a privacy officer who will have responsibility for the development, implementation, and enforcement of the organization's privacy policies and procedures (United States Department of Health and Human Services, 2001a; Federal Register, 2002).

The federal privacy rule supports the Supreme Court ruling in *Jaffee v. Redmond* and therefore accords, "psychotherapy notes" even greater protection than general medical information. The rule defines "psychotherapy notes" as notes that are "primarily of use to the mental health professional who wrote them, maintained separately from the medical record, and not involved in the documentation necessary to carry out treatment, payment, or health care operations" (U.S. Department of Health and Human Services, 2001a).

The federal privacy rule does not preempt state laws that are more stringent, nor does it supersede local courts' decisions, such as parents' rights to child custody or visitation. Neither does it conflict with other federal laws, such as the Privacy Act, which govern health care information that governmental agencies maintain. Therefore, psychotherapists should learn whether privacy provisions in their state statutes are more stringent than the federal rule. They must also be aware of other federal privacy guidelines that may apply to their practices (United States Department of Health and Human Services, 2001a).

According to the U.S. Department of Civil Rights, which is in charge of enforcing the federal privacy rule, "covered entities" are expected to take "reasonable" steps to comply with the rules (Office for Civil Rights, 2001). This implies some humane consideration for practitioners' financial ability to implement the regulations. The deadline for implementing the federal privacy rule is April 14, 2003. However, practitioners should inform themselves about provisions of the rule by reading the U.S. Department of Health and Human Services website or by consulting their professional associations and attorneys.

In chapter 5, I present suggestions for policies and procedures that are consistent with ethical guidelines as well as with provisions of the federal privacy rule.

DRUG AND ALCOHOL ABUSE TREATMENT

Two federal statutes protect confidential information disclosed in federally funded treatment of drug or alcohol abuse. The first is the Drug Abuse Prevention, Treatment and Rehabilitation Act of 1974. The second is the Comprehensive Alcohol Abuse and Alcoholism Prevention, Treatment and Rehabilitation Act of 1974. These regulations prohibit practitioners in federally funded substance abuse treatment programs from revealing the identifies of their patients unless their patients give specific written authorization. (United States Department of Health and Human Services, 2000).

STATE AND FEDERAL LAWS' EXCEPTIONS TO CONFIDENTIALITY

As noted above, while patients' right to confidentiality is critical, it is not absolute. The following are examples of state and federal laws' exceptions to confidentiality.

State Laws

LEGAL DUTY TO PROTECT

States "duty to protect" laws are exceptions to patients' right to privacy in that they require therapists to take reasonable actions to protect an identifiable potential victim from foreseeable harm. *Tarasoff v. Regents of the University of California* (1974), known as "Tarasoff I," dealt with the question of whether a therapist had taken sufficient action by reporting to the police his psychotherapy patient's threat to kill a female university student, Tatiana Tarasoff. Even after the therapist reported the patient's specific threat to the local police, the patient did end up killing Tarasoff, and her family sued the therapist and his clinic, claiming the therapist had not taken sufficient action to protect their daughter. The decision in this case created the legal precedent for seventeen states to enact their own statutes mandating that psychotherapists warn third persons that they are in danger of violence by a patient. The California Supreme Court modified this decision in "Tarasoff II" to a duty to protect potential victims which is predicated on the special relationship of therapist to patient. As one Justice wrote: "The protective privilege ends where the public peril begins" (*Tarasoff v. Regents of the University of California*, 1976). The duty to protect is a "well known fact of professional life" (Monahan, 1993). However, there is considerable variation among states and among professions within the same state regarding definitions of what constitutes a duty to protect, and how this duty is to be implemented varies between states and also within professions in the same state.

LEGAL DUTY TO REPORT SUSPECTED ABUSE (SUCH AS CHILDREN, VULNERABLE ADULTS)

Dating back to the 1960s and 1970s there has been widespread concern about the need to protect children from physical and mental abuse and neglect. All states have laws on reporting suspected child abuse. Because language varies, practitioners must know their own states' requirements for reporting of suspected child abuse.

Other types of reporting duties for suspected abuse also vary between the states. For example, only 17 states require therapists to report suspected sexual abuse by health care professionals.

Psychotherapists will learn the rules and standards of care for reporting duties by consulting local and federal rules and guidelines and professional codes of ethics, by attending continuing education offerings, and by discussing these topics with colleagues and consultants.

DUTIES TO REPORT HIV INFECTION

In most states, health care professionals are required to report cases of certain infectious diseases and sexually transmitted disease to their state health departments. This includes HIV or AIDS. State health departments, in turn, are required to report this information to the federal Centers for Disease Control and Prevention (CDC) in Atlanta, Georgia.

States have strictly limited practitioners' disclosures of these conditions to state health departments (unless patients have given authorization for release of this information to other parties) in order to prevent discrimination against AIDS- and HIV-infected patients, such as housing and employment. However, many state laws do have provisions that allow health care providers to protect other identifiable parties from infection. In these states, health care professionals may report instances of HIV or AIDS to spouses, sexual partners, emergency personnel, funeral directors, blood banks, and others who could be harmed unless they had knowledge of these conditions. Psychotherapists therefore need to consult their attorneys in order to clarify whether psychotherapists are covered by their state legal requirements relevant to reporting infectious and potentially harmful conditions without patients' authorization and, if so, how to appropriately implement these requirements.

Federal Laws

DUTY TO REPORT THREATS AGAINST THE LIFE OF THE PRESIDENT OF THE UNITED STATES

In 1917, Congress enacted a statute which defined threats of various kinds against the president and his successors as a felony (United States Code,

1917). In 1971, the purview of this statute was narrowed to three main issues: to protect the president from possible future attacks, to prevent the incitement of others to attack the president, and to prevent disruption of presidential activity (*United States v. Patillo,* 1971):

> Since the existence of a threat, even without further action, may lead to restrictions of the President's movements and requires that the Secret Service take protective action, the mere verbalizing of a threat against the President remains criminal because of its potential for disrupting the daily life of the President (Griffith et al., 1988).

Thus, if a patient threatens the life of the president, psychotherapists have a special duty to report the threat to the Secret Service (W. Menninger, personal communication, 1992). The Secret Service investigates threats and assesses their risk potential to the persons under protection (M. Coggins, personal communication, 1992).

OTHER CONSIDERATIONS

Consultations

Psychotherapists have an ethical duty to seek appropriate consultations (such as with clinical supervisors, consultants, or government agencies) when they have questions about whether it is necessary to disclose confidential patient-identifiable information without consent from their patients. When practitioners wonder, for example, whether or not certain types of parental behaviors trigger a legal duty to report suspected child abuse, they need to consult the appropriate child protection agencies' intake workers or supervisors. When practitioners request consultation about their reporting duties, it is normally unnecessary to disclose patient-identifying information.

Practitioners' Confidentiality Contracts

Practitioners make both implied and stated contracts with their patients about confidentiality. They need to follow their own confidentiality contracts. While I have personally never seen a malpractice case initiated primarily due to harm resulting from breaches in confidentiality, I have observed practitioners' failure to comply with their own confidentiality contracts emerging as a critical issue during the course of many malpractice lawsuits. Loss of confidentiality creates lack of safety and interrupts treatment.

SUMMARY

It is undisputed within the field of mental health that confidentiality is the foundation of effective psychotherapy. Unfortunately, the burgeoning "Information Age," with its giant technological arm, combined with a frightening increase in litigation, is insidiously eroding patients' rights to confidentiality and privacy. But the pendulum has begun to swing and the federal government is slowly responding to this formidable health care crisis. It has enacted a new federal rule aimed at protecting the privacy of patient-identifiable health information that is generated electronically and has promised stringent and consistent means of enforcement. Moreover, the rule is subordinate to stricter state rules that may apply in any given case and do not conflict with psychotherapists' legally mandated duty to breach confidentiality when there is a reasonable risk of harm to self or others. The federal rule also protects "psychotherapy notes" more than other types of health care records. Mental health organizations generally agree that state and federal laws need to go further to protect patient confidentiality, but see the federal privacy rule as the beginning of a uniform national standard that can be fortified by continued research and empirical data regarding the growing threats to patient confidentiality.

Policies and Procedures for Protecting Confidentiality

The previous chapter summarized the ethical and legal requirements for protecting privacy, confidentiality, and privileged information, explained how they constitute the infrastructure of effective psychotherapy, and cited their exceptions. The previous chapter also addressed the various ways in which each of these essential components of the therapeutic relationship has been eroded by electronic methods of communication, increasing litigation, and intrusions by managed care companies.

The purpose of this chapter is to address how practitioners can protect confidentiality and patients' right to privacy and appropriately manage their exceptions. Specific policies and procedures for maintaining the integrity of any information—whether it is oral, written on paper, or stored on computers—that identifies patients, their problems, or their treatment are provided. These recommendations are consistent with the ethics codes of mental health professions and the federal privacy rule. However, they are not legal or clinical advice for given situations. Practitioners should always consult their attorneys in order to clarify applicable state and federal laws and rules and whether their policies and procedures appropriately implement them.

SECURITY MEASURES

Security of Oral Communication

While other types of health care providers call their patients by name in the waiting room, the need for privacy in psychotherapy is even greater. Practitioners can protect their patients' privacy by not calling them by their names in waiting rooms or other occupied areas. For new patients whom the therapist does not know, an alternative is to ask, "Who are you here to see?" With known patients, an alternative is a smile, establishing eye contact, and saying, "Please come in when you are ready." Even when practitioners have authorization to discuss a patient or certain aspects of his or her case, they should make sure not to do so in the presence of nonauthorized individuals.

Security of Paper-Based Information

Practitioners should routinely check to see that a patient's identity is not visible to unauthorized users in one's private practice or other treatment center. Psychotherapists should scrupulously ensure that charts, assessments, intake questionnaires, and any other information on which patients' names may be seen are not left on counters, desks, floors, or in unlocked files or

drawers. All files should be immediately returned to locked filing cabinets. Buildings should be inspected for adequate fire alarms, extinguishers, and sprinkler systems.

Security of Computer-Generated and Computer-Stored information

Psychotherapists should protect computer equipment from unauthorized physical access and theft. The Ambulatory Care section of the American Health Information Management Association suggests the following security measures to protect information in computers from unauthorized access (Hughes, 2001):

- Use passwords to limit access during routine work and to prevent unauthorized access in the event the computer is stolen.
- Use floppy disks or compact disks or removable hard drives so that information can be transported and stored in a different location.
- Use at least seven alphanumeric characters to make it difficult to guess the passwords.
- Change passwords frequently and maintain any written notation of the password in a secure location away from the computer.
- Limit users to only one system log-on at a time.
- Program personal computers and work stations to log off automatically when they are inactive for a prescribed amount of time.
- Install anti-virus software to block external sabotage.
- Prohibit employees from loading unauthorized software onto the organization's computers.

Practitioners need to inform themselves of further safeguards that may be mandated by their state laws or by the evolving federal security standards. The United States Department of Health and Human Services publishes announcements of the status of proposed standards on its website.

PRIVACY MEASURES

"Routine" Uses and "Nonroutine" Disclosures

When developing privacy measures, it is helpful to distinguish between routine uses and non-routine disclosures of patient-identifiable health care information.

Routine uses of patient-identifiable information are those communications that psychotherapists make in order to develop diagnoses and treatment and to conduct other "necessary clinical operations," such as billing and consultations with patients' psychiatrists or other mental health team members. To be consistent with ethical standards, routine disclosures require initial consent from psychotherapy patients.

However, as psychotherapists know, billing third party payers is not always routine. Patients cannot know, for example, in the beginning of therapy what their diagnoses are nor what they will need to discuss in order for healing to take place. Even though patients provide initial consent to their therapists to provide minimal information, such as their diagnosis and dates of services, to third parties for reimbursement of services, they may be unwilling to reveal further information that third party payers may request later for reimbursement of continued treatment. Practitioners should therefore be certain that their patients are fully informed of specific disclosures being requested and that patients have authorized these in writing. Practitioners should then submit only the minimum necessary to payers.

Non-routine disclosures are those communications to third parties that are outside of the usual operations necessary for the delivery of treatment or billing. Examples of nonroutine disclosures include responses to requests for records from individuals or organizations outside of the treatment team, such as attorneys. Non-routine disclosures require written "authorization" from the patient to be consistent with mental health professions' codes of ethics (see appendix J).

It can be helpful for psychotherapists to maintain a record of all nonroutine disclosures. (See appendix I for a sample form that can be used to keep a record of nonroutine disclosures.) A record of nonroutine disclosures should be kept in the patient's file and should answer the following questions:

- date and time of disclosure;
- type of disclosure (e.g., electronic, telephone, fax);
- purpose of the disclosure;
- organization or individual, including address, to whom the information was disclosed;
- information disclosed;
- copy of signed and dated authorization for release of information.

Security of Fax Transmissions

Psychotherapy offices routinely use facsimile (fax) transmissions, which allow practitioners to exchange clinical information (e.g., with patients, insurance companies, other health care professionals, or attorneys) about their patients rapidly, conveniently, and precisely. There are risks in using fax transmissions that practitioners must take reasonable steps to prevent. For instance, fax transmissions can accidentally be sent to, or received by, the wrong party. Even when they arrive at the right machine, they might be read by a nonauthorized user. Psychotherapy practices therefore must develop and carefully enforce faxing guidelines that adhere to applicable laws for protection of patient-identifiable health information.

To protect confidentiality of faxed information, offices and organizations should adhere to the following precautions:

- Locate fax machines in a secure area with access only by authorized users.
- Limit faxed information to the amount necessary to meet the needs of the requester.
- Require written consent of the patient or his or her legal representative except in cases of extreme emergency or other legally authorized reasons.
- Include an attached cover page that states the following: **"This information is confidential. It is intended for use by the specified recipient only. If this fax has been received in error, please notify this office immediately."**
- Contact the recipient of the information to verify who will receive the fax and whether the information will be protected by necessary privacy and security measures.
- Keep a log in each patient's record of all fax transmissions.
- Designate one staff person to monitor incoming faxes, verify their completeness, and deliver them to the appropriate, intended recipients.

Privacy Officer

The federal privacy rule requires health care practitioners and organizations that are covered under the rule to designate a "privacy officer." The privacy officer must assume responsibility for ensuring developments, implementation, and enforcement of privacy and confidentiality policies and procedures. The federal rule does not specify criteria for the privacy officer. Thus psychotherapists in independent practices could choose to assume responsibility as privacy officers for their own practices.

Employee Screening, Privacy Training, and Security Agreements

The federal privacy rule also requires that employees be subjected to pre-employment background checks in order to verify history of reliability and that they receive security training. Training must teach staff how to protect the security of patient-identifiable health care information. The federal privacy rule also requires documentation of staff training activities.

All business associates, including employees, must sign a statement indicating that they understand and agree to the psychotherapy practice's policies and procedures for protecting patients' privacy and confidentiality. Computers and software that employees use need to be protected from theft, vandalism, and unauthorized access, whether the equipment is in the office or home-based.

Employers should give the following information to persons associated with their psychotherapy practice setting:

- the legal basis (state and federal) for patients' right to privacy and confidentiality;
- employees' responsibility for protecting confidential information;
- procedures to prevent or report breaches of security (e.g., unauthorized persons entering the office);
- notice that the psychotherapy practice's computer is protected against unauthorized access;
- consequences for failure to follow these policies, such as suspension, dismissal, or legal action.

Practitioner Agreements

When practitioners join the staff of a psychotherapy practice, they, too, should sign a confidentiality agreement indicating that they understand and will adhere to their professional ethics, state and federal laws governing patient privacy and confidentiality, and the psychotherapy practice's policies and procedures for protecting confidential information and patient privacy. The signed agreement should also include consequences for failure to follow the agreement.

Contractor or Vendor Agreements

Contractors, vendors, or other third parties that provide services to psychotherapy offices, such as copying, transcription, microfilming, destruction, or storage of records, must also sign the same kinds of contracts. These should indicate that they understand and agree to the office's confidentiality policies and procedures. Agreements should also include guarantees that these persons will not deliberately introduce software viruses or other hazards into the psychotherapy practice's computer system.

Communication With Patients About Privacy Practices

Conscientious psychotherapists have already been informing their clients about their offices' privacy practices. However, the federal privacy rule establishes uniform standards that psychotherapists who are covered under the rule must follow. Practitioners should present privacy practices information to patients in writing, preferably before an initial interview, in a form (such as a handout, pamphlet, or brochure) that patients can keep in their own records, discuss with their psychotherapists, and refer to as needed. In the initial appointment, therapists should attempt to obtain patients' written acknowledgment that they have received and read the privacy practices information. (See appendix B, "Client Information," which includes a statement on privacy practices.)

Because patients seek psychotherapy when they are emotionally distraught, oral and written communication with patients about confidentiality and exceptions to confidentiality should be clear, simple, and brief. Clients must be able to understand and incorporate this information within the context of building trust and a working alliance with the therapist. Opportunities for further clarification of procedures to protect confidentiality and to handle legally mandated exceptions to confidentiality often occur at various junctures during the course of treatment.

INITIAL WRITTEN COMMUNICATION

Practitioners must provide written communication about their privacy practices with answers to these questions:

- How does this psychotherapy practice use patients' information?
- What are the routine uses of patient information?
- Does this practice use patient information to remind patients of appointments?
- Does this psychotherapy practice report patient information to third party payers?
- What rights do patients have?
- What complaint procedure can patients follow if there are violations of the stated privacy policies?
- Under what circumstances and in which ways can patients amend information in their records pertaining to their care?

(See appendix B section "Your Right to Privacy and Confidentiality" for a sample statement that presents a psychotherapy office's privacy policies and procedures.)

INITIAL VERBAL COMMUNICATION

Verbal communication about privacy practices is necessary because it helps prevent misunderstandings and can be a vehicle for building trust and a strong therapeutic alliance. Some practitioners worry that having such discussions in the initial interview could intimidate, stifle, or intrude upon their psychotherapy clients. As with any other issue the therapist and patient address, the outcome depends on the method. If therapists rigidly dominate the initial interview with technical language and personal agendas about privacy matters, patients are likely to react with anxiety and trepidation. However, if therapists follow the age-old wisdom of "starting where the client is," a climate of learning and trust can be created in which the patient feels comfortable asking about and discussing a broad range of topics. Most patients, in my professional experience, have welcomed therapists' concern that they understand office-related procedures and how the procedures affect their treatment. In some instances, discussing innocuous rules and procedures reduces potential patients' anxiety about why they sought help in the first place.

Case Example. The following example illustrates how a therapist stayed sensitively focused on the primary goal of the first interview—understanding why the client is seeking help and establishing a beginning rapport and working alliance—while taking a few moments at the outset of the initial interview to communicate how information is protected and what the exceptions to confidentiality are.

Therapist: Today our goal is to talk about the problems that you have been having that have prompted you to seek my help. Before we begin talking about these problems, I wanted to ask if you received the client information I mailed and whether you have had a chance to review this information?

Client: [Indicates she has received it and has read it.]

Therapist: One of the most important items of information in that handout is how I will be keeping confidential what you tell me, and what the exceptions to your confidentiality are. [Pauses to see that client understands and appears agreeable to proceeding.] I must keep confidential what you tell me, unless you give me written consent to release your information or unless there are legally mandated exceptions to confidentiality.

Exceptions would include, for example, that if you are abusing a child I am legally required to report suspected child abuse, or if you tell me you are planning to kill yourself or someone else, I must act to protect you or the other person.

Client: [Nods, indicating she understands.]

Therapist: The handout also explains how I will be routinely using what you tell me. For example, I will be speaking with your psychiatrist about your condition for diagnostic and treatment planning. I also understand you are wanting me to bill your insurance company, so I would be sending in your diagnosis to the insurance company in order to be reimbursed. If your insurance company requires more information later, I will tell you what they are asking for so you can decide whether to release it to them or not.

Therapist: [Feels satisfied from the client's response that she has reviewed the written information and understands so far what the therapist has stated verbally.] Before I begin asking you about the problems that prompted you to come here and about the history of the problems and your life experiences, I want to give you a chance first to ask me any questions.

Client: [Is silent but contemplative, appears to be interested in the therapist's invitation to consider any questions she may have. After a few moments . . .] Well, yes, I do have a question . . . I am having problems with my husband, and I am wondering if you have experience working with marriage problems?

Therapist: [Answers client's questions about her professional background and waits for any further questions, but the client says she has no more questions.] Please don't hesitate to ask me any more questions that might occur to you later. If you're ready, let's move now into what brought you here today. What are the problems that have caused you to seek help?

ONGOING COMMUNICATIONS ABOUT CONFIDENTIALITY

While it is crucial to communicate with patients about confidentiality and exceptions to confidentiality before therapy begins, continuing discussions at various junctures in therapy may also be indicated. These may be helpful when third party payers request additional information beyond the diagnosis or when therapists receive a court order, subpoena, or third party request for records or must fulfill a legally mandated duty to report. Clinical tips for sensitively handling some of these situations are discussed elsewhere in this text. (See, for example, chapter 10, section on "Handling Attorneys' Requests, Subpoenas, Court Orders, and Search Warrants.")

PROTECTING PRIVACY AND CONFIDENTIALITY OF DIFFERENT CLIENT POPULATIONS

Treatment of Minors

Practitioners providing psychotherapy to children and adolescents must balance children's needs for confidentiality with parents' or legal guardians' needs for information. Parents or legal guardians generally have the right to see their minors' psychotherapy records, unless doing so could be harmful to the minors. Practitioners must therefore understand their legal obligations to disclose information to parents and legal guardians, while exercising good clinical judgment about whether doing so would undermine treatment or otherwise hurt children.

For example, a biological parent who has lost parental rights probably would not have access to the records unless the guardian gives permission. Also, minors who can legally give consent to treatment, such as "emancipated minors," normally have control over access to their records. Therapists should consult their state laws to learn the conditions under which children can become emancipated in their state. Practitioners must also learn whether their state statutes have provisions for withholding information from parents when it is in the child's best interest to do so. When there are no such provisions, practitioners should consider what is most helpful clinically to child and adolescent clients.

Parents and guardians generally have the right to review a child's record if the child is at risk for harming himself or others. Beyond this and a few other rare exceptions, practitioners often lack clear guidance as to when parents must be informed about their children. Schoener (2001a) suggests four parameters to consider when deciding whether to disclose information to parents:

- Weigh the pros and cons of telling versus not telling the parents, or any other given party.
- Attempt to assess whether the parent would be in a position to help protect the adolescent if he or she knew about the conduct.
- Determine whether the practitioner has advice to give the parent regarding what the parent could do to help prevent harm.

WORKING WITH PARENTS AND GUARDIANS

The degree of confidentiality and privacy needed to promote the best clinical outcomes for children depends to a large extent on the age and developmental stage of the children. Adolescents, for example, may request more privacy than younger children. In most instances, therapists can elicit the cooperation of parents and guardians regarding confidentiality when they explain the importance of confidentiality to the treatment outcome and solicit the opinions and advice of the parents or guardians.

Topics that practitioners should discuss with parents in order to gather important information, reduce anxiety, and increase cooperation include:

- their minor child's need for confidentiality in his treatment,
- the clinician's need to be able to make professional decisions about what it is necessary for parents to know,
- assurance that the practitioner will inform them of any risk with which they can help.

Sometimes parents can better understand the importance of confidentiality when practitioners explain it in black and white and parents can refer to it throughout the child's treatment. Developing a confidentiality statement that is signed by the parents, practitioners, and older children and adolescents not only increases understanding and promotes helpful questions, but helps to create an atmosphere of trust and support. Appendix G is a sample informed consent policy for parents and guardians and includes the following statement about the child's need for confidentiality:

> As a parent, I understand that I have the right to information concerning my minor child in therapy, except where otherwise stated by state and federal law and rule. I also understand that this therapist believes in providing a minor child with a private environment in which to disclose himself/herself to facilitate therapy. I therefore give permission to this therapist to use his/her discretion, in accordance with professional ethics and state and federal laws and rules, in deciding what information revealed by my child is to be shared with me. I understand that this therapist will inform me of any risk to my child with which I can help.

Issues regarding confidentiality involving minors can arise throughout the course of therapy. In most instances, therapists can abide by their ethical responsibility to "do no harm" and refuse to disclose information at any point during treatment if disclosure could cause serious harm to the minor. During therapy, practitioners should continue to reiterate the above principles and continue to weigh whether release of the information might cause serious harm. Whenever possible, therapists should promote direct communication between children and their parents or legal guardian regarding issues of concern to the parents or guardians.

Working with minors usually entails communicating with other professionals, which can complicate confidentiality further. Therapists should explain to minor patients (as appropriate, depending upon developmental stage) and their guardians that the child's therapy will involve a team approach in which the therapist will be conferring with the child's teachers and other school personnel. Therapists require consent from parents and guardians in order to share information with school personnel, except in emergency.

It is equally important for practitioners to keep in mind that discussions with teachers and principals can be risky. School professionals may not have the capacity to protect the confidential clinical information nor know how best to use it. I agree generally with Schoener's recommendations (Schoener, 2001a) that therapists limit discussions with teachers and principals to the following:

- information necessary for the child's safety (this should be shared with the child also),
- feedback that counseling is occurring,
- general information about prognosis, limited to such things as a statement that they are not likely to see change in the next few weeks,
- assurances that if this doesn't help, the practitioner will try something else,
- things the therapist would like school personnel to do to help the child (this should be shared also with the child).

Group Treatment

Trust that develops within group therapy depends not only upon clients' relationships with therapists, but also upon group therapy clients' relationships with one another. Because multiple clients are present during group treatment and practitioners have limited control over the behavior of clients after they hear one another's confidential disclosures, practitioners are unable to guarantee confidentiality of group clients' communications. Clients in group therapy therefore often feel a heightened concern about how the confidentiality of their private communications will be protected. Accordingly, group therapists have duties to individual group clients as well as the group itself to explicitly communicate and fully discuss their policies and procedures for safeguarding clients' confidentiality.

As with other forms of treatment, practitioners ideally should communicate expectations about protection and exceptions to confidentiality in writing as well as verbally in the intake sessions with individual group therapy clients as well as with all group members.

At the outset of the first group therapy session, while practitioners are reviewing the purpose and norms for the group, they should explicitly state

their own duty to safeguard group clients' confidentiality and cite the exceptions to confidentiality. Group therapists also should discuss the need for group members to make a contract with one another to refrain from discussing each other's identity and confidential communications outside of the group sessions as well as the consequences to group members if there are breaches of privacy and confidentiality. Group therapists need to ensure that all group clients understand and have pledged that they will adhere to the group rules regarding confidentiality.

The following is a sample privacy and confidentiality contract for group clients to sign after they discuss it in the first group session:

> I understand that in order to establish trust in group therapy so that group therapy can be helpful to me and other group therapy clients, it is essen-

tial that all group members' identities remain private and that all group members' confidential disclosures be protected. This means that while I have the right to choose to speak to others outside of group therapy about my own problems and my own participation in group therapy, I cannot reveal the identity of any other group members nor what any other group members have stated in any group session. I agree to take responsibility for protecting the confidentiality of other group members' identities and what they say in group sessions. I understand that should I breach this confidentiality and privacy agreement, accidentally or on purpose, my group therapist has the right to terminate my participation in group treatment.

Therapists can ensure privacy and confidentiality of group members by keeping an individual record for each group therapy client. Maintaining separate documentation in individual charts involves a few extra minutes after each group therapy session. However, it is the only way to guarantee adequate documentation and to protect group clients' privacy and confidentiality.

Family and Couple Treatment

The same wisdom that guides confidentiality for group therapy applies to couple and family treatment: Complete confidentiality is impossible. However, there is a mutual duty between the two members of a dyad or multiple members of a family to protect one another's confidential disclosures. As with other types of treatment involving multiple parties, practitioners should work ethically and systematically to safeguard confidentiality by imbuing treatment with a respect for the privacy of others and providing a role model for the ways in which that respect can be incorporated into the couple's or family's value system. Practitioners should provide written information regarding privacy practices as well as communicate these verbally to couples and family members.

When practitioners are responding to requests for family or couple records, identities and information from family members who have not given their consent for release of information must be omitted from any copies of the original record. In order to protect privacy and confidentiality and minimize later time-consuming record deletion problems, therapists may wish to keep separate records for each family member, as is done for group therapy clients. Practitioners should also document discussions about confidentiality and privacy expectations and clients' confidentiality contracts in their records.

Confidentiality After Death

Professional codes of ethics uniformly support the notion that confidentiality regarding therapeutic records extends after a person's death. Mental health professionals were alarmed when they learned that psychoanalyst Martin Oren released treatment records, therapy session tapes, and his recollections of his patient Anne Sexton to Sexton's biographer, Diane Middlebrook, after Sexton's death. Dr. Oren apparently believed that Sexton would have authorized him to release her communications in treatment to her biographer. However, the professional community maintained it was unethical for him to do so (Schoener, 2001b).

Despite ethical and legal requirements that protect clients' confidentiality after death, deceased clients' legally authorized representatives can act on their behalf and have access to their records. I suspect that most patients would feel alarmed if they were aware that relatives could eventually review their psychotherapy records. One therapist anticipated this possibility with his client after she developed a life-threatening illness. The client had spoken to the therapist in several treatment sessions about her decision not to tell her adult daughters certain details about her unhappy marriage with their father. Since the client's strong feelings about her wish for privacy had been a focus of her treatment, and she knew her physical prognosis was poor, the therapist inquired whether she might wish to consider the option of preparing an "advanced directive" that would indicate her wish to prohibit legally authorized representatives from having access to her records after she died. The client considered this option and decided to prepare a notarized statement to the effect that her wish was for no one to have access to her therapy records after her death. Her family members might still have a legal right to have access to her records after her death, but at least she knew the directive would inform them of her wishes for privacy.

Confidentiality in Mandated Reporting

As clients' trust in their therapists deepens, they may choose to disclose more sensitive information. In some instances, these revelations result in a duty to report illegal activities, such as suspected child abuse, which can sometimes result in disruptions to therapy. How practitioners handle a potential or actual reporting duty can make a difference. The best way to avoid disruption in therapy is to discuss with potential clients in the initial session the therapists' ethical and legal duty to report harmful activities to appropriate authorities. Knowing this from the outset can be a great source of support to clients. In many instances, clients are relieved to find a vehicle strong enough to help them disclose actions about which they are ashamed or over which they feel they have no control. Whenever possible, practitioners should consider whether and how they can involve their psychotherapy clients in making the legally mandated reports. Some clients have chosen to make the reports themselves, in the presence of their therapists. The goal is to balance clients' need for autonomy and control over their lives with society's need for protection.

For example, in states where practitioners must report health care practitioners' alleged sexual misconduct, clients have felt they have lost autonomy and control when therapists have reported previous therapists' alleged sexual misconduct. Even though these clients later stated they understood, and agreed with, the need for their therapists to report practitioner sexual misconduct in order to protect patients and even though they ultimately chose to make a report about the alleged misconduct to regulatory boards themselves, they still would have preferred having control over making the decision about whether and when to make a report.

Thus, when I learn that my client has experienced sexual misconduct by a former therapist but has not yet revealed the identity of that practitioner, I have found it helpful to inform clients of their options. "If you give me the name of a health care practitioner who has engaged in sex with you as his or her client, I am legally mandated in Minnesota to report to the appropriate licensure board what you have told me. If you don't want me to make a report or are not ready for me to do so, don't give me the person's name."

To be ethical when practitioners must make legally mandated reports, they should normally give only the "minimum necessary" to meet the purpose of the report. (See appendix J, which lists excerpts from ethics codes that emphasize this principle.) However, practitioners should also carefully weigh the possible outcomes in determining how much information to disclose. Schoener (2001c) has reported unfortunate instances where limited information in telephone calls to an identified potential victim of violence has led to potential victims feeling terrorized.

Suspected abuse reports to agencies, such as child protective services or regulatory boards, are easier because these involve calling a professional social services intake worker, not an identified potential victim of violence. These reports can be summarized briefly but precisely, and limited to the following:

- the reporting practitioner's name,
- the purpose of the report (including the legal duty that makes it necessary for the practitioner to make a report),

- name and address of the person alleged to have engaged in the abuse,
- name and address of the alleged subject of the abuse,
- specifically what the patient told the practitioner about the alleged abuse, specifically, "who allegedly did what to whom."

HANDLING THIRD PARTY REQUESTS FOR RECORDS

Principles to Consider

When considering third party requests for clients' confidential treatment information, practitioners must keep in mind the following principles:

1. the need to verify carefully the legitimacy of the request for disclosure of information;
2. the importance of ensuring that a client (or a parent or legal guardian where permitted by law) fully understands the request, its purpose, and has given consent for disclosure;
3. the importance of disclosing only the minimum necessary to accomplish the intended purpose;
4. the need to be informed of one's own state statutes and federal rules and to seek legal counsel from the practitioner's own attorney as needed.

It is important for the clinician to discern the type of the third party request for information they have received. Requests generally occur in one of three forms, and each type requires a different response.

A Third Party Request Without Signed Authorization (Type 1)

Psychotherapists may not release confidential patient-identifiable information without the adult client's or minor client's legal guardian's duly signed authorization to release the records, unless there are extenuating circumstances. Such cases include, but are not limited to, a legally mandated duty to report suspected child abuse or to protect an identifiable intended victim of violence. Thus, when practitioners receive telephone calls or letters from parties requesting client records without a release, prudent practitioners refrain from even acknowledging an acquaintance with the client by saying the following: "I am unable to acknowledge if I know or work with a client without a client's informed written authorization." Or, alternatively, "Without a client's signed informed authorization, I am unable to release confidential records."

A Third Party Request With Signed Authorization (Type 2)

This type of release of information is signed by a current or past client, or a client's legal guardian, to send records to another person or agency such as a social service agency, another therapist, or insurance company. Practitioners are more comfortable receiving requests for information when they are for purposes of sharing information needed for continuity of care, do not immediately raise the specter of legal action, and are signed by the patient or legal guardian. The relative informality of the form can, however, motivate clinicians to reproduce the entire record and send it as a matter of course to a person or the requesting agency. Practitioners must develop a more discerning response.

First, practitioners must determine whether the release of information form contains sufficient information to accurately determine the identity of the patient and specific purpose of the request and whether the release of information form is valid. For example, does the form contain adequate data to identify the patient, for example, date of birth or social security number, address, and telephone number? Does it state the specific purpose of the request and to whom the information will be sent? Does it include the patient's (or legally authorized representatitve's) signature and a date? Is the date of the signature recent enough to comply with state requirements? Is it possible to determine whether it was the client who signed the release and/or whether the client understood its purpose? Does it specify an expiration date (or event) for the authorization? Does it inform the patient about his or her revocation rights and any consequences of refusing to sign?

After determining that it is a properly executed and signed form and that the client understands its purpose, the practitioner should summarize only the information being requested (especially important in instances when the individual was seen in the context of conjoint, family therapy, or group therapy, and the names of other clients and their information must be protected). A summary allows the practitioner to aptly condense their perceptions of the relevant aspects of the clinical contacts for the person or organization receiving the summary. The general principle is to err on the side of sending too little rather than too much. If recipients want more information, they can contact the clinician.

If the record, however, contains information about drug treatment, federal laws protecting confidentiality supersede the release and no information should be released without specific consent on a federal form allowing the release and/or a court order.

Subpoenas (Type 3)

Subpoenas are another form of third party request for patient-identifiable information. In order to release information in response to a subpoena, just as with other third party requests, practitioners must obtain their patients' or patients' legal representatives' signed authorization for release of information. (For further information about subpoenas and how to proceed, see chapter 10, "Psychotherapists and Records in the Legal System.")

SUMMARY

Practitioners must develop policies and procedures to protect security and privacy of patient-identifiable psychotherapy information in all forms: oral, paper, and electronic. Policies and procedures must specify who will have access to what kind of information and how and when information may be accessed. Practitioners must limit access to confidential treatment information to authorized users who have access only to that information that pertains to their legitimate purposes. Patients need to be informed of policies and procedures pertaining to how their confidential communications will be protected and exceptions to confidentiality. This chapter presented practical tips that practitioners can use to develop their own policies and procedures.

CHAPTER

6

Retaining and Destroying Inactive Records

Imagine yourself in your office opening your mail. A life insurance company has sent you a request for a former client's records. You haven't seen this client in 10 years but know that his inactive record is still in your files. You look at his record. It is a mess. Mainly scribbles that don't make sense, even to you. Even though your former client has given consent for release of his records to the company, and you might be able to rely on your memory to write a report to the company, you don't want to have to write one more report this week to another third party. Hey . . . what about destroying the record since it's been a decade since you last saw him? How long must you keep records anyway? What do you do? You pick up the phone to consult a colleague.

There are no simple answers for how long to retain inactive records. It is essential that psychotherapists have systematic policies and procedures for retaining and destroying inactive client records. Here are the four general factors that help guide clinicians in this process:

- legal requirements,
- ethical requirements of professional organizations,
- needs of clients and continuity of care,
- issues associated with lawsuits and litigation.

This chapter addresses each of these factors and provides practical guidelines for how to effectively and efficiently maintain and dispose of clinical records.

FACTORS TO CONSIDER IN DETERMINING HOW LONG TO KEEP INACTIVE RECORDS

State and Federal Legal Requirements

Therapists should always consult the state statutes that govern their profession. Regulatory boards can direct therapists to the appropriate statute and often have copies that they distribute to therapists for a nominal fee. Not all states include statutes regarding the retention and destruction of records. Still, therapists should be familiar with state regulations pertaining to records. Especially important issues include how long records must be kept, and under what conditions, when and how records can be destroyed, and exceptions to statutory requirements. State laws vary. In most states, adult patients' files must be kept for at least 7 years after termination of services. Minor children's files must usually be kept at least until the child's 21st birthday.

The federal privacy rule does not govern how long psychotherapists must retain records after termination of services. It does specify requirements for security and safe destruction of records. The rule directs practitioners to adopt and apply whatever standards—state or federal—for safe storage and destruction of records are more stringent in a given state.

Professional Organizations' Ethical Guidelines

Most mental health professional organizations address the need for careful policies and procedures regarding retaining and disposing of records and emphasize the need to maintain client confidentiality in both practices. However, in most instances mental health organizations echo or defer to statutory requirements. Exceptions are the American Psychological Association's Specialty Guidelines for Clinical Psychological Services and for Counseling Psychological Services. (For excerpts from mental health professions' ethics codes' requirements for storage, retention, and destruction of records, see appendix O.)

Needs of Clients and Continuity of Care

While governmental regulations and ethical guidelines are two factors to consider when developing practice policies and procedures for maintaining and disposing of records, therapists should also keep in mind the importance of their patients' potential clinical needs and continuity of care. For example, a state statute may require therapists to maintain patient records for only 7 years after a case has been closed. But therapists may decide to keep records longer—even indefinitely—in case the patient seeks care again after 7 years, either from the original therapist or a different therapist located elsewhere. Similarly, a client who has terminated therapy may experience a crisis long after the 7-year retention requirement has expired and require additional mental health treatment. It can be tremendously helpful to therapists assessing the client's current needs to refer to previous records.

The following example is unusual because South Dakota state law requires psychiatric hospitals to retain records for an unusually long time: 30 years. However, it illustrates how helpful it was to a subsequent therapist when she was able to obtain the former psychiatric records more than 20 years after her new client's previous psychiatric hospitalization.

A 53-year-old South Dakota woman, mother of three adult children, who was suffering from depression and marital problems, sought psychotherapy again after nearly 30 years. She indicated to her new therapist that when she was 24, and her children were very young, she had become overwhelmed. At that time she developed a serious depression, became suicidal, was admitted to the psychiatric hospital, and received shock treatments. Because the law in her state requires hospitals to keep medical records for 30 years, the new therapist was able to obtain this patient's former records. Through reading the former psychiatric record, the new therapist had a deeper understanding of her new patient. For example, the new therapist was struck by the fact that while the patient had suffered a severe major depressive episode in the past, she had, nevertheless, been able to function reasonably well, free of depressive symptoms for nearly 30 years, had successfully raised her children, and had maintained friends and meaningful activities in her community. In this instance, the opportunity to review the former record gave the therapist valuable information—about both the patient's vulnerability to depression and her psychological resilience. It was also helpful to the new therapist and the patient to note that some of the patient's concerns in the past, as documented in her hospital record, were resurfacing in the present, so these issues could be clarified and become a focus in treatment.

Another 53-year-old woman, in a Southern state, returned for treatment with a psychotherapist whom she had initially consulted for premarital counseling 25 years ago. Intermittently over the past 25 years, the woman had returned for brief (3–5 sessions only) therapy in order to clarify her feelings of helplessness and her needs in her marriage. Each time, her presenting problems involved her wish to persuade her husband to take a job and contribute to the household expenses. When she turned 53, she became moderately depressed. She was tired of supporting herself and her husband. She wanted to be able to retire within 10 years. Her husband's increasing credit card debts were frustrating. Consequently, she felt alarmed that she would not have enough financial security in order to retire when she wanted to. When she returned to the therapist to work on these problems, she was shocked to hear excerpts from her record. Her therapist's notes revealed she had struggled with the same marital problems for over 25 years. The fact that her records were still available was helpful. From listening to excerpts from her records she was able to better see herself and her longstanding pattern of problems. The insights she gained strengthened her resolve to do things differently. As a result, she was able to establish and follow through on goals for her life.

Protection in the Event of a Lawsuit or Other Allegations

Another factor to consider when deciding whether and how long to keep inactive records, and the best manner by which to destroy them, is the possibility of lawsuits or other complaints. Complaints against therapists generally come through one of two vehicles: regulatory board complaints and malpractice lawsuits. If practitioners have kept clear, accurate, ethical, and comprehensive records, they can avoid suits or successfully defend their work on the basis of client files.

Since there is usually no time limit as to when patients can file complaints against practitioners through regulatory boards, some attorneys advise therapists to keep records indefinitely.

Malpractice suits are constrained by statutes of limitations, usually 2 years from the termination of therapy or from the time the patients realized that the practitioner's conduct harmed them. For these reasons, too, some attorneys have suggested that therapists maintain records indefinitely, or at least keep a summary statement of diagnosis and treatment, to be able to demonstrate the care they provided.

Inappropriateness of Destroying Records With Intent to Avoid or Influence Judicial Proceedings

It is never appropriate to alter or destroy records with the intent to avoid or influence judicial proceedings. The following case example illustrates a family court judge's anger, and a therapist's and mental health clinic's embarrassment, after the therapist destroyed a portion of the client's case in an effort to influence judicial proceedings involving his client.

A 30-year-old woman, who lived with her 7-year-old son in a Western coastal town, had been receiving psychotherapy in a private mental health clinic to deal with parenting and other adjustment problems following her divorce. After a year of psychotherapy, she decided she wanted to move to another city, a thousand miles from her home. Because the child's father had liberal visitation rights and lived in the same town, she needed to get the court's permission to move with her child away from the father. The woman therefore filed a petition in family court and the child's father disagreed, claiming the child needed more contact with him than would be feasible after the move.

The father was aware of the mother's previous problems controlling her anger, and the father's attorney decided to seek evidence of the mother's psychological imbalance to support the father's claim that it was in the child's best interest to remain geographically close to him. The father's attorney therefore served the private mental health clinic with a subpoena for the mother's records and asked the mother's therapist to testify in court regarding the mother's psychological status.

At the time she petitioned the court to move, the mother was psychologically stable and had been functioning well in her mothering of her young child for several months. She was worried, however, that her clinic record could potentially be harmful to her chances of gaining the court's approval to move away with her son. Initially, when she first sought help from the clinic, she was asking for help to control her impulsive behavior: She was hitting her son, causing bruises. Her clinic record contained a summary of these problems and a copy of the therapist's legally mandated report of suspected child abuse that the therapist had submitted to child protective services. The therapist's progress notes summarized the patient's treatment, which had focused on her goals of controlling her abusive behavior, and her excellent progress.

The therapist felt sympathetic to the mother's fears that the court would deny her request to move if the judge read references in her clinic record describing her previous abusive behavior with her child. Even though the therapist's documentation of the mother's abusive behavior was relevant and integral to the treatment plan, the therapist chose to delete the portions of the record pertaining to the mother's history of abusive behavior.

When the judge learned that the therapist had destroyed this portion of the record, he reprimanded the therapist, the mental health clinic, and its board of directors. He stated that the therapist's behavior was not only unprofessional, but it could also harm children. Even though the judge ruled in the mother's favor, permitting her to move with her child to the new city, the clinic's credibility and reputation were tarnished. As a result of this unfortunate incident, the clinic learned it needed a policy on retention and destruction of records.

POLICIES AND PROCEDURES FOR THE RETENTION/ DESTRUCTION OF INACTIVE RECORDS

Security of Inactive Records

Practitioners should protect the confidentiality and physical integrity of inactive records as carefully as they do active records. All too often, files end up in flimsy cardboard boxes in inadequate storage spaces where they are subject to destruction by the elements or access by unauthorized users. Paper records should be kept in strong, locked, fireproof containers and stored in secured, climate-controlled facilities.

Destruction of Inactive Records

Equally important is the need to have safe destruction procedures. I have heard of disturbing situations that could have been prevented with more careful planning. For example, a private practitioner who was moving to another office told me that his secretary "accidentally" shredded a box of current patients' active files rather than the box of his former patients' inactive files that he was ready to destroy. In another instance, a mental health clinic manager told me she had conscientiously chosen a reliable company to pick up and shred her clinic's psychotherapy records, but the company's procedure was to ask her to leave closed boxes of records to be shredded in the alley behind the clinic so that the truck driver could retrieve them and take them to the company's shredder. Even though she felt confident that the company was reliable, she was concerned that confidential records could accidentally spill out of the boxes when the driver loaded them onto the truck or that passersby in the alley could get into the closed boxes. She knew that her clinic, not the company, was responsible for safeguarding their patients' confidentiality.

In another example, practitioners in a private practice were diligently collecting psychotherapy records that needed shredding, but leaving them in piles on counters in their office where they were visible and accessible to anyone visiting the office, including evening cleaning staff. The cleaning staff had no clear job expectations for assuring privacy of records. Even the owner of the office building, who was not a mental health professional, became concerned about the lack of security. Patients, too, felt uncomfortable as they entered the suite of offices, wondering if someone could carelessly glance at their own charts once they had ended treatment.

Staff Security Agreements and Consequences for Violations

The federal privacy rule includes requirements for staff security agreements. Even if practitioners are not covered under the rule, the procedures that follow make common sense.

All staff, including independent contractors, should be informed of, and sign, confidentiality agreements in order to protect the security of inactive files. Agreements should include consequences for staff for violations of security policies. When psychotherapy offices hire independent contractors to retain or destroy inactive files, these persons, too, must agree to policies and procedures for protecting privacy and security of inactive records. Policies and procedures should include the following:

- clear job expectations to protect privacy of inactive files for all staff, including support, cleaning, independent contractors, and professional staff;
- consequences for staff for violations of inactive record privacy expectations;
- signed confidentiality agreements by all staff and independent contractors obliged to protect privacy of inactive files;

- secure place for keys that unlock cabinets that contain inactive files;
- length of time inactive files will be kept;
- method for destruction of inactive files (e.g., will they be burned or shredded?);
- manner in which clients will be informed of record retention and destruction policy.

See appendix B, "Client Information," for record security, retention, and destruction section on "Right to Read your own records," which includes a statement regarding policy and procedures.

SUMMARY

Four factors that practitioners need to consider when determining how long to retain records, and when they can destroy them, are legal requirements, ethical requirements, clients' needs, and issues associated with lawsuits and regulatory board complaints. Therapists are cautioned never to destroy records with an intent to alter judicial proceedings, but instead to develop consistent policies and procedures for record retention and destruction. The federal privacy rule requires practitioners to have privacy agreements (with consequences for violations) for all business associates, including independent contractors. I have offered sample policies and procedures that can be used with staff and with patients that are consistent with the mental health professions' ethical guidelines and the federal privacy rule. Practitioners should always consult their own attorneys and regulatory boards to learn about legal requirements for given situations.

Using Patients' Records as Therapeutic Tools

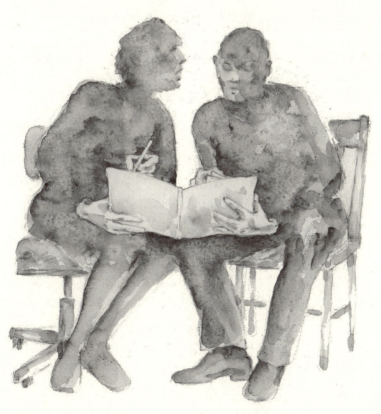

My colleagues' eyes usually glaze over when I enthusiastically mention using record keeping as a therapeutic tool. Most therapists see record keeping as a necessary evil—a boring burden that distracts them from the heart of their work. I have felt the same way. But as I developed as a therapist and learned to use every aspect of the therapeutic relationship, I saw that faithfully creating a chronicle of clients' courageous and often arduous journey is a powerful tool that hastens their healing. Seeing and discussing records validates their hard work and allows them to see themselves, their problems, goals, and gains. Reflecting on notes ratifies their role as collaborators in the therapeutic process. Involving clients in the chronicle of their work enhances self-determination, insight, responsibility for healing, and the integrity of the therapeutic relationship. Record keeping thus can be a dynamic aid to therapeutic intervention and an indispensable tool for growth.

Though involving clients in observing and using the record-keeping process can be valuable, therapists must be aware of several issues. Therapists are responsible for creating the records and maintaining them in their offices. They must be judicious in deciding how, when, and to what extent to use records in therapy. Timing is crucial. Therapists must use professional discretion when responding to clients' requests and be keenly attuned to clients' mental and emotional status in order to make good decisions about whether or not to employ notes and records as a tool at a particular juncture. Finally, when choosing this or any other therapeutic tool, they must stay true to their own style.

This chapter will examine (a) the history of clients' access to records, (b) use of records as a therapeutic tool, and (c) management of complex, challenging situations, such as when patients request that portions of their records be deleted, or when they insist their therapists keep no records.

HISTORY OF CLIENTS' ACCESS TO RECORDS

The U.S. Freedom of Information Act of 1966 and Federal Privacy Act of 1974 introduced patients' right to examine and comment upon their own records in federally funded institutions. This caused therapists great consternation. They worried that opening up records to clients' scrutiny could harm the therapeutic process, result in loss of practitioner control over the record, and even "degrade the helping relationship by introducing argumentation and disagreements" (Freed, 1978). However, a few pioneering practitioners in social work, psychiatry, and marriage and family therapy embraced the idea and endeavored to use the new rule as an opportunity. They were surprised to find the process of discussing records with clients to be helpful. Most of their trepidation was unfounded. Some of the positive outcomes of allowing clients to examine their own records included increased communication between clients and professionals and clients seeing this demystification as a symbol of mutual trust, acceptance, and interest (Freed, 1978; Townes, Wagner, & Christ, 1967). Indeed, Freed astutely suggested that fears associated with not using records in the therapeutic process were a paper tiger and a missed opportunity for better treatment (Freed, 1978).

Patients' legal right to access their own records is now commonplace in the United States. Many state laws, as well as the new federal privacy rule, require psychotherapists to allow their patients to examine and comment upon their own records upon their request, unless the contents of the record could be harmful to them. However, despite clinical and authoritative evidence suggesting that engaging clients in record keeping is not harmful and can be therapeutic under most circumstances (Grange, Renvoize, & Pinder, 1998), practitioners have continued debating the issue. For example, Furlong (1998), a psychoanalyst, warns against patients reviewing their own records. He views the clinical record as "analytic mental space," the privacy of which "must be respected . . . even by the patient whose discourse contributes to it, in order for it to function effectively." Yet, others within the analytic community have noted that therapists have a professional responsibility to establish clear goals and state these goals in language that can be understandable to the patient and to others (O. Renick, personal communication, 2001).

Interestingly, many of my patients have expressed no desire to see or discuss their psychotherapy records, even when I have invited them to do so. However, a large proportion have taken an active role in examining and discussing my clinical notes. With few exceptions, clients have experienced no harm from seeing their records, but instead have found the process to be an evocative learning tool. In my own professional experience, sensitive, factual, nonjudgmental records can inspire clients to greater curiosity about themselves and their problems and enhance their participation, sense of safety, and security in the therapeutic relationship.

The debate over the efficacy of involving clients in record keeping is not likely to be resolved in the absence of a significant paradigm shift. For the purposes of this discussion, I will focus on the ways that records can become therapeutic tools.

HOW RECORDS ARE USED AS THERAPEUTIC TOOLS

Evaluation Phase

The initial evaluation records help establish a treatment alliance, set the stage for the work ahead, and continue to be of benefit to patients and therapists throughout the course of treatment. Records can be used therapeutically in the following ways.

TO PROVIDE A GUIDE FOR AN UNPREDICTABLE JOURNEY

Psychotherapy is a process of discovery, much like writing a book. Even when authors have an outline, there is no certain way to anticipate all that lies ahead. For therapists, too, it is not possible to predict the course of therapy with each unique patient, even when therapists have knowledge and previous clinical experience treating a variety of people suffering from similar kinds of emotional and mental disorders. Therapy parallels writing in that "Putting an idea into written words is like defrosting the windshield: The idea, so vague out there in the murk, slowly begins to gather itself into a sensible shape" (Zinsser, 1988).

Psychotherapy, thus, is largely an inductive process in which records become a map that shows where one has been and where one should go. The initial evaluation starts the process of charting the patient's problems, goals, and progress. With each session, information becomes more detailed, helping to illuminate a path that practitioners and clients may rely upon together.

TO HELP ORGANIZE AND PROVIDE A SUPPORTIVE "CONTAINER"

Typically, patients with mental health problems experience extreme anxiety, especially in the initial evaluation, about how they may effectively express themselves. It is common for clients to report feeling overwhelmed or as if they were in a vacuum. They fear they will sound disorganized or incoherent, and wonder how a therapist could possibly understand the complexity of their problems and their debilitating confusion and fear.

Recording what our patients say about their problems and life experiences helps therapists start to identify and organize what initially may sound like disjointed fragments of information. To use Winicott's concept, records can help create a "holding environment" for our patients' experience, providing strength to us and our patients. Seemingly disparate experiences and symptoms gradually congeal into a language that can be understood and used. The record helps clarify our patients' needs and goals; what they have tried before, successfully or not, to solve their problems; and what might or might not be helpful to them. It helps us further define our respective roles and responsibilities in their treatment.

TO PROVIDE A BRIDGE TO FURTHER EXPLORATION

When we can refer to our notes on a previous session and ask our patients about their subsequent thoughts, we build bridges between sessions. Concepts and experiences discussed in previous sessions become the basis for further exploration and also may point to additional information or assistance we may require in order to better formulate accurate diagnosis and treatment plans. It also makes real for patients that even therapists need tools like record keeping to build a bridge because they are human, too, and need material aids to remember.

TO ENHANCE TRUST AND CONFIDENCE IN THE THERAPEUTIC PROCESS

On hearing their therapists refer back to what they told in a previous session, patients usually are relieved to learn they have been understood. Records can become a reflection of their successful communication, increasing their self-esteem and their confidence that they have the skills to help heal themselves.

Similarly, clients benefit from seeing their therapists use consulting notes. To my follow-up survey question about what was helpful in therapy, patients mentioned the mutually respectful collaboration between professionals. They said it was helpful to them to watch professionals pool knowledge and skills to help them solve problems; the interdisciplinary collaboration honored the complexity of their problems and taught them how they, too, could ask others for help and benefit from collective wisdom (Luepker, 1999).

TO PROMOTE ACCURACY OF RECORDS

Equally important, clients can help themselves and us along the way by correcting factual inaccuracies in our notes. Therapists are learning the "story line" for the first time. Understandably, we can misreport some facts, especially in initial evaluations when we are inundated with information. When patients review their records, they can identify factual mistakes and make a list (on a separate page) of corrections that can be inserted into their record. In addition to ensuring the accuracy of records, this exercise conveys our commitment to thoroughly understanding our clients and making them an integral part of our learning process.

TO PROMOTE SELF-DETERMINATION IN ESTABLISHING TREATMENT PLANS

Using the record to establish treatment plans with our patients promotes client self-determination and assures that treatment contracts are mutually understood and agreed upon. Participating in the process encourages patients to clarify what they want to work on and what they are not ready to work on and illuminates other important clinical information, such as what they believe about themselves and their lives.

After we have enough information from our evaluations to develop diagnoses and treatment plans, we can summarize with our patients the problems, diagnoses, goals, objectives, procedures, and estimated time for treatment. Keeping it as clear and simple as possible, staying away from jargon and close to our clients' own words, we can usually complete treatment plans on one page that anyone can readily understand. (See appendix C for a sample treatment plan form and appendix D for a sample revised treatment plan form.)

We may choose to write treatment plans prior to sessions or during sessions. Either way, by enlisting our patients' participation in clarifying and documenting treatment plans, we promote their self-determination and strengthen the treatment alliance.

Here is an example of a discussion between a therapist and client as they jointly developed a treatment plan:

Therapist: As we discussed last week, I think we are ready to establish our treatment plan. Here is a one-page treatment plan form I have found useful to document problems, goals, procedures, and outcome in treatment. It is like a road map that helps us stay clear and focused in our work together, and able to see what progress we are making toward your goals. I got started before you arrived today and began by writing down the problems you described in our first two sessions that you said you would like help with. Here they are [reads them to client]. Are these correct? Did I leave anything out?

Client: Yes, these are all the problems I told you. But I think I want to start only with the first four problems and put this last problem on hold for now. I think this is all I can manage to work on right now.

Therapist: That makes good sense to me given what you've told me. You can always decide later when and if you want to tackle this last problem. I think you are wise to clarify what you feel is manageable now and to consider timing and pacing yourself.

Therapist: Let's look at the goals now and put them in your words. As you look at these problems, what are you are hoping can be different in your life . . . or exactly what would we be seeing if you achieved the goals you described?

Client: Well, looking at the first problem, 'trouble deciding whether to stay married,' I want to be able to make a decision . . . whether to stay in my marriage and try to salvage it or else divorce my husband.

Therapist: O.K. [Writes down goal: "Make decision whether to try to salvage my marriage or divorce husband."]

Client: That sounds fine.

Therapist: You also said that you were anxious having your husband in the house because he chooses to remain involved with the other woman;

that you have been having trouble thinking clearly, focusing, and concentrating; have been unable to get to sleep and stay asleep; and that you cannot eat. Did I understand these problems? [Client indicates they are accurate and therapist writes them down on the problem list.]

In my experience with similar situations, before we can help you clarify what to do about your marriage in the long run, the first task is to work together to help you help feel more comfortable and be able to eat, sleep, and think clearly. Do those goals as a priority make sense to you? [Client agrees.] O.K., so I will write those down as your first goals. [Therapist writes down goals to "think more clearly; to be better able to focus and concentrate; to be able to get to sleep and stay asleep and to eat." Client agrees.]

From what you have told me, it sounds like your husband's living in the home is a constant hurtful reminder that he is being unfaithful to you and you therefore feel you could feel more secure if your husband were not in the home, and you have decided you would like to ask him to move out. Is that your goal? [Client agrees.] O.K., so I'll write that asking him to leave is one of your goals too.

Let's look at self-care. We talked about how caring for yourself is crucial in feeling less anxious and depressed. You mentioned you are not getting any exercise these days because you have been feeling so bad. Getting exercise a minimum of three times a week is important for everyone to maintain good mental health. But when anxious and depressed, people require more. It is important for you set goals that you feel you can really manage so you will have success. Do you feel you can begin doing something this week in the way of exercise? [Client indicates she could.] What shall we put down as your goal for this coming week?

Client: Well, I like to walk, and I think I could set a goal to walk two times this week. [Therapist adds: "self-care: walk 2X/week" to list of goals.]

Therapist: Now that we've completed the problems and goals, let's turn to diagnosis. A diagnosis is simply a name for a problem. It helps us to know what is going on and gives us ideas about possible remedies. Your insurance company also requires diagnosis in order to pay for treatment.

It looks like your distress started when you found out about the affair your husband was having with another woman. You said you were hurt, anxious, felt betrayed and confused, and started to feel really down in the dumps. You said it was like the floor dropped out from under you. You were hit from left field and now you are trying to adjust to the sudden change in your understanding of yourself, your husband, and your marriage. This constellation of problems or "symptoms" is most consistent with a diagnosis called adjustment disorder with anxiety and depressed mood. I think we should start with that to see if it is the best fit.

If you want me to bill your insurance company for your treatment, this will be the diagnosis I will use. If we need to change the diagnosis as we go along, we'll use what we are learning to fine-tune our hypothesis.

Client: [Indicates agreement with this diagnosis to be sent for billing purposes to her insurance company.]

Therapist: Now, turning to our procedures column, I am recommending we continue with 50-minute sessions once a week. Do you feel comfortable with that? [Client agrees and therapist writes that down.] If we need to change it later, we can, but let's start there.

Also, as we discussed last week, I would like to see if some of your symptoms, such as trouble focusing, concentrating, sleeping, could be caused by depression. I recommended that you consult my psychiatrist colleague for an evaluation to see if you are depressed and, if so, whether an antidepressant might help. [Client agrees and therapist writes down in procedure column: "Referral for psychiatric evaluation to clarify diagnosis and options."]

We also talked last week about the importance of my being able to routinely consult with your psychiatrist about your treatment so she and I can clarify your diagnosis and treatment planning. I would like to write that down in the procedures list and ask you to sign a form that authorizes me to consult with her as needed.

Now, looking at the section of our treatment plan that says "estimated time": It is always difficult for me, based upon my experience with similar kinds of cases, to predict how long treatment will take. So what I would like to do is for us to put a question mark here. We can assess our time frame as we go along. You can always choose to end treatment at any time. If you are making no progress or getting worse, I would have an obligation to end treatment or refer you to more appropriate help. My best guess is that you will make good progress in solving these problems, and that the time it will take to get you where you want to be will continue to come into focus as we work toward your goals.

In regard to billing, I understand you will be using the Fortunate Insurance Company, which does not require me to send in periodic requests for further sessions. Therefore, only we will be in charge of assessing what you need, and we will also be considering your psychiatrist's recommendations, too. The only information the insurance company requires is your diagnosis, so I would request that you sign this form giving me permission to send your diagnosis to them for billing purposes.

Client: O.K.

Therapist: I think this completes our treatment plan. But I also wanted to mention our outcome section here on the right side of the page. We will periodically be noting the progress you are making on solving these problems in this column. It will be helpful for us to be able to see tangible evidence of progress. We will regularly reevaluate your goals and keep track together of whether the work we are doing is helpful to you, or what we might need to be doing differently.

Client: O.K.

Therapist: I ask my clients to sign the treatment plan and I'll sign also, to show we have mutually agreed upon this plan. I will keep the plan in your record, but you are always welcome to have a copy. Would you like to have a copy now? [Client indicates it's enough just to have it in the record, does not need a copy.] Therapist places the treatment plan in the record.

Treatment Phase

After laying the groundwork in the evaluation phase, records continue to be useful throughout treatment. During treatment, practitioners can use records to enhance therapy in the following ways.

TO MONITOR PROGRESS

Progress notes allow us to see tangible progress. In the example above, the therapist appropriately realized her patient could not benefit from treatment until she was feeling more secure and physically and mentally stable. To assess the client's progress, the therapist referred to the initial treatment plan and discussed with the client how the plan was working.

Therapist: Our first goals were to help you feel more secure and to improve your sleeping, eating, and concentration. You had decided you would ask your husband to leave the home since he was choosing to remain involved with another woman; your other steps were to begin caring for yourself by beginning to get some exercise, and to consult my psychiatrist colleague about the possible need for an antidepressant. I understand that you did ask your husband to leave, that he has taken an apartment, and that you and he are cooperating in taking care of your children. It sounds like you have made good progress in that area. Have you had a chance to make an appointment with the psychiatrist yet?

Client: Yes, I have. My appointment is scheduled for next Thursday.

Therapist: [Recording that progress in the record.] Good for you. Were you able to begin exercising?

Client: I was able to walk three times this week.

Therapist: How did that feel?

Client: Walking made me feel better . . .

Therapist: Good.

In subsequent sessions, this therapist continued inquiring about and documenting her patient's sleeping and eating habits and her ability to focus, concentrate, and think clearly, all of which gradually began to improve. Even though the patient was still having marital problems, the visible signs of improvement in her symptoms of depression helped her appreciate how she was choosing not to be a victim and was more in control of her life. She and her therapist were then able to make use of therapy to explore her feelings about herself and her marriage.

TO SERVE AS A BRIDGE BETWEEN SESSIONS

Keeping progress notes after each session (even only a paragraph) provides continuity from one session to the next. A chronicle of interventions and progress allows us to move more quickly and efficiently to the next step of treatment. It creates a context within which both the client and therapist can understand the client's problems from different perspectives and make better decisions about priorities. Having a bridge between sessions also helps clients internalize their therapy and thus be able to make use of it between sessions.

In the following example, the therapist has been working with a patient who has suffered from lifelong fears of abandonment and difficulty stating her true feelings and needs to others. She had come to therapy to build self-confidence and develop communication skills so she could express her feelings and needs to her husband rather than continue to protect her true self. Before the client arrived for her appointment, the therapist reviewed progress notes from the previous session. When the client arrived, the therapist noted themes from the previous session as a bridge to identifying and exploring topics of discussion for the current session.

Therapist: I recall in our session last week, you were exploring what you wanted to say to your husband . . . as you were walking into the office today, you seemed tearful and said you were feeling anxious.

Client: I did follow through with my decision to tell him what was really on my mind, how I was feeling and what I needed. I realized after our session last week that I couldn't live anymore with myself if I didn't tell him what I was really feeling. It was hard, but I got it all out and felt relieved. But it was his response that made me upset and anxious. He became very angry and cold. It took a lot to get the courage to communicate honestly, and now I feel rejected and alone. That's why I am upset today.

TO OFFER "MIRRORING" OPPORTUNITIES

Our patients may be ashamed of their problems or feelings of helplessness. In their minds, going to a therapist only confirms their defect. What's more, they may believe the therapist can "see" them as inept and weak. Because they give clients a chance to read the therapist's factual, nonjudgmental language, records can be invaluable in reframing erroneous assumptions. This allows clients to view their problems more objectively, serves as a model for self-acceptance, and encourages more openness.

Reviewing the record with our patients also reveals differences between therapists' perceptions of patients and how patients see themselves. For example, the record may reflect that the therapist has more confidence in the patient's problem-solving skills than the patient. This may lead to discussions about the different perspectives and open doors for the client to see himself or herself in a more positive and generous light, especially when the therapist gives examples of how the client has demonstrated good problem-solving skills. It may also lead to opportunities to explain how cognitive distortions are associated with the client's major depressive disorder, or trigger questions about how she learned to discount her own value.

A striking scene in the French movie *The Little Thief* illustrates dramatically how records can become a mirror that helps shape identify development. The protagonist, a troubled adolescent girl with a history of maternal abandonment, other childhood trauma, and compulsive stealing, finds herself alone at night in the director's office of a juvenile detention center. She discovers her record on the director's desk and reads the notes. As she silently absorbs the adjectives, she sees herself through the eyes of others. This experience was life-changing for the girl because it allowed her to see herself in an entirely different way.

TO PROVIDE PERSPECTIVE

As narratives, records can help patients gain perspective and develop distance from the gripping immediacy of their distress. Patients suffering from traumatic stress, for example, often say they experience the memories of the traumatic events as though they are occurring in the present (Herman, 1995). In self-protection, they reflexively avoid speaking, feeling, or thinking about the traumatic events. Detailed narratives of traumatic events are essential to trauma patients because when the facts are made explicit through language, the patient is free to move through a gamut of emotions and grieve for unspeakable losses. Narratives, both verbal and written, allow patients to gain control over the events by creating distance from the trauma.

The usefulness of the therapists' notes can be enhanced by having clients write a specific account of the traumatic events or draw pictures of the traumatic events to place the trauma in a linear context of before, during, and after. Externalizing trauma—naming it—diminishes its timeless hold over clients and expands clients' perspective about what happened. Moreover, when clients feel ready to allow therapists to bear witness to their pain and suffering, therapists' attunement to feelings and creation of records can help validate clients' experiences and promote healing.

TO REVEAL LACK OF PROGRESS OR DETERIORATION

Records assist therapists in identifying when patients are not responding to treatment or are getting worse. In either of these circumstances, we have a responsibility to recognize the problem, reevaluate our professional services, and determine what alternative action we may need to take in our patients' interest.

In one case example, a practitioner was able to make good use of his notes to explore why his client had been deteriorating. The therapist noticed that his client's relationship with his wife had been deteriorating over a few-week period after a remarkable period of increasing intimacy between the client and his wife. By reviewing the client's treatment record, he was able to pinpoint the onset of the client's marital tailspin. He was able to ask his client what had been going on at that time that may have precipitated the deterioration in his marriage. This kind of "tracking back" helped the client reveal events that had precipitated his hopelessness in his marriage, which became the focus in treatment.

When practitioners cannot find ways to help clients make progress, options include obtaining consultation, ending treatment, or referring patients for an alternative intervention. Many therapists have asked me how to handle difficult treatment situations with patients, such as when patients are not complying with their part in the treatment contract. Many times they have found the answer in the records. By tracking patients' lack of compliance with their treatment plans and the reasons behind noncompliance, therapists have been able to open meaningful discussions with patients and determine the best option to pursue.

For example, one practitioner made a contract in which her patient agreed to be honest with the therapist. When the practitioner discovered that the patient was not being honest, but instead was secretly continuing the very behaviors for which the patient was asking the therapist for help, the therapist called the problem to her patient's attention. The therapist reminded her that therapy could not work if the patient continued these behaviors: If the patient chose to continue to conceal her behaviors from the therapist, therapy would need to end. The patient acknowledged the problem and agreed to be honest. The therapist documented the problem and renewed the contract in writing in the record, and gave a copy to the patient and to her psychiatrist.

When the therapist discovered later that the patient was continuing to conceal the truth about her behaviors, she felt surprised. Because of her countertransference feelings (disbelief in her own perception of reality, and wanting to continue to work with the patient), the therapist momentarily forgot she had already warned the patient that therapy could continue only if the patient complied with her part of the treatment contract.

Fortunately, by reviewing the record, the therapist was better able to see the patient's pattern of deception in treatment and that she and the patient had already renewed the patient's contract to be honest in therapy. The therapist realized she had no choice but to terminate treatment. Fortified by knowledge from the record, the therapist consulted the patient's psychiatrist, who agreed that therapy was untenable under the circumstances and suggested to the therapist a safe transition for the patient. The psychiatrist agreed to continue providing medications and to handle emergencies as needed, but supported the therapist's plan to initiate termination of therapy. The therapist contacted the patient, offered a closure session, presented referral options, and documented the status of the termination for the record, with copies for the patient and her psychiatrist.

Termination Phase

Bringing closure to treatment in a sensitive manner is as important as a good beginning. Records play a vital role in termination. Many patients have never had an opportunity in their lives to end a relationship constructively, which, in part, includes expressing what the relationship has meant to them. The termination phase provides a key therapeutic opportunity to review with our patients what has transpired in treatment, the extent of their progress, and what they found to be the most useful part of treatment. Documenting the status of termination with our patients, just as we created the initial or subsequent treatment plans together, is a vital part of this therapeutic task. By encouraging active participation, we help patients to conclude treatment effectively and to feel free to return to treatment in the future if they need to. (See appendix E for a sample closing summary form.)

MANAGEMENT OF COMPLEX, CHALLENGING SITUATIONS

In most instances, patients understand that records are an integral part of professional services. However, on rare occasions, patients demand at the beginning of initial evaluations that therapists keep no records. Sometimes, patients who are in the midst of treatment request that their therapists omit facts from their records. We need to make it clear to our patients at the outset the reasons for record keeping and why, therefore, neither option is acceptable or ethical. Establishing appropriate professional boundaries with our patients regarding the purposes and protocol for record keeping establishes and maintains a safe therapeutic relationship and protects practitioners from the appearance of impropriety.

SUMMARY

Record keeping has therapeutic value. When patients choose to have access to their own records, and when therapists can use records as a routine part of therapy, practitioners can promote patients' self-determination and enhance their participation in healing. Reflecting on records helps patients feel understood. They help practitioners and patients remain focused on the patients' problems and treatment goals. They help clinicians and clients see progress or lack thereof. Records serve to clarify our respective roles, boundaries, and responsibilities, and provide a vehicle for communicating, bridge building between sessions; they contribute to our patients' positive self-image.

Clinical Supervision Records

Imagine you are a clinical supervisor in an out-patient psychiatry depart-
ment of a university teaching hospital. One of your interns, a graduate stu-
dent with training and experience working with infants and children, is
providing supportive treatment to a 30-year-old married man. The client's
wife was recently admitted to the psychiatric unit of the hospital and diag-
nosed with major depressive disorder that began 12 days after the birth of
their first child. Her husband reported she had become disorganized, unable
to care for the baby, and ultimately attempted suicide. The client is distressed,
tired, and overwrought. He is attempting to care for his infant son, while
working full-time as an insurance agent in an office in his home. For reasons
that are unclear to you or your intern, the client has declined offers of help

from relatives. Your primary concerns are the father's ability to competently care for the child and whether further intervention is needed. You therefore pay careful attention to your intern's evaluation and treatment of the client and his family crisis. You are satisfied with your intern's meticulous assessment of the client's mental status and descriptions of his feelings toward daily activities with his child. You concur with the intern's conclusion that the client is adequately coping with the considerable stress associated with his wife's condition, the needs of his infant, and his job demands. Your intern follows your recommendation to encourage the client to accept the assistance of home visits from a public health nurse. He complies with this suggestion and a nurse routinely assesses the client's and baby's needs. Your intern confers with the visiting nurse and reports to you that despite the unexpected adversity, the client appears to be coping adequately. As a result, you are stunned when the chief resident in psychiatry informs you the client has been arrested for the death of his child and the client's family members may file a lawsuit against you and the clinic for mismanagement of the father's treatment and negligent supervision of an intern. You are devastated about the death of the child and filled with fear and self-recrimination when you realize you have not documented your conscientious, detailed, and consistent supervisory conferences with your intern. What do you do now?

Supervisors are responsible for their supervisees' work, unlike consultants, whose contractual arrangements are voluntary and without liability for their consultees' performance (Schoener & Conroe, 1989). In fact, inadequate or improper supervision is among the most common causes for disciplinary actions by regulatory boards (Association of State and Provincial Psychology Boards, 1998; Reamer, 1995). It is also a growing cause of action in malpractice lawsuits. Nevertheless, many clinical supervisors are unaware of fundamental tasks associated with competent supervision. Among these are the need for written, signed contracts between the supervisor and supervisee that explicitly detail the requirements for mastery of learning objectives, including protecting confidentiality and developing relevant treatment plans. Most supervisors do not put their supervisory contracts in writing, even though misunderstandings about expectations can arise between supervisors and supervisees (Kaiser, 1997). In addition to the lack of contracts, supervisors routinely fail to document supervision sessions in which they describe the client's assessments, treatment plans, and progress, as well as the supervisee's performance and where remedial efforts may be needed. Lack of documentation is a serious clinical concern. Without a written chronology of the scope and effectiveness of supervision, supervisors cannot show their reasoning and efforts to improve clients' emotional and mental health, and, most important, to prevent harm to clients. As an experienced family therapy supervisor recently lamented: "Supervisors are at the same place psychotherapists were twenty years ago—they don't understand the importance of document-ing their supervision" (W. Bera, 2001, personal communication). The pur-pose of this chapter is to describe the responsibilities of clinical supervisors, demonstrate how record keeping helps supervisors fulfill their responsibili-ties, and clarify the characteristics and contents of good supervisory records.

CLINICAL SUPERVISORS' RESPONSIBILITIES

Mental health professionals use the apprenticeship model to teach psycho-therapy. At all levels (graduate student training, internships, and prelicensure practice) trainees and new therapists learn under tutelage of trained super-visors who are responsible for overseeing and directing supervisees' assess-ment and treatment of patients. Clinical supervisors must be accessible to help supervisees assess patients' problems and needs, plan appropriate inter-vention, and handle emergencies. Good supervisors carefully identify supervisees' strengths and weaknesses and foster an open, supportive learn-ing environment in which supervisees can explore, grow, and develop confi-dence. This requires a foundation of trust so that supervisees can feel free to discuss any concerns or dilemmas about their work, no matter how simplistic or embarrassing they may seem. At the same time, supervisors are an au-thoritative source for their supervisees. Integral to good supervision is pre-senting a role model for exemplary professional boundaries and conduct. This is accomplished by reviewing supervisee records, requiring supervisees to discuss all of their cases in detail and provide rationale for their clinical decisions, and by providing feedback and recommendations to improve pa-tient care. Supervisors also regularly evaluate their supervisees, both ver-bally and in writing, and discuss their evaluations in supervision. Finally, they provide references and make employment recommendations, such as whether to retain or promote supervisees.

While the foregoing goals of clinical supervision are standards of care that supervisors need to know and implement rigorously, often this is not the case. Many supervisors lack sufficient time, funding, administrative support, or skills essential to training competent clinicians and ensuring proper care of patients. This is an area in which mental health organizations need sys-tematic review and the means to encourage and evaluate competent supervi-sion skills.

Because supervisors have great power over their supervisees, they have a fiduciary duty to take proper care of supervisees and supervisees' patients. Mental health professions' ethics codes therefore establish guidelines for training and supervision. Ethics codes hold supervisors responsible for hav-ing sufficient knowledge and skill in the clinical field they are supervising and for refraining from exploitation of their supervisees to meet supervisors' personal needs. The legal doctrine of "vicarious liability" also creates the expectation that clinical supervisors are legally accountable for providing appropriate supervision to their supervisees. Under this doctrine, if supervisees or patients can show that supervisors had a professional responsibility for them, but harmed them due to supervisory negligence, they can, in theory, sue supervisors.

HOW CLINICAL SUPERVISION RECORDS HELP SUPERVISORS FULFILL THEIR RESPONSIBILITIES

Supervisory records benefit supervisors and supervisees in many of the same ways that psychotherapy records benefit practitioners and patients. See Table 8.1 for a list of parallels between benefits of psychotherapy records and benefits of clinical supervision records.

CONFIDENTIALITY OF SUPERVISION RECORDS

Since supervision records are confidential, they must be stored with the same security procedures as psychotherapy records. Parameters of confidentiality, including exceptions, must be discussed with supervisees. When supervision records are destroyed, it may be useful to retain a brief summary of supervision activities in the event of a subsequent malpractice claim or other legal action. The same standards used to guide the destruction of clinical records apply to supervision records. Supervision records are never altered or destroyed to influence a judicial hearing.

CHARACTERISTICS AND CONTENTS OF GOOD SUPERVISION RECORDS

As with clinical records, supervision records should be clear, concise, specific, germane to the supervision plan, and free from conjectures and value judgments. Contents of good supervisory records include the following.

Face Sheet

The face sheet includes important identifying information such as the supervisee's full name, address, phone numbers, name and address of the referring organization and its relevant representative, (e.g., academic insti-

TABLE 8.1
Parallels Between Benefits of Psychotherapy Records
and Benefits of Clinical Supervision Records

Benefits of Psychotherapy Records	Benefits of Clinical Supervision Records
Help clarify presenting problems and histories of patients	Help clarify supervisees' professional strengths, weaknesses, previous professional training, experience
Help psychotherapists clarify treatment goals for clients that logically flow from clients' presenting problems and history	Help clinical supervisors establish supervisory goals and learning plans that logically flow from assessment of supervisees' learning needs
Assist psychotherapists and patients to formulate and mutually agree upon treatment plans, including treatment goals and procedures	Assist clinical supervisors to formulate and mutually agree upon learning plans, including supervision goals and procedures
Help assess progress or lack of progress in meeting treatment goals	Help assess progress or lack of progress in meeting supervisory goals
Help foster treatment alliance	Help foster collaboration in supervisory relationship
Help evaluate efficacy of treatment	Help evaluate efficacy of supervision
Provide summary of progress and outcomes of treatment and recommendations that can be used later for continuity of care	Provide summary of progress and outcomes of clinical supervision and recommendations for supervisory evaluations and letters of reference
Help psychotherapists show what they did so they can respond to a financial audit	Help clinical supervisors show what they did so they can respond to a financial audit
Help psychotherapists show that their services met the standard of professional care for psychotherapists in their professional community in the event of a regulatory board or legal complaint of psychotherapist negligence	Help clinical supervisors show that their supervisory service met the standard of professional care for clinical supervisors in their professional community in the event of a regulatory board or legal complaint of supervisory negligence

tution and academic advisor) name and professional address of the supervisor, supervision fee and billing arrangements, if any, and person to contact in case of emergency.

Supervision Contract

Just as written treatment plans help therapists and their patients assure mutual consent and appropriate attention to treatment goals, so can written contracts assist supervisors and their supervisees to assure mutual agreement and focus on supervisory goals. Written supervision contracts should always include identifying information, purposes, parameters of supervision, and the rights and responsibilities of supervisor and student. They should be signed by all relevant parties. For example, for students and interns, supervisory contracts should also be signed by graduate school representatives. For new professionals who require supervision to meet regulatory board requirements, contracts should be signed by regulatory board representatives and, if applicable, by employers who are permitting the employee to use outside supervision. For professionals who require clinical supervision to meet employment contracts, employers should sign the supervisory contracts. (See appendix K for a sample clinical supervision contract.)

Learning Needs Assessment

A key component that informs a supervision contract is the learning needs assessment. Just as psychotherapists begin by documenting the basics (such as reasons for treatment, therapists' role, and to which practitioners confidential information will be disclosed), so should supervisors document the basics. Basics include: (a) purpose for the clinical supervision, (b) number of required supervision hours, (c) types of clinical cases needed, (d) criteria for supervisory evaluation, (e) when the supervisor will need to conduct a formal evaluation of the supervisee's work, and (f) to whom the supervisor will send a written evaluation. (See sample clinical supervision contract, appendix K.)

Second, just as psychotherapists begin by documenting an assessment of client strengths and needs, so should clinical supervisors document their assessment of supervisees' professional knowledge, previous training and experience, and learning needs. (For a list of information to include in the supervisor's assessment of learning needs, see appendix K sample clinical supervision contract.)

Supervision Progress Notes

Just as psychotherapists need to document what transpires during treatment, so should supervisors document what transpires during clinical supervision. Supervisors should document the cases they discuss with their supervisees. They should include in their records specific issues and problems, clinical decisions, options considered, and recommendations to prevent risk of harm, such as suicide, violence, or sexual revictimization. Clinical supervisors should also document supervisory discussions and recommendations regarding clinical decisions that have professional boundary implications (e.g., gift giving, client invitations to social events, home visits). They should also document all discussions regarding policies and procedures for protecting confidentiality and privacy and informing clients of exceptions to confidentiality.

In psychotherapy supervision at the Medical College of Pennsylvania, Hanneman School of Medicine, Whitman and Jacobs have used written outlines of problems and goals, including estimated times for reaching goals, to foster good treatment (Whitman & Jacobs, 1998). Also, Bridge and Bascue designed a useful "Supervisory Record Form" which permits supervisors to document each psychotherapy supervisory session. Their form includes the date of the supervisory session, name of case, supervisee's concerns, supervisory goals, supervisory activity, and recommendations for each supervisory session (Bridge & Bascue, 1988). The form assists supervisors to remain focused on specific cases and on supervisees' problems and needs with their cases, and to document supervisory interventions that promote good quality care to patients.

Consent Forms

Two types of consent forms initiated at the beginning of the supervisory process should be included in supervisory records. The first type include statements that inform patients who is responsible for their care and what is involved in supervision of their care, such as supervisory discussions and supervisory review of records or audio- or videotapes. These statements can be incorporated into the notice of privacy practice. They include a list of names of all persons who will have access to patient-identifiable confidential information for supervision and how frequently cases will be reviewed. Patients' signatures are needed on these forms.

The second type of consent forms are those that inform supervisees about information shared with other persons or institutions such as graduate schools, regulatory boards, and employers. These consent forms should include the inclusive dates, name of supervisee, content, and purpose of supervisory information to be sent, and the name of the person or organization to whom the supervisory information is to be sent. These forms should be signed by the supervisee.

At the end of supervision, a third type of consent form may be needed. This type involves subsequent requests for supervisors to authorize release of their performance evaluation information. In lieu of consent forms, former supervisees should put all such requests in writing and sign them. Supervisors should maintain these requests and copies of letters or reports regarding supervisees in their files.

SUMMARY

Clinical supervisors are ultimately responsible for the care that their supervisees provide to patients, yet supervisors often overlook the importance of maintaining supervisory records. There are many parallels between the benefits of good psychotherapy records and the benefits of good supervision records. Clinical supervision records are helpful because they document supervisees' learning needs, supervisory contracts, and dates and content of supervisory contacts. They clarify supervisory goals, monitor and evaluate progress in supervision, and indicate whether supervisory interventions were timely, promoted good quality care, and reduced risk of harm to patients.

Teaching Record Keeping

Imagine you are the graduate student intern described in the previous chapter. You are horrified when the chief resident in psychiatry grimly appears at your office door to inform you that the police are charging your client with the murder of his infant son. Your heart pounds when you learn the client's family members could sue you for this incomprehensible tragedy. The resident instructs you to retrieve the client's record. You are stunned to see you did not document your detailed assessment of the client's ability to cope with strenuous job demands, being sole caretaker of his baby, and the stress of his wife being treated on an in-patient ward of a psychiatric hospital. Moreover, there is nothing in your record about your recommendations, such as enlisting the public health nurse for well baby care or developing a support network consisting of family members, friends, neighbors, and church members to reduce the client's severe stress. As your head swirls, you recall that while your supervisor was very supportive in this case, you and she never discussed the critical need for meticulous records.

Graduate students, interns, and new professionals acquire competent psychotherapy skills not only through intensive course work, but through rigorous hands-on training and clinical supervision (Krasner et al., 1998). The purpose of supervision is to help students and new professionals to apply conceptual knowledge to clinical settings. This includes making sure that students and trainees understand the relevance and necessity of systematic documentation. However, most graduate school curricula lack instruction in record keeping and clinical supervisors rarely teach it. In a study of psychology faculty providing psychotherapy supervision, respondents reported that only 10% of supervision time involved reviewing records (Tyler, Sloan, & King, 2000). The purpose of this chapter, therefore, is first to emphasize the need to make competent documentation of clinical treatment central to all training, and second, to provide specific methods of teaching record keeping. This chapter's general advice is meant to be used in conjunction with the formats, models, and examples presented in the other chapters of this text.

WHY TEACHING RECORD KEEPING IS ESSENTIAL

As we saw in the example of the overwhelmed client who killed his infant son, well-written records are essential for protecting clinicians from false allegations, as well as for proper diagnosis, treatment plans, and clinical intervention. In the event of a lawsuit or complaint to a regulatory board, a good record is the only way supervisors and supervisees can demonstrate professional and good-faith efforts to assist the client. Thus, one of the more valuable contributions instructors and supervisors can make is teaching students and trainees the importance of maintaining accurate, succinct, and germane records.

There is no substitute for routinely collaborating with students and trainees about patient records. This activity helps students and trainees as well as instructors and supervisors. It helps instructors in practice methods and in ethics courses to teach applications of clinical and ethical principles to case management. It enables supervisors to identify patients' problems and progress and helps supervisees develop appropriate goals and objectives for therapy. Repeated review of supervisees' records also improves supervisory skills and insight and expands the supervisor's repertoire of interventions with both supervisees and clients. In short, good records help instructors and supervisors become better teachers and help students and supervisees become better therapists.

METHODS FOR TEACHING RECORD KEEPING

Obtain Informed Consent From Clients for Supervisory Review of Records

Clinical supervisors must make sure that supervisees provide a written notice of privacy and practices and tell their patients in the initial session that a licensed, experienced clinician will be supervising the psychotherapy sessions, will discuss the case regularly with the supervisee, and will review and sign all records. If sessions are to be videotaped or viewed live by the supervisor and other trainees, clients must be informed and give written consent prior to the use of electronic equipment. Requiring informed consent for supervision further defines the limits of confidentiality and allows clients to determine their own boundaries of safety and privacy. Explicit discussions regarding supervision establish a foundation of trust with clients and respect in the therapeutic relationship, and they foster clients' sense of control and self-determination.

Assess Record-Keeping Knowledge and Create Learning Objectives

Teaching of record keeping in the classroom or in supervision should be systematic. The first step is to find students' or supervisees' baseline knowledge of the topic. This can be done through pre-assessments. Assessments ask students and trainees to list what needs to be included in competent records and to describe their philosophy about record keeping and rationale for their position. Assessments show learning gaps and identify what ideas influence students' and supervisees' values and beliefs about the role records play in therapy. After completing the learning needs assessment, the next step is to establish learning objectives. Instructors should include the following in their course syllabi and clinical supervisors should include these in their supervision contracts:

- record-keeping learning objectives
- activities which the learning objectives require
- standards for mastery of the learning objectives
- methods instructors and supervisors will use to evaluate successful completion of the learning objectives

Clinical supervisors should be sure that supervision contracts routinely include careful review of, and feedback about, the interns' or new professionals' records. (See chapter 8 for further discussion of supervision contracts). Supervisees should be encouraged to read sample records and evaluate their own record-keeping abilities. Progress toward increasingly effective record keeping should be discussed and noted. Similarly, persistent problems should be addressed throughout supervisees' training.

Use Contemporaneous Case Material

Teaching record keeping during hands-on experience with clients is generally more direct than what can be offered in the classroom. Supervisors have access to contemporaneous notes. Also, the content of records need not be altered to protect confidentiality. An added benefit of teaching record keeping during direct supervision is greater control over the standard of care and over records for which supervisors are ultimately professionally responsible. However, classroom instructors can use disguised case notes and ask students to critique and rewrite the notes more appropriately. Or, they can present videotaped therapy sessions and ask students how they should be documented. For example, the HBO series *The Sopranos*, which can be purchased in stores that sell videotapes, depicts numerous therapy sessions. These case vignettes can be used in practice methods and ethics courses to evoke record-keeping exercises.

Provide Outline for Record Keeping

Instructors and supervisors should provide supervisees or students with an outline of what to include in, or exclude from, records. For example, chapter 3 presents a detailed discussion of characteristics and contents of good records. Supervisors should use categories from the outline, give specific examples, explain the basis for each point, and emphasize that consistency in record-keeping format makes clinicians' jobs easier and pertinent information more accessible.

Begin With Supervisees' or Students' Observations

Supervisory sessions should begin with what supervisees or students have experienced or observed during their sessions with patients. The ways in which supervisors structure their questions about the supervisees' client interviews can help supervisees learn ways to organize interview data into a useful format to increase their understanding of clients' needs and the best plan for treatment. Once supervisees have freely discussed an initial case, it can be helpful for supervisors to consider with supervisees how supervisees can state the interview material in their records. Teachers can take a similar approach, basing classroom discussion of potential approaches on disguised process notes of a psychotherapy case or on a videotaped interview suitable for classroom use.

Guide Supervisees in Putting Observations in Outline Form

Once supervisees and students have had an opportunity to discuss their observations of the case, the supervisor can guide the student to consider how observations can best be stated in written form. Referring to the beginning of a model record-keeping outline, which is presented in chapter 3, for example, supervisors and teachers can ask their supervisees or students to tell them who the client is: name, age, marital status, race, ethnicity, or other characteristics, occupation, and who referred the client. Supervisors should then ask how supervisees or students would succinctly record that kind of *identifying information* in writing in the record. Supervisors or teachers might give examples of how they record identifying information in their own records.

Moving on to the next category in the model outline presented in chapter 3, supervisors or teachers can ask supervisees and students to state what the client states are his problems or reasons for needing help. They then should ask how these *presenting problems* could be stated in the record.

Proceeding to the next category, supervisors and teachers can ask supervisees and students to tell the *history of problems*, starting with their onset, circumstances surrounding onset of problems, and how they would succinctly document the history of problems in the record.

Provide Continuous Realistic Feedback

Continuous realistic feedback promotes learning. When supervisees or students identify appropriate information to include in the record, the supervisor should reinforce the importance of the students' points and note why these are good record-keeping practices. Supervisors and teachers should always validate supervisees' inclinations to record information that supports their diagnoses and treatment plans.

Reflect on Characteristics and Contents of Good Records

Supervisors should help supervisees or trainees to distinguish between relevant and irrelevant and useful and not-useful language by continually reflecting upon a list of characteristics and contents of good records (see chapter 3). Unlimited opportunities exist for supervisors to seize "teachable moments" to help students become proficient in writing clear, relevant professional records.

For example, if students include irrelevant information in a record entry, supervisors can return students' attention to the outline presented in chapter 3: "Let's refer back to our record-keeping outline that tells us what we state in a record must be limited to what is relevant to the patient's diagnosis and treatment. How is the information you included relevant to the patient's diagnosis and treatment?" Supervisors should let supervisees work to learn how to discriminate. Struggling with tough questions is an invaluable learning tool. Supervisors should probe for the basis of the students' decisions and let them explore even better options.

Supervisors should explain that direct quotes from clients are preferable to paraphrasing because quotes are concrete statements that are less likely to be misinterpreted.

It is critical also for supervisors to teach beginning therapists how to discriminate between problem-centered and value-laden language. Considering examples of each type, and inviting discussion of them, is a good teaching tool. When supervisees or students use jargon or potentially detrimental language, supervisors can turn this into a learning experience by asking further questions to steer them away from this practice.

For example, if supervisees use a comment that sounds prejudicial, supervisors can ask supervisees to consider the following: "What does our outline in chapter 3 say about the importance of value-free language? How can we determine whether the language in our records comes across as judgmental or prejudicial?"

Supervisors can let their supervisees generate answers, then expand upon these, using follow-up questions: "What happens to our choice of words when we write from the perspective of being in our client's shoes?" "Could the same information be stated in another less biased way? How would you do that?"

Supervisors should clarify when even relevant material, such as the gender of a client's partner, may be unsuitable to include in the record. Supervisors should help supervisees consider alternative ways to address sensitive information in the record.

Instructors and supervisors should also help students and trainees discriminate between information that is important to discuss in supervision yet may be inappropriate to include in patient records. For example, it is crucial for supervisees to feel free to speak in supervision about all feelings toward their clients, including sexual attraction. However, stating countertransference feelings in the record is not necessary or helpful. Instructors and supervisors can use the discussion about inappropriate contents in chapter 3 as a resource in the classroom and in supervision.

SUMMARY

Writing and maintaining good clinical records are central to effective psychotherapy and ethical practice. However, graduate schools rarely teach these skills. For this reason, most student and post-graduate therapists enter supervised clinical experiences with no theoretical or practical framework for understanding or implementing competent record keeping. This lack of skills carries over to institutional settings, where inattention to records deprives patients and students of best quality in professional services.

The purpose of this chapter is to make students, professors, graduate school administrators, and supervisors outside of the academic setting aware of the need for systematic instruction on why and how to write and maintain effective clinical records. Included are examples of the broad implications of inadequate records and methods for teaching specific skills inherent in competent clinical record keeping.

Psychotherapists and Records in the Legal System

Imagine a process server arriving at your office door with a subpoena for a client's records. Now what do you do? Your client has asked you to disclose his records in his legal case. But you believe that sharing his records with his attorney could be harmful to the client. What are your options?

Psychotherapists often have trouble answering these kinds of questions because they lack knowledge of the legal system. Consequently, even seasoned practitioners lose their bearings. They begin questioning their clinical judgment and struggle with how to respond when they receive subpoenas or when attorneys pressure them, telling therapists they are "obliged" to release their patients' records. One practitioner told me he became so anxious in response to an attorney's demands that he lost his usual composure and handed over his client's entire original record to the attorney. He needed help thinking through his options before acting. He is not alone. Nearly all conscientious practitioners worry about the personal and professional ramifications of being pulled into litigious situations.

Information about the legal system helps practitioners to better serve their clients and to protect their practices. It allows them to identify options for appropriate professional relationships with patients and attorneys. Knowledge of the legal process helps therapists form their policies and be more systematic about goals, interventions, and documentation regarding clients. When practitioners have patients' authorization and when they conclude, based upon their professional judgment, that they should disclose records in a legal matter, therapists can learn to incorporate the legal experience into the therapeutic relationship. Accruing knowledge and skills about therapists' proper roles in the legal process builds confidence and reduces anxiety. In short, with knowledge, neither practitioners nor their clients need to be victims of the legal system.

This chapter provides an orientation to the legal system. It provides practical information and methods to help practitioners function more comfortably inside or outside of the system. The first section gives an overview of what makes therapists worry about the legal system. The second section stresses the importance of practitioners clarifying their roles. The subsequent section offers information and guidance to practitioners for handling various types of requests for patient records, such as attorneys' calls, subpoenas, and court orders. The fourth section presents information about interactions with the legal system and how practitioners can conduct themselves appropriately. The following section describes the process of preparation for testimony in depositions and the courtroom. The next section summarizes techniques for giving testimony, and the final section discusses the management of clinical issues that arise when patients are in legal disputes and when therapists become involved in their patients' legal cases.

THERAPISTS AND THE ADVERSARIAL PROCESS

Why Practitioners Worry: Clinical and Ethical Reasons

The following are clinical and ethical reasons why psychotherapists worry about becoming involved in their patients' legal cases:

LOSS OF CONFIDENTIALITY INTERRUPTS THERAPY

Therapy is no longer confidential when practitioners release psychotherapy records to the attorneys who are representing their patients in a legal matter. When confidentiality ends, therapy is interrupted. As a result, there are privileged communication laws that give patients the right to decide whether their confidential disclosures in therapy are revealed to courts.

A celebrated example of a client's right to privileged communication in federal courts was upheld by the U.S. Supreme Court in the *Jaffee v. Redmond* (1996) case. This case involved Karen Beyer, a clinical social worker, and her psychotherapy patient, Chicago police officer Marylu Redmond, who was charged with violating the constitutional rights of Ricky Allen, Sr., a man whom she killed on duty responding to a fight at an apartment complex. Attorneys for the deceased victim's family demanded access to Redmond's psychotherapy record, hoping to unearth further evidence of Redmond's guilt. However, Beyer refused to release her patient's record because Redmond

had not authorized her to do so. Beyer's attorneys argued that Beyer had acted lawfully in refusing to release her patient's record without the patient's authorization. Under Illinois law, they noted, communications between clinical social workers and their psychotherapy patients were "privileged," providing patients with the legal right to choose to keep their psychotherapy records out of court. The lower court agreed with Beyer's position, but a federal appeals court overturned the lower court's ruling. Ultimately, the U.S. Supreme Court heard the case. Numerous mental health professions rallied to support Beyer's position and submitted respective *amicus* briefs with detailed reasons why patients required confidentiality in psychotherapy.

The U.S. Supreme Court recognized the necessity for confidentiality in psychotherapy. Writing for the Court, Justice Stevens noted that "Effective psychotherapy depends upon an atmosphere of confidence and trust, and therefore the mere possibility of disclosure of confidential communications may impede development of the relationship necessary for successful treatment" (*Jaffee v. Redmond*, 1996). The Court therefore upheld Beyer's patient's right to withhold her psychotherapy records in federal court. Justice Stevens stated that "The federal privilege which clearly applies to psychiatrists and psychologists, also extends to confidential communication made to licensed social workers in the course of psychotherapy."

HARM CAN ARISE FROM DUAL ROLES

Psychotherapists also understand their ethical responsibility to refrain from engaging in dual roles that could harm their clients. When therapists serve as witnesses in their patients' court cases, they take on a dual role. Sometimes engaging in the roles of both witnesses and therapists can be harmful, at other times it is less harmful, and in some instances it may not be harmful at all. In all instances, it can interrupt the work of current therapy.

EXAMPLES OF POTENTIAL HARM IN DIFFERENT TYPES OF LEGAL CASES

The following types of legal cases give examples of various levels of potential harm and how therapy is interrupted when therapists release records and engage in dual roles by becoming witnesses in their clients' legal cases.

Child Custody and Visitation Lawsuits. Parents who are divorcing frequently ask their children's psychotherapists to release their children's records or to testify in custody and visitation disputes. It potentially can be harmful to the child and the family to do so even when both parents give the therapist permission to release their child's therapy records and to testify. During the crisis of their parents' marital dissolution, children under psychological stress require their therapists' supportive neutrality. When therapists testify, parents and children perceive therapists as taking sides or making judgments. This has a chilling effect on children's comfort in therapy. Judith Wallerstein, an acclaimed researcher on the effects of divorce on children, strongly asserts that children's and parent's mental health records are usually "irrelevant" in child custody and visitation cases (J. Wallerstein, 2002, personal communication). If courts require mental health evaluations, they should appoint independent examiners.

Personal Injury Lawsuits. Testifying regarding the facts of diagnosis and treatment in personal injury cases also interrupts therapy. However, it can be potentially less harmful for two reasons. First, in personal injury cases it is routine for the courts to review all medical records. When patients choose to claim damages in a personal injury case, courts must examine all past and current records to determine whether the alleged "events" have caused harm to the patient or have exacerbated pre-existing conditions. Therefore, attorneys for patients and defendants gather and review all of the patient's medical records. Sometime they also request that therapists provide reports or testimony regarding their patients' diagnoses and treatment. Patients' attorneys hope that records will provide evidence of psychological damage. Defense attorneys hope to prove that the patient's problems are unrelated to the alleged charges.

Second, unlike children in custody and visitation cases, patients are in control of whether or not to file personal injury suits. If they choose to continue with the lawsuit, they must give their therapists permission to release their psychotherapy records. If they do not want anyone to see their records, they can choose not to file the personal injury claim.

However, even when patients are in control of deciding whether to file the lawsuit and ask their therapists to release their records or to testify, psychotherapists have good reasons to worry about the potential negative impact on therapy when their clients' records are used in the adversarial system. Defense attorneys attempt to use the information in the records to argue against clients' claims and clients end up feeling on trial themselves. Psychotherapists sometimes also feel manipulated by patients and attorneys whose apparent primary goals are to "use" testimony about therapy in order to provide supporting evidence that the patients have required therapy to treat the "damage." When a positive outcome of their legal case is their first priority, patients often discontinue therapy once the legal case is over.

Capital Mitigation Cases.   In capital mitigation cases, the question before the court is whether to confer a sentence of life imprisonment or of death. These cases are rare examples of times when patients have little to lose by authorizing the release of their records. Defense attorneys must be able to find evidence of trauma and mental illness or other impairment to develop "mitigating factors" which would augment their arguments against the death penalty. Defense attorneys, therefore, often ask their clients' therapists to testify regarding their knowledge of clients' life history, diagnoses, and treatment. Thus, unlike other circumstances, it may be unethical to refuse to release records or testify in capital mitigation cases when patients have requested that their therapists do so.

Why Therapists Worry:
Parallel Universes of Attorneys and Therapists

Even beyond ethical and clinical conflicts, therapists also feel anxious because the legal system is unknown terrain. The following describes some of the vast differences between attorneys and psychotherapists.

Therapists and attorneys have different goals and different methods of achieving their goals. The goal of the legal system is to arrive at the "truth." The process is an adversarial process in which there is a "winner" and a "loser," where each "side" declares its position to be "right." The aim is to "win" by proving the merits of one's case and by exposing weaknesses in the opposing party's argument.

By contrast, the goal of psychotherapy is to increase the client's well-being by ameliorating unwanted symptoms. The process is a cooperative one that constructively promotes patients' ability to act in their own best interests and improves patients' mental health and interpersonal relationships. Effective psychotherapy sometimes involves confrontation, but it is not adversarial.

Lawyers are often confused by therapists' jargon and the inexactness inherent in psychotherapy. They become frustrated when psychotherapists answer their questions with "It depends . . ." and then begin a lengthy discussion about the conditions under which x or y would be true. For their part, therapists cannot understand attorneys' insistence that they "cut to the bottom line" and "get to the point." One attorney told a therapist: "If you have a point, I'd appreciate it if you got to it soon."

Therapists see people and their problems as complex. In their view, life cannot easily be assigned to the narrow areas of black and white, but must be lived in the interminable shades of gray that require constant scrutiny and redefining. Therapists lament feeling pressured or "manipulated" by attorneys while attorneys see this as simply "achieving goals." Therapists often feel that lawyers are being "argumentative" while lawyers insist they are merely "discussing issues" and telling therapists "not to take it personally."

Most therapists either feel that forensic work is in conflict with therapeutic goals, or they simply dislike the adversarial process. They do not want the stress of public scrutiny and the risk to their reputations or livelihoods. At best, working in the legal system is a challenging experience. At worst, it is an overwhelming ordeal. Mental health practitioners who serve as witnesses in depositions or in court are subjected to professional slurs ("How much are you being paid for your testimony, doctor?"). Also, their testimony is memorialized on transcripts and used in subsequent testimony to undermine their credibility ("Isn't it true that in the Smith vs. Jones case that you said . . . ?").

Growing Trend Toward "Forensic" Specialization

Still, a growing number of mental health professionals do elect to engage in specialized forensic work. Such work includes conducting evaluations for custody, adoption, divorce, personal injury, competence, and sanity. Psychotherapists are more motivated now than ever before to expand into other areas, including forensics, to supplement what they can earn providing psychotherapy. The influence of HMOs and the trend toward biomedicine have resulted in increasing emphasis on psychopharmacology and on brief treatment. Large business-oriented companies are limiting therapy to 4–20 sessions and requiring therapists to "justify" additional sessions, even for patients with complex conditions. Thus many psychotherapists have become "refugees," looking for alternative career opportunities.

Some practitioners also see other, more altruistic benefits in forensic work. For these professionals, it is rewarding to use their professional knowledge to educate juries about highly complex matters. For example, a mental health professional who has conducted mental health evaluations and provided testimony in capital mitigation cases feels she has made a difference by informing courts about the impact of pervasive developmental delays and the effects of chronic childhood abuse and neglect on children's loss of control over their violent impulses. Another mental health professional has found it rewarding to educate juries about the effects of psychological trauma in personal injury cases.

Psychotherapists' Need for Information

Even when practitioners are not pursuing forensic specialization, it is important that all therapists have a basic understanding of the adversarial process. Because of the increasing litigiousness in the United States, many experienced practitioners have told me they are receiving subpoenas or letters from attorneys for the first time. Practitioners can now assume that sometime in their careers they are likely to become involved in a legal case. Knowledge is their best tool.

DEFINING ONE'S ROLE

Understanding and Communicating Practitioners' Roles to Patients

When practitioners wish to minimize their involvement in court cases, they should make their policies clear to their patients at the outset. If clients are involved in legal proceedings, or believe they will be, practitioners may best serve such patients and themselves by referring them to therapists whose practice includes forensic work.

Even when psychotherapists circumscribe the boundaries of their practices, this does not guarantee that they will not become involved in a legal case that may arise years later. Patients may become embroiled in legal matters years after termination of their therapy. The following is an illustration of a former patient's legal case and need for records arising years after the patient ended therapy.

A psychologist who meticulously guards her patients' privacy and confidentiality had treated a patient 5 years before the patient opted to leave an emotionally abusive marriage. In desperation, the patient's spouse made erroneous allegations regarding her mental instability. The patient feared that these unfounded allegations could plant doubt about her in the minds of the court-appointed child custody evaluators. She and her attorney therefore asked her former therapist to write a letter about her psychological status during her previous treatment. The patient's former therapist agreed to summarize the minimum necessary to fulfill the intended purpose in a letter to the patient's attorney, which proved extremely helpful to the patient. Nevertheless, even when such circumstances cannot be foreseen, clarifying policies about forensic involvement does help to define practitioners' areas of expertise and professional focus.

Distinctions Between Treatment Witnesses and Evaluation Witnesses

In addition to clarifying policies regarding their involvement in legal cases, it is crucial for psychotherapists to understand (a) what an expert witness is and (b) the distinction between experts who are treatment witnesses and those who are evaluation witnesses. The following defines *expert witness* and discusses the respective roles of treatment and evaluation witnesses.

EXPERT WITNESSES

Expert witnesses are persons who, by virtue of training and experience, can provide an opinion about a specific topic or question that the court requires in order to make a determination of fact. Mental health practitioners are used as experts in legal matters because of their professional education, training, and experience in social sciences or medicine. They generally fall into one of two categories: treatment experts or evaluation experts. Most therapists who testify in court cases are treatment experts.

THE ROLE OF TREATMENT WITNESSES

Psychotherapists are often called as treatment or "fact" witnesses because they have worked to assess, diagnose, or treat the client. In this capacity, they may be asked to testify about their assessments of, and interventions with, the client and about the client's progress and prognosis. Treatment witnesses' testimony is limited to such facts pertaining to their assessment and treatment of their clients.

For example, in a disputed custody case, a mother alleged that the father had a history of having made numerous suicide attempts in front of their preschool-age child. She believed this adversely affected the father's capacity to care for the child. The court requested information from the father's therapist to help determine whether contact would harm the child: including how the father was referred to the therapist, his diagnosis, progress in treatment, the therapist's opinion regarding the father's mental condition including risk for suicide, and his prognosis. The father gave his therapist permission to disclose the information requested by the court. The therapist complied with the mother's attorney's request to submit written answers under oath to the attorney's questions ("interrogatories") and also cooperated after receiving a court order to testify in a court hearing about her diagnostic opinions and the course of the father's treatment.

It is important for therapists to clearly define with their clients and their patients' attorneys their role in legal proceedings. Practitioners have often told me, for example, that they feel "responsible" for whether their patients "win" or "lose" their legal cases. It is easy for clients, also, to feel confused about their therapists' role. Patients and therapists alike need to understand that the patients' attorneys, not the therapists, are responsible for advocating for patients in the legal system. The therapist's role is limited to providing professional opinions based on their professional training and experience and to answering questions about information contained in the clients' privileged file with the minimum necessary.

Even when therapists carefully define their limited role in a legal case, therapists' professional opinions may be inconsistent with the goals of the legal case or with the client's expectations. When this happens, it may cause serious problems in the client–therapist relationship. This is one more reason why it is critical to discuss candidly with clients throughout the course of therapy the therapist's impressions regarding diagnoses, treatment, and progress, as well as the limits of confidentiality. (See chapters 5 and 7 for further discussion of these issues.)

For example, if a client with a diagnosis of narcissistic personality disorder files a personal injury claim and requests that his therapist produce a copy of his records to his attorney, he is likely to become upset if he learns only through court proceedings the nature of his diagnosis and how it may be perceived by the jury. The therapist, client, and client's attorney must be open and honest about the information the therapist will reveal and how it will be presented. When cases go to trial, all parties need to be prepared for both direct examination by the client's lawyer and for cross-examination by the opposing attorney.

It is difficult if not impossible to continue therapy when clients are aware that their records will be used in court and that opposing attorneys will attempt to use all of the information in their records against them. It is easy to see how these two roles—therapists as clinical advocates and therapists as treatment witnesses—may work counter to one another and how therapists' assuming both roles can seriously strain even the strongest therapeutic alliances.

THE ROLE OF EVALUATION WITNESSES

There are many ways that the role of evaluation experts differs from the role of treatment witnesses. Unlike treatment witnesses, evaluation witnesses' clients are either the attorneys or judges who have hired or appointed them. Unlike therapist witnesses, their job is to systematically review all records, past and current, in order to formulate professional opinions pertaining to the questions in the legal case. Even though their mental health examinations are similar to those conducted by therapists, evaluation witnesses' focus, unlike the therapists' focus, is on information required to answer questions in the legal case. Unlike therapists, evaluation witnesses also know from the start that they cannot promise confidentiality to their evaluees. Their job is to either consult with attorneys or to prepare and send their evaluation reports to the attorneys who have hired them or to the courts that have appointed them. Finally, evaluation witnesses cannot predict whether their findings will be adverse to their evaluees' legal case.

Therefore, to be ethical, the evaluation witness needs to inform the evaluee of the purpose of the evaluation prior to beginning the evaluation, including parameters and limits of confidentiality. The evaluation witness should then obtain informed consent to conduct the evaluation and release the findings. Evaluation witnesses should provide an informed consent form for evaluees to read prior to the evaluation and discuss and sign at the first meeting with the evaluation witness. (See appendix L for a sample consent form used by evaluation witnesses in personal injury cases.)

The court (judge) can appoint evaluation witnesses to answer questions posed by the court (such as competency or sanity) or to confidentially assist either litigant in preparing their cases. In some instances, attorneys may privately hire experts. This is often true in civil litigation, when clients have the means to hire their own attorneys. However, a large proportion of criminal cases involve indigent clients who cannot afford to retain private attorneys.

Evaluation witnesses range from educational diagnosticians to psychiatrists. Evaluation experts assess the evaluee. All licensed mental health practitioners who are trained in the diagnosis of emotional and mental disorders can conduct mental health evaluations, but different specialties may use different assessment techniques in a case. A psychologist, for example, may conduct cognitive or personality testing. A neuropsychiatrist may administer the Halstread-Retan Neurological Battery. A psychiatrist may look for medical causes of behavior. A clinical social worker may conduct a lengthy psychosocial evaluation.

Evaluation witnesses provide their results and professional opinions to the attorney who has appointed them, not the evaluees, and they bill the attorneys or the court for their time. The attorney decides whether the information is helpful. If so, she decides how to incorporate it into the case; if not, she discards it. Courts use evaluation witnesses' findings as a basis for their legal rulings. If the attorney decides to use the confidential expert's information, the results must be divulged to the other side prior to going to court under rules of "discovery."

In some instances, there may be two or more evaluation experts evaluating a client. Some cases boil down to a "battle of the experts," where experts from each side offer different opinions. In a recent homicide case a psychiatrist and psychologist had very different views about a client's competence to stand trial. The psychiatrist, who had seen the client for only 7 days at a local hospital, opined that the client was depressed but able to understand the charges against him and to assist his counsel. The psychologist, who had visited the client for a longer period and had seen him under a variety of circumstances, including a period when he was hearing voices and tried to commit suicide, said that the combination of his low I.Q. (69), his severe childhood neglect and abuse, and his escalating depression rendered him unable to assist his counsel meaningfully or act in his own best interest. When such a conflict occurs, it is left to the judge or jury to decide what to believe. In this case, the judge said the client was competent and the trial proceeded.

Evaluation experts have a very different kind of professional relationship with evaluees than do the treatment experts. It is short lived. The process can be synthetic and intrusive. The two are not working together to achieve the client's goals or to alleviate the client's suffering. Rather, evaluation experts are objectively observing and assessing evaluees. This may involve asking evaluees to arrange colored blocks or discuss intimate details of their childhoods. Evaluees know that the information will be given to their attorneys or to the courts. In either event, evaluees are not providing information at their own pace, in the context of a trusting relationship that has developed over time, and the information will not remain privileged. Moreover, evaluators may reach conclusions that may or may not be adverse to the client's legal case and which evaluees may perceive to be incorrect, hurtful, or embarrassing.

However, practitioners who assume the role of evaluation experts should not leave their clinical skills at the door of the evaluation office. They have the same ethical duty to protect the dignity of clients as do treating experts. They must carefully inform the evaluees at the outset of their role and the nature of the evaluation, including the fact that it is not possible to predict whether the evaluation findings will be adverse to the law case. Evaluation witnesses and referring attorneys must decide which of the two will reveal the results of the evaluation findings to the evaluees and how and when this will occur. Evaluees should not have to learn for the first time in court that they have trouble understanding complex situations. They should not hear the details of their sexual abuse in a public setting without first having an opportunity to receive information or explanations about the nature and importance of the evaluation experts' testimony.

HANDLING ATTORNEYS' REQUESTS, SUBPOENAS, COURT ORDERS, AND SEARCH WARRANTS

Requests for patients' records or for therapists' professional opinions or testimony come in many forms. The following are frequent types of requests and ways that therapists can handle them.

Calls and Letters From Attorneys

For both treatment and evaluation witnesses, it is imperative to continuously observe the boundaries of confidentiality. Unless psychotherapists have a signed authorization with specific instructions from their patients, they cannot communicate with anyone, including their clients' attorneys, about them. Evaluation witnesses cannot communicate with anyone except the attorney who has hired them without the evaluees' authorization. Therapists and evaluation witnesses should say, "I can neither confirm nor deny knowledge of this person without signed authorization." Therapists should then talk with their clients (or previous clients) about the calls or letters. Evaluation witnesses should speak with the attorneys or courts who have hired them about the calls or letters.

Practitioners who serve as treatment or evaluation witnesses may talk with an independent forensic consultant at any stage of a legal case—and it is often immensely helpful to do so—as long as they do not use names or reveal privileged information. For example, a therapist might say:

> I have been treating a client for five years, and she has recently decided to file a lawsuit about her employer's sexual harassment, which she claims has caused her to lose her job. Her attorney just telephoned me and insists that I send my client's complete file to him. I feel I cannot acknowledge that I even know this client to callers without her authorization, and I do not want to send the records. There are embarrassing details in her file, so I think her records could be harmful to her lawsuit. What do I do?

Subpoenas

A subpoena (the word officially means "under pain of") is a legal mandate, issued in the name of the court, but generally signed by an attorney or clerk of the court. Subpoenas may be requests for copies of records only, and the practitioner isn't asked to appear in person. Other subpoenas (called *subpoena duces tecum*) are requests that the practitioner appear at a legal hearing (e.g., deposition or court hearing) and bring whatever records are specified.

Subpoenas are a process that allows attorneys to collect information and develop their cases in a number of different circumstances with the professional expectation being that they will not abuse this right.

While all subpoenas require a response from the clinician in order to avoid contempt of court charges, a subpoena is only a type of third party request. Therefore, subpoenas should not be responded to in an automatic manner. Patients are not requesting the information, so subpoenas do not necessarily supersede the clinician's responsibility to protect their patients' or clients' confidentiality. A subpoena, for example, isn't sufficient to open substance abuse treatment records and shouldn't be enough to open privileged mental health records. Substance abuse treatment records, for example, require a court order signed by a judge to release them. Other treatment records that might require a court order signed by a judge are outlined in individual state statutes.

Therefore, when clinicians receive subpoenas, they should contact their clients to determine the following: whether they are aware of the subpoena and understand its purpose, whether the psychotherapy records are actually needed (for example, psychotherapy records may not be required in personal injury civil lawsuits if the plaintiff's psychological condition is not an issue), and if they wish the information to be released. If the patient or client indicates that he or she wants the information released, the practitioner should obtain a signed release from the client before submitting the information to the requesting person or agency. If there are delays in obtaining informed consent, the practitioner should respectfully contact the person issuing the subpoena to explain the need for time.

Even when clients have signed authorizations for releases of their psychotherapy records in their attorneys' offices, often patients do not understand the implications of what they are signing. Therefore, practitioners can help by suggesting that patients seek clarification from their attorneys about how their treatment records will be used in their legal cases. Only with adequate information can clients give informed consent for release of their psychotherapy records and even for pursuing their own legal cases.

In matters involving a subpoena, if the client or patient indicates that they do not want the information released, then the clinician should contact the attorney representing the patient or client and have this attorney fill in the papers required to quash the subpoena. *Quash* means to "squash," and is the legal means by which to avoid honoring a subpoena. There must be grounds to quash a subpoena, such as confidentiality.

Practitioners should carefully read the subpoena in order to determine the date by which they must respond to a subpoena. When timing is a problem—for example, there isn't sufficient time to contact clients for authorization to release their confidential information or if clinicians have compelling clinical or personal duties that conflict with the timing of the requested appearances—practitioners may exercise the option to respectfully request that the attorneys or court reschedule their appearances.

When practitioners submit confidential treatment information in response to a subpoena, clinicians should compile a summary of the treatment: condensing the information so as best to comply with their ethical duty to provide the minimum necessary. This process, and all communications such as telephone calls or letters, should be documented in patients' records. With their summaries, practitioners should enclose copies of authorizations of releases of confidential information signed by their patients or clients.

Therapists should never release their clients' original records to anyone. They should release only copies. Both treatment and evaluation witnesses should always document any releases of copies of records—for example, what they have released, and to whom. Documentation of release of treatment records should include dates of treatment covered.

Two final words to the wise: First, it is always important for practitioners to use their professional judgment regarding whether release of records could be potentially harmful to their clients. Second, therapists also need to determine whether the subpoena is bona fide. In rare instances, clients have created and issued false subpoenas. The following case example illustrates how a therapist used her professional judgment to protect her client's welfare and paid attention to detail in the subpoena.

A father who had allegedly physically abused his son obtained his son's former treatment records from the boy's former therapist by issuing a fake subpoena to the former therapist. The boy's former therapist erroneously believed that the subpoena was real and mailed copies of the boy's records to the name of the person on the subpoena. Later the father woke the boy in the middle of the night and read the boy's former therapist's notes to him. The father appeared subsequently in the boy's current therapist's office, with another bogus subpoena, asking for her clinical notes. The current therapist had, in the meantime, learned from the boy how his father had misused the boy's previous records. She suspected that this subpoena was also fake. She reminded the father that she had already offered to meet with him to discuss his questions. She stated she could not, however, release the boy's records because she understood he had misused the boy's records before. She stated that, therefore, in her professional judgment, it could be harmful to the boy to share the boy's records with the father. The current therapist also stated she believed the subpoena was not bona fide. At this point, the father backed down and said he would "tear up the subpoena" and did so. Clues to the boy's therapist that the father's subpoena was bogus: (a) it was printed on regular copy paper instead of the heavier bond paper, and (b) when the therapist called the court to check if the case number was active, the court clerk informed her it was not.

Court Orders

A court order is a legal mandate signed by a judge. Generally practitioners respond to the request of the judge in the manner indicated in the court order. A clinician cannot quash a court order, because it is the judge making the order. To get the court order reversed, the clinician would need to appeal the judge's decision to the next higher court. Generally, the clinician must have good legal grounds to do so because higher courts look with disfavor on "interim" appeals, i.e., appeals in the middle of the case. Also, appealing the order could anger the judge, which may strategically be unwise, depending upon what the case is. When clinicians choose to appeal a judge's decision, they should consult legal counsel.

However, judges are available for discussion, or are at least in a position to read a letter. When clinicians are concerned about sending the information in the form requested by attorneys or judges, clinicians may respectfully explain their concerns to judges. This can be done by telephone or in the form of letters. When practitioners respectfully and clearly express legitimate ethical and clinical concerns, practitioners have discovered that judges generally try to heed their concerns.

For example, psychotherapists in several states throughout the country have respectfully written to family court judges about their ethical concerns in becoming involved in custody and visitation disputes of their minor child patients, even at the request of both parents. They have informed judges in the form of a letter about their ethical duty to "do no harm" to their clients. Psychotherapists have explained how they were hired by the family members to serve in a neutral role as therapist. Practitioners have clarified how, in their professional opinion, becoming involved in a custody battle would require them to step out of their neutral role and thereby potentially harm the family. Judges have, in most instances, responded affirmatively to psychotherapists' respectful letters explaining ethical dilemmas and potential harm to children. (See appendix M for an example of a letter to a judge.)

Some practitioners have protected their child patients from potential harm by exercising the option to request that the state's attorney file a motion to "show cause" why the parents should have their psychotherapy records. Practitioners have chosen this option, for example, in instances when a parent is accused of suspected child abuse and issues a subpoena for the child's records through his or her attorney as a way to seek information to discredit the child. In this way, judges can become aware of a parent's intent and be in a position to explore the potential harm to the child and whether or not the parent's request should be allowed.

In attempting to respond appropriately to these various types of requests for information, clinicians must recognize the dual standards that are at issue: confidentiality and the discovery rules governing criminal and civil action in the courts.

Search Warrants

Search warrants are documents based on "probable cause" that a psychotherapist has evidence germane to a legal case, making it necessary for police or other investigative officials to enter the psychotherapy office and search for information. Agencies, such as prosecuting attorneys or police, write the search warrants and judges must review them and sign them in order for them to be valid. Search warrants include a list of specific items needed.

When judges sign search warrants and police or other investigative officials arrive at therapists' offices to look for records, it is extremely disruptive and can be frightening. Therapists should try to remain calm and be a role model to their patients, who are also alarmed by sudden intrusions of officials arriving unexpectedly with search warrants. Therapists have the right to read the search warrant to see what the police are looking for, to monitor what the police remove, and to respectfully ask for an inventory of what they remove, but they must allow the police to proceed. In the case of a substance abuse program, however, a search warrant is insufficient to open records. Most police departments do not know this. Therefore, having a copy available of the federal statute governing substance abuse treatment records to respectfully show the police is important (Schoener, 2001a).

Altering Records: A Cautionary Note

It is never proper to alter or destroy records with the intent to influence a judicial proceeding (Weintraub, 1999; Brooke, 1994). Practitioners can best protect their clients, themselves, and the professional relationship by adhering to appropriate record-keeping procedures (see chapter 3 for discussion of contents of good records and chapter 6 for discussion of retention and destruction of records). In short, psychotherapists must document that which is relevant to the treatment and also adhere to a policy regarding record retention and record destruction.

Sometimes clients request that the practitioner either keep relevant information out of the record or omit information that they believe will be "harmful" to them. Therapists can be helpful by discussing with their client the purposes of record keeping, why material relevant to treatment cannot be deleted, as well as options to protect the client.

Summary

In response to legal requests, practitioners must keep in mind the following:

1. the need to verify the legitimacy of the request for disclosure of information;
2. the importance of ensuring that a client (or a parent or legal guardian where permitted by law) has fully understood the request and its purpose and has given consent for disclosure;
3. the importance of disclosing only the minimum necessary to fulfill the intended purpose;
4. the need to inform oneself of applicable state statutes and rules and to seek legal counsel from the practitioners' attorneys (not clients' attorneys) as needed.

AFTER BECOMING INVOLVED IN A LEGAL CASE, NOW WHAT?

Here is a road map for interactions practitioners can expect to occur once they have decided to play a role in a legal case. It offers ideas for handling oneself appropriately as a mental health professional.

Communication With Attorneys

DEFINE PROFESSIONAL EXPERTISE

After therapists have decided it could be appropriate for them to serve as treatment experts, or when they are determining whether it is appropriate, it is essential to define for attorneys exactly what the expert does. Never assume that attorneys are familiar with mental health professions. Some attorneys are well informed and use mental health professionals regularly in a variety of capacities. Others have never worked with a mental health professional and have many misconceptions. In fact, it is not unusual to hear attorneys use the terms psychiatrist and psychologist interchangeably, or to refer to clinical social workers as psychologists. Mental health professionals get lumped into one generic group. Some attorneys are unaware that many types of professionals are licensed in their states to diagnose and treat mental and emotional disorders. A clinical social worker, for example, informed an attorney about recent court cases that had recognized clinical social workers as mental health professionals who were qualified by their professional education and experience to diagnose and treat emotional and mental disorders (*Jaffee v. Redmond,* 1996) and to testify regarding their diagnoses (Court of Appeals of Maryland, 1999).

To avoid this confusion, practitioners must be clear about the boundaries of their knowledge and expertise. They must explain their training and experience and always provide the attorney with an up-to-date resume.

A few words about resumes. In some cases, witnesses have several different resumes because they have emphasized different skills or training in order to apply for different jobs. Practitioners should be sure to tell attorneys if they have done this so attorneys can preempt any questions in a deposition or court about practitioners' veracity. Practitioners should never change or delete information from their resumes for the purpose of testifying. In one case a naive witness significantly altered her resume at the request of an attorney. On the witness stand, opposing counsel supplied her with a copy of her unedited resume and questioned her about it for over an hour. By the end of questioning, the witness's credibility had been destroyed.

DISCUSS FEES FOR EXPERTS' TIME

Psychotherapists who must appear at depositions or in court or who must write reports for their patients' legal cases have often asked whether they can bill for their time and, if so, what they should charge. Nothing can ruin professional relationships or practices so quickly as not being reimbursed for one's time. Kern states that both types of witnesses are entitled to be paid for their time (Kern, 1996). Witnesses should never work without a contract with an attorney or without a court appointment. Practitioners may choose to donate their time (this is called *pro bono* work, which translates as "for the good," i.e., free), but this decision should also be stated clearly in a contract. Witnesses should explain their fees and billing procedures with attorneys during the first conversation and establish a verbal agreement or contract on how they will be paid for their time in the case. Practitioners should then request a letter from the attorney or court which sets out the fee arrangement. The letter should include the specific type of request, the practitioner's fee, for what types of time the fee will be paid, and when the fee will be paid (on receipt of the witness's bill or within 1 month). Treatment and evaluation witnesses should state to attorneys that it is unethical for mental health practitioners to enter into contingency fee agreements, whereby practitioners are paid for their time only if the attorneys' clients win their cases.

Experts normally bill for any time they must spend in a case: reviewing records; meeting with attorneys; traveling to and from depositions, hearings, or trials; and waiting to testify in court. Frequently, therapists charge more for their time in legal cases than they charge for their time providing treatment in their clinical cases. They do this because legal cases involve more pressures, more knowledge, inescapable deadlines, and interruptions to therapists' schedules.

Litigating fees: This is the last place experts want to end up. Usually attorneys are reliable in complying with payment contracts they make with their witnesses, but occasionally it may be necessary to file a claim in small claims court or through other avenues.

MEET WITH ATTORNEYS REQUESTING EXPERTS' TIME

Whether practitioners are serving as potential treatment witnesses or as evaluation witnesses, it is helpful to meet with the attorneys who are requesting their services. Setting aside time to talk communicates the importance of the matter and a mutual commitment to understanding the issues involved and it clarifies what role practitioners could appropriately have in the cases.

In some instances, meetings with potential mental health witnesses can help attorneys realize that the practitioners are not the best persons to use in their cases. In one case, for example, an attorney representing a man in criminal court met with two practitioners, a psychiatrist and a clinical social worker, who were treating his client. He had presumed that the psychiatrist could best help the jury to understand how his client's egregious history of abuse and neglect and how his mother's severe mental illness had arrested his development and contributed to his problems with perception, judgment, and behavior. Though the psychiatrist was highly esteemed and experienced both in clinical and in forensic matters, he lacked knowledge of the adverse effect of cumulative psychosocial stressors on development. Moreover, the psychiatrist's manner was offensive and he appeared biased. During the meeting, he also appeared to dislike his patient and was argumentative and sarcastic as he discussed the case. By the second meeting, the attorney came to believe that this psychiatrist was not the treatment witness for the job. Instead, the attorney asked the clinical social worker to testify, and her testimony went very well.

Meetings also give potential treatment or evaluation witnesses an opportunity to get answers to necessary questions such as, What the case is about? What does the attorney expect the witness to do? What knowledge does the witness have that could help or hurt the case? Do the attorneys' expectations jibe with the witness's scope of knowledge, training, and expertise?

WITNESSES' RESPONSIBILITIES TO STATE POTENTIAL ADVERSE EFFECTS

In addition to addressing the limits of their expertise and their commitment to remain within the facts that they have, potential treatment or evaluation witnesses should also speculate with their clients or evaluees and their clients' or evaluees' attorneys about how exposing sensitive information could be counterproductive to the clients or evaluees in the long run. What is the gain if one wins the battle but loses the war? Consider the case of a 22-year-old female patient who sought therapy for trauma resulting from a date rape and who, while in treatment, decided to sue her rapist.

The patient had revealed to her therapist that she had been sexually abused as a child, had become promiscuous in her teens, and had, like many victims of sexual abuse, abused alcohol and drugs to numb her emotional pain. Her moods were mercurial and she was often angry, fighting with friends and neighbors. The therapist had diagnosed her with both posttraumatic stress disorder and borderline personality disorder.

After intensive psychotherapy over approximately a 2-year period, the patient had made tangible progress. Most of her flashbacks were gone; she was no longer cutting herself; she was working; she was attending a 12-step program and remaining sober; and she was no longer having unprotected sex. Her rages were under control and she was sleeping more comfortably with the help of antidepressants prescribed by her psychiatrist. The focus of her clinical work had progressed to resolving her enduring grief. During this phase of her psychotherapy, she was moving back and forth between debilitating sadness and revenge fantasies. In this context, she was feeling upset about her date rape and learned that she could file a personal injury case against the man who had raped her.

In the therapist's professional judgment, the patient was at a sensitive juncture in her therapy and might be displacing her grief and anger onto the date rape incident. The patient was convinced she could get relief from her emotional pain if she were to win this case. Yet the therapist wondered if filing a lawsuit would serve her. Being preoccupied with her legal case would likely interrupt her therapy, and when the legal case was over, the enormous sense of loss and abandonment might still loom over her.

The therapist understood that all of the patient's records would be needed in court in order to determine whether the date rape had caused new problems or exacerbated old problems. With her client's authorization, the therapist reviewed her client's treatment records with the attorney. She showed him where the patient had recounted previous drinking binges and blackouts, periods of uncontrolled rage, convictions for shoplifting, and episodes of chronic lying, all of which predated the rape. Would it serve the case, the therapist asked the attorney, if these events were to come out in court? If the client's attorney did not bring this information in, is it possible that the opposing attorney would? Equally important, would the court process itself serve to re-traumatize this patient? Would she feel harmed again if she lost her case?

Attorneys may be interested only in the law. In most states a rape victim's prior history cannot be used against her, but there are many cases in which such information finds its way into the record. Therapists may be looking at the case through different lenses than do attorneys. Therapists are concerned only with the client's emotional welfare. Practitioners therefore have a responsibility to share with their clients and their clients' attorneys their professional thoughts and concerns about harm their clients could experience as a result of clients' legal cases.

Whether to file a legal complaint is up to patients. But when practitioners share their perspectives, they can help clients and their attorneys develop a broader view of the case. Such a conversation may have therapeutic implications as well. Helping clients articulate their aims may help them see other alternatives that do not pose as great a personal risk. Jeannette Milgrom, a clinical social worker, found that a "wheel of options" helped her clients visualize other options available to them to address injustices (Milgrom, 1989).

CAREFULLY UNDERSTAND THE REFERRAL QUESTIONS

It is very important for both treatment and evaluation experts to know what the attorneys are asking them to comment on. Therapists therefore need to elicit from attorneys what the attorney will be asking and what treatment information they will need to present. Evaluation witnesses must know what questions they are being expected to answer and what they will need to develop and to present. Both types of witnesses must make ethical decisions about whether the attorneys' requests are appropriate and whether they can accomplish the tasks when it is clear what attorneys are asking for.

Typical questions that attorneys ask potential treatment witnesses are:

How was Ms. X referred to you?

What problems did Ms. X describe to you?

What were her goals for therapy?

Did you develop opinions or diagnoses about her problems? If so, what were these?

Did you develop a treatment plan? If so, what was your treatment plan?

Have you or anyone else referred Ms. X for testing or any other kinds of assessment?

If so, what were the reasons for the referrals and what were the results of that testing?

Have you consulted anyone else about Ms. X? What did they say?

What has been Ms. X's progress? What evidence do you have about that?

Do you have an opinion about Ms. X's prognosis? If so, what is it? And what is the basis for your opinion?

When did you see her and for how long?

Attorneys' questions may not become clear to witnesses until they have learned enough about the case. As they talk further with attorneys and their clients, the issues become more focused. Practitioners should always reflect back to attorneys and their clients what they believe attorneys are asking them to do, and tell them whether or not they can offer the opinions they are seeking. Some cases are uncomplicated and have clear questions; it really boils down to reporting the news. Other cases are more complex. For evaluation witnesses, whose roles are broader than treatment witnesses, there can be many turns and twists as the investigation proceeds. As the emphases of the cases change, so can the evaluation witnesses' roles.

Sometimes therapists and evaluation witnesses have wisely requested consultation from professional colleagues familiar with legal work because they are confused about what an attorney is asking them to do. They mistakenly think the source of their confusion is a lack of legal knowledge. This usually is not the case. More often than not, the source of the problem is that the attorney does not yet have a clear vision of the case, and the therapist or evaluation witness has not asked enough questions.

REPORTS

Whether attorneys request that experts write reports depends on a number of variables, including whether there is likely to be an out-of-court settlement, the jurisdiction in which the case is being litigated, and whether there have been depositions. The purpose of a treatment witness's report is usually to summarize the client's diagnosis and treatment. The purpose of the evaluation witness's report is to delineate findings and professional opinions that answer the attorneys' or courts' questions. Most states require evaluation witnesses to provide a written report for the opposing attorney in order to avoid surprises at trial. Either type of witnesses' reports likely will become the basis for their testimony if they are called as witnesses in depositions, hearings, or trials. Witnesses should follow their ethical requirements and include the "minimum necessary" to fulfill the purpose for their reports.

Depositions

In some jurisdictions, attorneys can take depositions, which are sworn statements of potential witnesses. Since most cases are settled out of court, the likelihood of treatment or evaluation witnesses testifying in depositions is greater than the likelihood of their testifying in courtrooms. The purpose of a deposition is to get information about what a witness from the other side ("adverse witness") might say in court. In the deposition, the witness is questioned in the presence of attorneys from both sides.

Both treatment and evaluation witnesses can receive subpoenas for depositions from opposing counsel that include the following: the date, time, and place where the witness is to appear. If the subpoena is *duces tecum*, experts are required to bring their patient's records. Usually dates of depositions are not set in stone. Most attorneys will work to accommodate practitioners' schedules. Depositions may take place at a courthouse, in one of the attorneys' offices, or even in practitioners' offices. When attorneys take depositions from experts who live in distant locations, they typically travel to the experts' locale and the experts choose where to have the deposition. If cases originate in a different city, depositions may take place in hotel suites, borrowed offices of local attorneys, or offices of court reporters.

Depositions usually take place around a conference table. The attorneys requesting the deposition and their client sit on one side of the table. The witness who is being deposed, the attorneys who have retained the witness, and the attorneys' client sit on the other side. A court reporter sits at the end of the conference table and records *verbatim* what is said.

While depositions may appear less intimidating and less formal than a courtroom, looks are deceiving. Depositions are taken seriously. Witnesses' deposition testimony is an important factor in attorneys' decisions of whether or not to settle cases out of court. If the case goes to trial, opposing attorneys rely upon witnesses' deposition testimony in developing their defense arguments. They attempt to find inconsistencies and errors in the deposition testimony. Therefore, witnesses should take extreme care in depositions, as in the courtroom, to answer questions honestly and to base their answers solely

on their professional experience and training and on the facts that are available to them. They should always remember that they are only witnesses; they are not responsible for winning the case.

As part of the discovery process in depositions, federal rules require that treatment and evaluation witnesses state names of all legal cases in which they have given deposition and courtroom testimony. Therefore, witnesses should come to depositions prepared with a list of their previous testimony.

Court rules require that experts have an opportunity to read the transcript prepared of their deposition testimony in order to verify its accuracy. Mental health witnesses should request the transcript of their deposition, read it carefully, and enter corrections on the page provided for corrections. Since attorneys rely on witnesses' deposition testimony during trial, evaluation and treatment witnesses need to be certain that deposition transcripts are accurately recorded.

Witnesses may feel uncomfortable the first time they read their own words. They can use this as a teaching tool. Most witnesses notice that some of their responses look different on paper than they had intended. Because mental health witnesses come from the culture of therapy and speak a very specific dialect, they use shorthand that another therapist would immediately understand but that is confusing to "aliens." That's all right. Practitioners will get the hang of how their testimony may be used in direct and cross-examination and in the ways they can improve their responses.

Court

Practitioners may be called as witnesses either at preliminary hearings or at trials. The purpose of hearings is to resolve issues integral to a case. Rulings by a judge on issues taken up at a hearing help to define the legal contours of a case. For example, if practitioners are evaluation experts they may be called to testify as to competency or sanity. If practitioners are treatment witnesses, they may testify as to their previous or current clients' past or current mental status. The judges may take their testimony into consideration when they rule on issues.

Hearings may be open or closed to the public. Depending on the situation and the judge's policies, they may be held in open court or in a judge's chambers. For example, in custody suits, it is common for judges to hear testimony confidentially in order to protect children's identity and emotional welfare. This means that the press is not privy to the testimony, although the court file will reflect that the hearing occurred. (For example, the O.J. Simpson criminal trial was open to the public, while the proceedings in his custody battle were closed.) If a hearing is *ex parte* (away from the party) it means that only one side will be heard by the judge. This is much more common in federal court than in state or local courts.

Out-of-Court Settlements

Most cases are resolved before trial. Once the issues are clarified and the parties learn what they stand to lose, and the amount of time, money, and emotional energy involved, they may elect to compromise and settle their dispute out of court. Resolutions often occur after depositions and pretrial hearings.

The proliferation of mediation and restorative justice illustrates the increasing emphasis on out-of-court settlements. In fact, in some states (Florida, for example) people seeking to divorce must take a "divorce class" that focuses on, among other issues, communication, conflict resolution, the legal and economic consequences of divorce, and the effects of divorce on children. Similarly, Florida residents are required to participate in mediation before a divorce is set for trial.

Interestingly, most mediation results in agreements that are similar to what the parties' lawyers predicted would be gained at trial. Moreover, mediated agreements result in better compliance since the parties generate the terms of the agreement instead of having the outcomes imposed upon them by a judge.

The only alternative to settlement is trial. If a case is tried, practitioners will receive a subpoena for trial (this is different from a subpoena for deposition or a hearing). If practitioners are working with attorneys where the agreement to come to court is implicit, they may choose to ask that the attorneys serve them with a subpoena so they can verify for their records that they were called to court. Subpoenas are also helpful if practitioners work in a clinic or agency; they are "excused absences," so to speak. Going to court under subpoena obviates the need to use sick leave or vacation time.

PREPARING FOR DEPOSITION OR COURTROOM TESTIMONY

Whether witnesses are testifying in depositions or in the courtroom, careful preparation is essential. Here are some simple tips practitioners can use to reduce their anxiety and reinforce their professional skills.

Schedule

Witnesses should clarify when their testimony will be needed. Attorneys attempt to consider practitioners' clinical and personal demands on their time when scheduling witnesses' court appearances. Practitioners should therefore be sure to inform attorneys or courts who have hired or appointed them about times they will not be available

Organize

Witnesses should systematically organize their files so they know where to find any documents they may be asked to discuss. It can be stressful to be interrogated, thus it is important for practitioners to know where to find the information they will need in order to answer the questions. It is helpful to use folders with two internal flaps so documents can be easily compartmentalized. For example, a face sheet and consent form is attached to the inside left flap, and records from previous treatment are attached to the opposite flap. Tests and other diagnostic information are kept on the left-hand side of the second flap, across from which is attached correspondence. Progress notes are kept on the left-hand side of the second flap, and billing information is attached to the inside of the back of the file. Practitioners should find the filing system that works best for them and make sure the file is in order as they are preparing the case. It is important to remember that any notes experts take with them to a deposition or to the witness stand must be made available to the opposing lawyer when he or she asks to see them.

Visualize

Practitioners should reread the file with a fresh perspective. What questions would someone ask about the records who wasn't a therapist or who didn't know the client? Are there any gaps or missing documents? Are diagnoses and the bases for the diagnoses properly noted? Have practitioners memorized any conversations with other professionals whom the client has seen, and do they have in their possession signed and dated release forms to show their clients' or evaluees' authorization for these discussions? Practitioners should be sure each entry in the progress notes is dated and signed and that any errors are crossed through, corrected legibly, dated, and initialed.

Practitioners should not worry if their files are not perfect; no such files exist. They should simply be aware that attorneys may ask them questions that either are unanswered in the records or they aren't prepared to answer. They can make a note of these questions to discuss with the attorneys with whom they are working or with professional colleagues who have more experience in depositions or in court testimony (such as provided by members of the Clinical Social Work Federation's Committee on Clinical Social Work and the Law).

Treatment witnesses should be able readily to find in their records how and when they first met the patients; their patient's evaluation, diagnosis, treatment, and progress; how and when they became involved in the case; and other relevant treatment information.

Memorize

Testifying in court is like having a highly structured conversation. The more witnesses know off the top of their heads, the better and quicker will be the flow of information. However, during their testimony, it is always appropriate for witnesses to look at their records in order to refresh their memories. It is far better to take the time to do that than to attempt to give an answer that may be inaccurate from one's fading memory. Witnesses should try to commit to memory basic facts they may be asked, such as:

- a definition of their professions and certifications (What is a clinical social worker? A clinical psychologist? What does it mean to be board certified in clinical social work? In clinical psychology? In psychiatry? What are the requirements for board certification? Is an exam required for board certification or licensure?);
- the first and last times they saw the client;
- the referral source;

- the presenting problems (for therapist witnesses);
- the referral questions (for evaluation witnesses);
- the diagnoses of the client or evaluee;
- number of hours of therapy (for treatment witnesses);
- number of hours of the evaluation (for evaluation witnesses);
- any changes in diagnoses (for treatment witnesses).

A greater command of these and other facts (or at least where to readily find them) not only reduces witnesses' anxiety but communicates their credibility and authenticity either in depositions or in the courtroom.

Verbalize

It is usually impossible for therapists to grasp all facets of a legal case without help since the legal system is often foreign to them. However, treatment witnesses can effectively learn their way through the process by using the same techniques they teach their clients. In the same way that they show clients how to examine problems from different perspectives, psychotherapists benefit from learning the assumptions, biases, and filters that attorneys, judges, and juries bring to a case. Mental health practitioners know from their therapeutic training and experience that talking helps people gain insight, expand their point of view, and identify options.

Practitioners can simply transfer this knowledge to their forensic cases. When they have been called by an attorney and have agreed to testify, they should talk with the attorney about their questions and concerns. It is also helpful to find a mental health practitioner mentor with experience in the legal system who can shed light on the next step along the path. The only unhelpful question is the one that goes unasked. The more practitioners can ask, the more they learn and the more mastery they attain. It's like a big jigsaw puzzle: First turn over all the pieces, then start fitting them together. The more practitioners can put together, the more confident and knowledgeable they can become. If they remain curious and stick with it, they will eventually clarify the whole picture. Each time treatment witnesses go through the process, or help their clients to do so, they learn a little more. In time, expert witnesses become as fluent as natives, able to navigate this "dark continent."

Have an Anticipatory Overview

When practitioners are ready to "cross the border" into the courtroom, it can be helpful to get a preview of where they are going. They can ask their patient's or their evaluee's attorney to help them visualize the courtroom where they will be testifying. Some practitioners have even asked the attorneys who have hired them to show them the courthouse. When practitioners are court appointed, they may wish to find an attorney who is not involved in the case to help them with this task. They can usually find a vacant courtroom at lunchtime or during recesses.

When they visit courthouses, practitioners learn the layout. Where is the witness room where they will be asked to wait until they are called to testify? Where is the jury room (witnesses must always avoid contact with jurors)? The telephone? The rest room? The cafeteria? Where are the judge's chambers in the event they are asked to testify *in camera* (judge's chambers)?

Practitioners can then go to the courtroom where they'll be testifying and examine the room from all vantage points. It helps to note the location of each counsel table and where the jury will be seated, and to sit in the witness seat. What do you see and how do you feel? Practitioners' conversations with the attorney may have been limited to telephone calls or discussions at a desk. The courtroom is a very different environment. Attorneys may seem remote as they speak from a podium or behind the counsel table. It can be helpful for practitioners to think about their testimony while either visualizing or actually sitting in the witness chair. Practitioners might develop new questions or areas of concern as they visualize or sit in the courtroom. They should not be shy. They need to discuss these questions with attorneys with whom they are working. Now is the time for witnesses to ask.

Practitioners should notice any equipment in the courtroom they will be using to illustrate their testimony, such as an overhead projector or other audiovisual aid. Although many courts have new, very sophisticated machines that are used to show evidence, these don't always work well. If practitioners will be asked to demonstrate or discuss evidence (e.g., testing results, copies of records or genograms), practitioners should request that attorneys make sure it works and what the information will look like on the screen that the judge and jury will be viewing. In order to prevent unnecessary interruptions in the trial, attorneys should also make sure there are extension cords and extra light bulbs for the projector.

Prepare for Necessities

Treatment and evaluation witnesses should start with the basics. Witnesses should know where the building is, where to park, how early to arrive, where to report, and what they need to bring with them for their personal needs. Many witnesses, for example, have had to run in and out of court to put money in a parking meter because they didn't know there was a parking lot around the corner or that they could be exempt from parking charges. In one case, an expert actually stopped in the middle of his testimony to tell the judge that he had to go "feed the parking meter," which is unacceptable "court etiquette." Another expert who knows he feels less alert in the middle of the morning or afternoon, puts a plastic wrapped peeled orange and bottle of mineral water in his briefcase before heading off to a deposition or courtroom. While waiting to testify, or during breaks, having an orange segment and sip of water helps him maintain his focus.

Make Realistic Preparations for Being Away From the Office

Prior to depositions, hearings, or court trials, practitioners should always ask the attorneys involved how much time they can expect to be out of their offices. Then double the time. In most instances, attorneys underestimate the time that will be needed to accomplish a task in a legal case. Sometimes lawyers try to put a positive spin on what is involved and so tell practitioners that they'll "be in and out in an hour." Other times the judge is called away to an emergency hearing. In still other cases, practitioners may be called to testify out of order to accommodate another witness. Sometimes the testimony of a previous witness may take much longer than anticipated. Whatever the reason, practitioners can avoid disruption in their offices by planning for extra time.

Practitioners should never schedule important appointments or activities immediately after they "think" they'll be finished with a court-related duty. Things rarely go as planned. In fact, one of the most important tools in legal cases is patience, followed by flexibility.

Practitioners should be sure to inform patients who are scheduled on the day of their testimony that while they expect to return to the office in time for their appointments, they could be delayed and may need to contact them. Therapists should verify where and how the patients can be reached if necessary.

Dress Appropriately

Practitioners should select clothing that is consistent with the somber atmosphere of the legal system. Dress matters. It can either enhance or erode mental health witnesses' credibility. Comfortable but subdued professional attire is appropriate. Women should wear conservative business suits, simple jewelry, and closed heels. Men should also wear conservative business suits and ties. The following example illustrates the importance of appropriate dress: A psychologist who was testifying in a courtroom as a treatment witness in her client's sexual assault case recalled how uncomfortable she had felt because of her clothing. She was wearing a two-piece suit, in a shocking pink color. She became aware during her testimony that her stomach was in knots. She was not sure why, since she had experience testifying in similar cases. She gradually realized she was feeling out of place next to the judge, who was wearing a long black robe. She felt she was standing out like a sore thumb in the subdued climate of the courtroom. Her discomfort had distracted her from her testimony. She wished she had put on her tailored dark blue suit that morning.

Bring Along Amenities for Comfort

Witnesses should consider whether it would be helpful to bring healthy snacks, such as nuts or sandwiches, in their briefcases. They should always bring with them any prescribed medications that they may require. It can also be helpful for witnesses to have reading materials to keep occupied while waiting to testify.

TESTIFYING

"Swearing In"

Whether practitioners are testifying as treatment or evaluation witnesses in a deposition, hearing, or trial, they will be asked to swear that the testimony they give is the complete truth. From the moment they begin their testimony until they are dismissed from the deposition or witness stand, a court reporter will record their every word and verbal expression ("uh-huh") and most of their nonverbal responses ("witness nods"). If treatment or evaluation witnesses are testifying in depositions, they will most likely be sitting around a conference table with all of the attorneys, their patients or evaluees, and a court reporter. In the event they are called to testify at a hearing or trial, they will be directed to the witness stand or judge's chambers.

Becoming Qualified as an Expert

In the courtroom, treatment and evaluation witnesses will first be qualified as experts. *Qualified* is a legal term that means that the witness professional experience and training "qualify" them to render certain types of professional opinions that will be helpful to the court in understanding the case.

Attorneys who have hired mental health witnesses begin by asking the witnesses questions about their professional qualifications. Questions are sometimes more extensive for evaluation witnesses than for treatment witnesses. Questions include: graduate schools attended, clinical internships, field work placements, or residencies, current and past titles and professional work experiences in clinical or academic settings, organizational affiliations, licensure and other legal or professional certifications, hospital affiliations, honors, and publications that are relevant to the legal case. All of these areas should be detailed in practitioners' resumes. The resumes are then entered into the record. The attorney also asks witnesses to tell how they became acquainted with the plaintiff or defendant and what types of professional opinions they have been asked to provide.

Opposing counsel may elect to cross-examine witnesses about their qualifications as experts. Or opposing counsel may "stipulate" (agree) to their expertise. After hearing from both sides the judge will decide whether witnesses can testify as experts. Experts are usually qualified without comment or argument.

Experts must be careful to delineate what kind of testimony they are qualified to give. Treatment experts, unlike evaluation witnesses, cannot provide a professional opinion in a personal injury case regarding whether an alleged event has "caused" psychological damages. (In their role as therapists, they have not been in the role of forensic evaluators.) They can state facts limited to their findings from treatment: that the client sought treatment on a particular date for getting help for a psychological problem, the onset of which began after the alleged event. They can testify to the history the client has reported, including whether the client stated that the alleged events exacerbated previous problems. They can testify to the fact that treatment has focused on psychological problems related to the alleged event. Unlike evaluation experts, their knowledge is limited generally to what their clients have reported to them and does not include "corroborating evidence" to support the "truth" of what their clients have reported. In contrast, evaluation experts will have formulated professional opinions, such as (in personal injury cases) whether the alleged events have caused new damages or exacerbated former psychological problems. They will base their professional opinions on their review of data that are normally beyond the scope of therapists' purview in treatment.

Direct Examination

The purpose of direct testimony is to reveal what mental health witnesses believe or know through a series of questions and answers. Treatment witnesses will testify about the course of treatment and their diagnoses. Evaluation witnesses will testify about how they were asked to do a forensic mental health examination and their professional opinions regarding the case. Attorneys who have hired either type of witness will ask them questions in a direct examination. Some questions will require only brief answers, while others will be open-ended questions which allow witnesses to provide a longer narrative answer.

Mental health witnesses should prepare their direct testimony well in advance of the time they will be presenting it. They should work with attorneys who have hired them, or, if the court has appointed them as experts, they should work with consultants. When mental health witnesses work with attorneys, they should keep in mind that the way attorneys help mental health practitioners prepare for direct examination depends upon a number of factors: attorneys' experience, how much they've worked with social science and related experts, their personality types, their attitudes about experts, their understanding of and confidence in the subject matter and in the experts' conclusions, and whether there are other experts in the case who will provide supportive data. Some attorneys are very structured and collaborative and will develop very detailed testimony with practitioners. Others do not meet with or work with experts until just before a hearing or trial, and then discuss expert testimony very generally. In one case an attorney asked the expert as they were walking to court, "So what are you going to say in there?" Unless mental health witnesses assert their needs, they may never hear the questions until they are in court.

In direct examination, the attorney who has called the expert as a witness cannot ask leading questions, that is, questions that suggest an answer. "Did you attend the University of Colorado?" is an example of a leading question. A more proper way in direct examination for the attorney to inquire about his or her expert's educational background is: "Where did you do your undergraduate work?" Or, "Did there come a time when you were asked to evaluate the Plaintiff?" is more appropriate than, "When did you conduct an evaluation of the Plaintiff?" Prior to the trial, therefore, an expert needs to clarify all the information the expert and the attorney believe to be relevant to the case so that the expert will be prepared and the attorney will not have to ask leading questions.

Cross-examination by opposing counsel is different because leading questions are allowed. These court rules presume that the expert has discussed the case with an attorney who has hired the expert and that the expert will know what to volunteer. Working with attorneys to use clinical information in court is like importing a rare product into a foreign country. Mental health professionals are the experts about the content, while the attorneys know the route. Practitioners can make the journey smoother by helping attorneys to formulate questions that will elicit the most relevant, accurate information from them. They should continually educate the attorney about the limits of their purview. They must be clear about what they can and cannot say and why. Once mental health witnesses know and understand the questions the attorneys will ask, they should check to see if their "story line" flows coherently. Both treatment and evaluation witnesses should be sure they know the attorney's overall objective during the questioning so they can remain focused.

Mental health professionals always need to let professional ethics be their compass. It is not their job to ensure that the testimony they provide is "good" for the client's legal case or helps the client "win." Mental health witness job is to report honestly and clearly what they know and how they know it. As a psychologist who testifies regularly says, "Just look them in the eye and tell them what you know."

Basic Rules of Thumb for Testimony

LISTEN CAREFULLY

It is crucial that witnesses listen carefully to the questions and never answer if they don't understand. Many times attorneys roll two or three questions into one, or give circuitous lead-ins to questions. Mental health witnesses need to use their professional skills and take a moment to reflect on the words and make sure they understand the question. If they are confused, they should use reflection or paraphrasing to ask questioners whether they understand the question: "I'm not sure what you are asking me. Are you asking me if he went to school?" Or simply say, "I don't understand the question" or "I don't know the answer." Or, "Please rephrase." Or, "I can't answer the question in the way you have asked it. I would need to answer it in two parts. Would you like me to answer?"

USE PLAIN AND SIMPLE LANGUAGE

Witnesses should keep their audience in mind and speak plainly so that juries and judges can understand. Mental health professionals know exactly what is meant by "the patient presented with auditory hallucinations, echolalia, and paranoia," but this is unfamiliar to most people. Instead they should say, "The client was hearing voices or noises, was repeating what other people said, and was suspicious and fearful of others." The word "affect" is typically not known. Witnesses should substitute the word "emotion."

ONLY ANSWER WHAT IS ASKED

Less is better, especially on cross-examination. Mental health witnesses often err on the side of offering more information than they are asked. Unless attorneys who have hired them have asked them ahead of time to elaborate, the best answers are usually "yes," "no," "I don't know," and "I don't remember."

AVOID HUMOR OR ARROGANCE

In courtrooms or depositions, humor can backfire and arrogance is out of place. Thus, speaking in a pleasant, nondefensive, straightforward, and professional manner is best.

REMAIN CALM AND RELAXED

It can be difficult for witnesses to remain calm and relaxed when they are fully aware that the job of opposing attorneys is to undermine their credibility. One evaluation witness found it helpful to use meditation techniques both while she was waiting to testify and when she was on the witness stand. It helped her to remind herself that she was only there as one of many parties in the legal matter who held an opinion. She reminded herself that she was there not to "win" the case, but only to give her understanding of reality.

When there was a brief interruption in her testimony so that the attorneys could argue an objection in front of the judge, she used the respite to breathe deeply, focus on her out-breath, and relax her facial and shoulder muscles. When the attorneys resolved their dispute and she resumed her testimony, she felt composed and her mind was clear for the attorney's next question. She felt so relaxed, in fact, that when the attorney began to yell at her, making it impossible to concentrate on the attorney's questions, she calmly said, "It would help me if you would not yell at me." The attorney yelled back, "I am not yelling," but immediately lowered her voice, to which the witness quietly said, "Thank you." By remaining relaxed, the witness was able to retain her composure in the courtroom, just as she remains calm in tense psychotherapy sessions with her therapy clients. Her calm demeanor in the face of the aggressive lawyer gave her more credibility with the jury.

Cross-Examination

The goal of cross-examination is to elicit the truth and expose weaknesses or errors in the witness's testimony. Thus, it is an attack. Witnesses must respond professionally and gracefully, not defensively or aggressively. They need to understand that opposing attorneys are "only doing their job" to undermine their testimony and credibility. It sometimes helps to think of it like a game, or to remember that the more personal the attacks, the more successful the witness has been. There are many techniques that attorneys use in cross-examination to accomplish their goals of exposing weaknesses or errors in the witness's testimony.

Attempts to Undermine the Witness's Credentials

In the following example, the treatment witness remained calm and did not respond to the attorney's slurs. She simply replied to the opposing attorney's questions.

Attorney: Ms. Jones, are you just a social worker?

Witness: I am a clinical social worker.

Attorney: You don't have a doctoral degree, do you?

Witness: No, I do not have a doctoral degree.

ATTEMPTS TO SHOW WITNESS IS A "HIRED GUN"
AND "PAID FOR TESTIMONY"

In the following example, the witness understood the opposing attorney's tactic to portray him as a "hired gun." The witness was able to make an important distinction between being paid for his testimony and being paid for his time.

Attorney: Dr. Smith, have you testified before?

Witness: Yes.

Attorney: How many times would you say you have testified?

Witness: Approximately 20 times.

Attorney: Are you being paid for your testimony today, Dr. Smith?

Witness: No, I am being paid for my time.

ATTEMPTS TO SHOW WITNESS IS BIASED

Another tactic is to attempt to show that witnesses are biased because they have testified solely for plaintiffs' attorneys or solely for defendants' attorneys.

In the following example, the opposing attorney was unsuccessful in using this tactic to demonstrate that the evaluation witness was biased. The witness had consulted to both plaintiffs' and defendants' attorneys. Had the witness not had both types of experiences, he nevertheless should have simply responded to the question in a nondefensive manner.

Attorney: Dr. Anderson, you testified earlier that you have testified in similar cases over the past 20 years. Were the cases plaintiffs' cases or defendants' cases?

Witness: I have testified in both.

A wise strategy to deal with questions on cross-examination designed to discredit or embarrass the witness is to have the attorney who hires the witness ask these questions during direct examination: "Are you being paid for your time?" Or, "Do you testify for plaintiffs or defendants, or both?" When the attorney who hired the witness asks these questions, it disarms the opposing counsel and takes the sting out of the issue.

ATTEMPTS TO DEMONSTRATE INCONSISTENCIES

Another tactic is to "impeach" witnesses by demonstrating inconsistencies between their previous testimony and current testimony or between their

testimony and other facts. The following example illustrates how an opposing attorney "impeached" (discredited) a treatment witness by demonstrating a lack of foundation for her professional opinions regarding her patient's
diagnosis (this example underscores again how important it is for therapists
to continuously reassess the accuracy of their patients' diagnoses during the
course of treatment):

Attorney: Dr. Smith, you have testified today that your diagnosis of Ms. X
was major depressive disorder with postpartum onset specifier. Is that
true, Dr. Smith?

Witness: Yes.

Attorney: Dr. Smith, you testified in your deposition that the patient first
began suffering from symptoms of major depressive disorder four months
after the birth of her baby. Is that correct?

Witness: Yes.

Attorney: Dr. Smith, could you please tell the jury by when depressive symptoms must begin in order to meet the criteria for a postpartum onset
specifier?

Witness: It is written in the DSM-IV, but I don't recall the exact criteria.

Attorney: I have here a text that may refresh your memory, Dr. Smith. Do
you recognize this text?

Witness: Yes.

Attorney: Please tell the jury what the title of the text is and explain to the
jury what it is.

Witness: The title is DSM IV. This text delineates symptoms and criteria for
diagnoses of mental and emotional disorders.

Attorney: Dr. Smith, on page 386 of this text, do you see the section called
"Postpartum Onset Specifier"?

Witness: Yes.

Attorney: Dr. Smith, please read for the jury the first sentence in that section.

Witness: [Looks at the page listing criteria for diagnosis for depression with
postpartum onset specifier and sees, to his dismay, that onset of symptoms must fall within 4 weeks after the birth of the baby, not within four
months, as he had stated in his earlier testimony.]

Attorney: Thank you for reading that section to the jury. Now, after refresh-
ing your memory, Dr. Smith, is it still your professional opinion that the
patient's major depressive disorder had postpartum onset specifier?"

Witness: No, my earlier testimony was incorrect.

"Tricks" That Attorneys Use

In order to undermine witnesses' credibility, opposing attorneys employ a variety of questions that they hope will confuse or disarm treatment and evaluation witnesses during cross-examinations. Witnesses must be aware of these techniques so they can carefully listen to questions and avoid falling into traps.

Some opposing attorneys attempt to disarm witnesses or cause them to say things they might not otherwise say by being overly informal and friendly. One case involved an interaction between a public defender and an experienced therapist who had never testified in court before. The legal case involved the therapist's patient, a 9-year-old girl who had been sexually assaulted by an adult neighbor and friend of her family.

The friendly, engaging public defender smiled warmly at the treatment witness as she walked through the courtroom door: "Oh, hello, Ms. Jones. I understand you do a lot of work with children." The witness, taken by surprise by the public defender's warmth and informality, replied, "Well, yes, I do, but most of my clients are adults." In an effort to demonstrate that the therapist lacked qualifications to testify as an expert witness in a child's law case, the public defender began the questioning with: "I understand, Ms. Jones, that you mostly work with adults." Ms. Jones had realized earlier that her off-the-record comments to the public defender had the potential of creating an erroneous perception of her practice. She therefore had immediately informed her minor patient's attorney of the informal interchange with the public defender so that he could be prepared to present her many years of experience treating children.

Another tactic attorneys use is to make statements about events that never took place and to ask witnesses to comment on them. Insecure witnesses can become flustered and try to act like they have knowledge about the events even though they never occurred. This underscores the importance of being familiar with the case record.

Attorneys may, in addition, also phrase questions in a confusing or negative manner, making implications that are unfounded. For example, one attorney stated to the witness: "I understand from your deposition that you were unable to distinguish between Ms. Brown's childhood abuse and the abuse she experienced during her treatment with Ms. Y."

Attorneys may also appeal to the witness's vanity. For example, an attorney might question: "Wouldn't someone with your outstanding credentials and in your position be aware that . . ." when, in fact, the witness would have had no reason in his professional capacity to be aware of that particular incident.

Sometimes attorneys incorrectly paraphrase or misquote the witness's previous testimony. Mental health witnesses must therefore be constantly vigilant in clarifying what they actually said.

Another tactic attorneys use is to ask vague questions, such as, "Dr. Smith, have you been testifying for a long time in lawsuits?" Mental health witnesses must be careful to specify details rather than answer a vague question. A specific response might be: "I have served as a mental health witness in legal cases since 1990."

Sometimes attorneys will imply in their questions that the mental health witness has engaged in unprofessional conduct. For example, "Dr. Smith, is it true that you have been providing psychoanalysis to this patient even though everyone knows that psychoanalysis has been discredited for years?" Following such questions, attorneys who have retained the witness should object.

Sometimes attorneys ask questions that challenge the adequacy of the witness's professional conduct (such as in malpractice cases or instances of duty to protect) even when the professional has acted appropriately and within the standard of care.

Sometimes attorneys attempt to trap witnesses into saying that they can do things that no mental health professionals are able to do, such as predicting dangerous behavior with certainty.

By using double negatives, attorneys can confuse witnesses and the jury. For example, the question, "You did not ask whether he was not planning to kill himself, did you?" could lead an unwary witness to answer incorrectly. Witnesses need to keep in mind that two negatives add up to a positive. Witnesses should clarify the meaning of the question for the jury. "I don't understand the question" is the best response. Witnesses should wait until the question is clear before they answer.

When attorneys preface their questions with "If you remember," it frequently causes witnesses to forget what the question is about! "If you remember, Dr. Smith, your patient came to you with symptoms of depression. What was the first thing you did to help her?"

Also, when attorneys preface questions with "To your knowledge," or "As far as you know," it can confuse the witness about the meaning of the question. It can also be hazardous for witnesses to preface their answers to such questions with "To my knowledge." For example, "Dr. Smith, to your knowledge, did your receptionist contact the patient to remind the patient of her appointment with you on July 8, the day she made her suicide attempt?" If Dr. Smith replies, "Not to my knowledge," then it is unclear to the jury what happened. Does Dr. Smith's answer mean that the receptionist did not make a reminder call to the patient? Or does the answer mean that Dr. Smith does not know whether the receptionist did or did not? A better answer would be precise: "I do not know whether the receptionist called the patient or not."

Attorneys also use the tactic of asking witnesses whether they agree with a long series of oversimplified statements that appear to be entirely true. Attorneys attempt to lead witnesses into agreeing with many such statements with the goal of trapping them into making conclusions that are untrue. A cautious witness can avoid being entrapped by asking attorneys to clarify their questions.

Sometimes attorneys intimidate their witnesses by remaining silent for several minutes, causing the witness to erroneously surmise they should be making further responses. Mental health witnesses should show that they are not afraid of silence. They should not volunteer anything that attorneys do not ask.

In depositions, attorneys may ask witnesses if they have stated everything they know on the subject. Witnesses need to be careful to leave the door open to their future testimony in the courtroom. In order to be cautious, they should say: "I have told you all I can recall at this time." Or, "Can you please be specific with your question?"

Re-Direct Examination

The purpose of re-direct examination is to present further information that will confront or minimize the impact of the cross-examination tactics and strengthen the witness's credibility and testimony. The initial attorney returns to question the witness on issues that were developed in cross-examination.

MANAGING OF CLINICAL ISSUES DURING LEGAL CASES

Negative Effects of Legal Cases on Patients and Therapists

Litigation is a stressful process that requires time, money, and energy and can cause myriad feelings for patients, including sadness, anger, confusion, shame, betrayal, and intense preoccupation. Being involved in a legal case and evaluated by a mental health professional (evaluation witness) places a person under a microscope, magnifying each deficiency, tearing scabs off old wounds, and leaving patients exposed to those with uncharitable intentions. The two experiences together would tax even the strongest among us and can be life-changing for clients who are emotionally or mentally burdened.

Similarly, it takes a toll on practitioners. For therapists, too, litigation leaves them exposed to those with uncharitable intentions whose role is to undermine their credibility. Thus therapists' management of their own problems related to their clients' legal cases is of utmost importance.

Techniques for Handling Anxiety

Litigation can become the basis of good therapeutic work. It can be used to develop problem-solving skills. Clients may learn just how courageous and capable they are, and therapists may confront demons only to learn that they were paper tigers.

ANTICIPATE TESTIMONY AS A THERAPEUTIC TOOL

When cases involve clients with whom therapy is ongoing, therapists can use their potential testimony as a therapeutic tool to strengthen their relationship with and empower their clients. They teach problem-solving skills and lend ego strength to clients when they are forthright and realistic.

Because lawsuits are extreme stressors, they typically feel overwhelming. Clients therefore must be able to speak freely with their therapists about their lawsuits, just as they speak about other problems in their lives.

Therapists therefore should talk about their clients' understanding of the lawsuit (all legal cases are lawsuits, whether civil or criminal), where they think they fit in, how going through a legal process is similar to or different from other experiences in their lives, and how they feel about the litigation. Therapists should ask their patients what they would like the outcome to be and, more important, what they will feel or do if the outcome is not what they would like. If the case isn't decided as they hope it would be, what will they decide to think about themselves, the legal system, and their therapy? Have clients make distinctions between what they are and are not in control of and what therapists who serve as witnesses are and are not in control of. These discussions can be very powerful forces in reducing anxiety and helplessness and demonstrating essential interpersonal skills. Clients can turn the "thorns of their crowns" into the "jewels of their crowns" by maintaining an internal locus of control and honoring themselves as they face difficult challenges. Sticking with them through a legal process may be one of psychotherapists' most valuable contributions.

Therapists should document only what is relevant to treatment. They should never record details of discussions their clients have reported having with their attorneys. Specific statements in their records about clients' discussions with their attorneys could undermine clients' attorney–client privilege when the records are seen in court. The following is an example of how a therapist met the requirements of record keeping in a progress note, without recording details that could potentially sabotage her client's privileged communication with attorneys.

12/1: Jane Doe indicated her lawsuit continues to be a major stressor. She discussed her feelings about the lawsuit. We explored her goals and feelings about possible outcomes. She stated that going through her legal case has meaning for her regardless of outcome: "Even if I lose the case, I know in the future I will feel better about myself knowing that I stood up and spoke the truth of what happened to me."

HANDLING THERAPISTS' OWN ANXIETY

When psychotherapy clients ask practitioners to provide information to their attorneys, practitioners may be ethically obligated to do so, even when the prospect is distasteful or causes them to feel anxiety. For example, as discussed previously, clinical information may be necessary for defense attorneys to develop arguments in order to save lives, such as in capital mitigation cases. The following case example illustrates how a therapist's anxiety about court impaired her objectivity and ruptured her solid treatment alliance with her former client.

A defense attorney representing a man who was facing the death penalty in the sentencing phase of his homicide trial contacted the therapist of the client's mother. The mother had formerly been in treatment with the therapist for over a year. The information the therapist could provide about the mother was critical. The severe abuse and neglect her son said he had suffered at his mother's hands was a key component in her son's legal arguments against the death penalty in the sentencing phase of his trial. With the help of her son's attorney, the mother respectfully sent her former therapist a signed, notarized release form and asked her by phone to provide information about her condition that was to be used in her son's legal defense.

Initially, the therapist complied with her former client's request. She talked freely with the attorney's investigator over the telephone, electing to return calls and to discuss the mother's previous problems. The therapist remembered the mother well, especially the mother's childhood sexual abuse and her diagnosis of dissociative identity disorder, for which the mother had sought treatment from the therapist. She remembered the mother's progress in treatment and her remorse over her maltreatment of her son, which had replicated her own severe childhood abuse.

In an unfortunate turn of events, the son's attorney failed to inform the therapist, as he should have, that he would be including the therapist's name on a witness list and that the opposing attorneys therefore would eventually be contacting the therapist. When the opposing attorney saw the therapist's name on a witness list, he sent the FBI to interview the therapist, which shocked the therapist. The therapist responded by becoming uncooperative.

She refused to return phone calls from the client's attorney, her former client, or the county child welfare social worker, who also needed the therapist's information.

When the judge intervened and ordered the therapist to submit a report to the judge of her treatment of the mother, the therapist became anxious about the prospect of having to provide a report. She replied to the judge with a scathing letter. Even though the therapist had never asked the attorney, the investigator, the mother, or the county social worker to stop calling her, she claimed that all of them had "harassed" her.

The therapist's former client felt hurt and stunned. She could not understand why her therapist would characterize her phone call asking for help in her son's trial as "harassment." She did not know why the therapist, who had been helpful to her in weekly sessions for over a year, was refusing to return her phone calls. The former patient not only faced her son's potential death sentence but perceived herself as being abandoned by her former therapist.

The therapist's anxiety over the adversarial nature of the legal case and the unexpected visit from FBI investigators is understandable. Quite likely, the therapist's distress could have been prevented had the son's attorney prepared her for what she could expect. Nevertheless, a more professional and helpful approach to her former client's needs would have been to remain calm and to consider her ethical duty to her former client, who had requested that the therapist release her confidential information to the court, and her legal obligation to comply with the court order. The rule of thumb is to not overreact to court procedures. Don't create unnecessary battles.

THE NEED TO RECOVER AFTER COURT TRIALS

It is helpful for practitioners to know that their patients and they need to "recover" after legal cases have ended. Just as patients typically experience a psychological "letdown" after their legal cases are over, it is also common for practitioners to feel exhausted, demoralized, even depressed following a court case. This is understandable. Many patients do not realize, until the legal case is over, how much energy they have expended in surviving the legal case. Mental health witnesses, too, are not used to the adversarial system and may have experienced attorneys' questioning as personal or degrading attacks. Knowing that these are understandable reactions can be helpful. Just as practitioners assist their patients in caring for themselves in the aftermath of a legal case, so should practitioners care for themselves. They need to seek support from colleagues and employ whatever methods help them to soothe themselves.

SUMMARY

Even the most experienced psychotherapists become anxious and confused and don't know how to respond when they receive calls or subpoenas from attorneys requesting that they release their patients' records or testify in their patients' legal cases. For therapists, the adversarial system is like a foreign culture: They do not understand its language or its customs. Even worse, they are unclear about their roles and do not understand their options. However, with information and ongoing consultation from colleagues who have experience with the legal system, practitioners can clarify their roles and become more confident in their interactions with the legal system. This chapter answered the most frequent questions practitioners have asked me about their roles in the legal system. It defined the differences between treatment witnesses and evaluation witnesses, discussed methods for handling subpoenas or other requests for records in legal cases, and presented strategies for handling clinical issues that arise in therapy during legal cases as well as ways to clarify one's role and provide testimony in depositions and in court.

Planning for Interruptions or Closure of Psychotherapy Practice

Imagine yourself in this nightmare: You are a successful psychotherapist in a busy solo private practice and are taking a much-needed ski vacation with your husband and children in Utah. On the second day, you decide to try skiing down a more difficult slope. Suddenly, unexpectedly, you hit a tree. The accident leaves you seriously injured, without speech. Your career as a psychotherapist is abruptly interrupted. You cannot contact your patients yourself, and no one else knows their names, nor where you keep the keys to your files, nor the password for your computer in order to access your patients' records. You cannot help your patients deal with this tragedy and sudden loss of your services, nor can you help them consider alternative solutions to meet their needs for ongoing treatment. You are especially concerned about those who have experienced deaths of parents when they were very young. For them, losing you without preparation or discussion with you will likely feel like another abandonment. You always take care to prepare your clients for your vacations. You had planned to prepare them in advance of your retirement, too. Now what will happen? How will your patients have access to their records so other professionals can take over their care? Your husband and adult children are helping you get the urgent medical care you need. But it has always been inappropriate for them to know your patients' names and see their confidential records. They cannot help with your professional emergency. What do you do?

Practitioners are clinically, ethically, and legally compelled to take reasonable steps to assure continuity of care for patients when their practices are temporarily suspended or permanently closed. Nevertheless, many practitioners in independent practice and other settings are unaware of how to carry out this critical responsibility in advance of an interruption in services, such as in the tragic circumstances above. Often they have not developed policies and procedures to ensure the ongoing clinical care of their clients, adequate protection for the confidentiality of client records, or access to those client records by appropriate agents after clinicians' retirement, incapacitation, or death. Professional organizations have only recently begun to give attention to the urgent need for policies and procedures in this area (North Carolina Society for Clinical Social Work, 2000; Salomon et al., 1997). Establishing proactive procedures for management of tasks involved in suspensions or closures of practices is essential, as it protects and comforts everyone who is directly and indirectly involved with the clinician's practice.

The purpose of this chapter is to help practitioners anticipate and make plans for records prior to interruptions or closing of their practices in order to promote continuity of care. The first section summarizes the clinical, ethical, and legal reasons why it is critical for practitioners to make contingency plans for patients' records. The second section presents specific procedures practitioners can use to prevent problems with records during temporary suspension or closing of practices, and provides a sample written plan.

CLINICAL, ETHICAL, AND LEGAL REASONS
FOR HAVING PLANS FOR RECORDS

Clinical Reasons

Continuity of care in psychotherapy is essential. Effective therapy depends largely on the stability and dependability of the therapeutic alliance. In most instances, the therapeutic relationship gradually becomes an extremely important source of strength and validation. It increases the client's self-esteem, confidence, and insight and reveals a novel understanding of the power of shared wisdom.

While continuity of care is critical, it is impossible to prevent interruptions or even permanent cessation of clinical practices. In most instances patients experience interruptions due to planned events, such as vacations or minor medical procedures. Longer hiatuses include maternity or paternity leaves, prolonged but curable illnesses, therapists returning to school for advanced degrees, or changes in organizational staffing patterns.

In exceptional circumstances psychotherapy practices are permanently closed. Therapists may move to distant locations, change vocations, or leave private practice to work in agencies that do not provide direct therapeutic services. In still other cases, the income of practitioners has become so limited by managed care and other changes in health care politics that they are unable to earn a living wage. Retirement explains another portion of closed practices. A substantial number of mental health professionals are over 50 years old. Many of those who have not yet retired are now preparing for ending their practices. In rare instances, therapists die from illness, are in fluke accidents, or must suspend their practices due to regulatory board sanctions.

Clients who receive treatment in institutions (such as academic settings, clinics, employee assistance programs that use interns, or larger mental health organizations) generally have fewer concerns about breaks in treatment or changes in therapists. They know in advance that these settings are geared toward high turnover of practitioners. They know that other staff can help them have access to their records as needed. Still, patients have many of the same experiences as private practice clients, and clinical and administrative issues should be acknowledged and treated with equal care and concern.

Clients are not alone in their difficulties regarding suspended or closed practices. Clinicians often face the same complex issues from the reverse side. They must evaluate each client as to how to approach and work through the effects of interruptions or cessation in treatment. Additionally, they may have the added burdens of finding appropriate practitioners to whom to refer clients, working with bureaucratic protocols, properly dispensing records, and wading though morasses of financial matters. Shared practices present complex problems. Losing a colleague to life changes or death involves enormous financial, clinical, and administrative responsibilities that may take months or years to resolve.

Even family members can be affected. They should not have to take responsibility for clinical management of records. However, spouses of deceased practitioners have called me with the following kinds of questions: "My husband was in solo private practice and died of cancer a few months ago. He left all of his psychotherapy patients' records in his office. It is not my psychotherapy practice, but he did not designate anyone to manage his records. Am I responsible for holding onto his records? If so, for how long? What do I do?" Another distraught spouse called me to say: "My wife died last year and one of her former psychotherapy patients has called me, asking for a copy of her record. What should I do?" Family members should be protected from having to deal with clinical emergencies whenever possible.

Ethical Guidelines

Because clinicians are well aware of the negative effects of a sense of abandonment, all professional associations' ethics codes unanimously agree that practitioners must take steps to prevent abandonment and assure continuity of care in the event a practitioner can no longer provide services. The following excerpts from four ethics codes illustrate this professional commitment:

1. American Counseling Association (1996) Code of Ethics and Standards of Practice, Section A: The Counseling Relationship, #11. Termination and Referral. a. "Abandonment Prohibited. Counselors do not abandon or neglect clients in counseling." 1.7. "Counselors assist in making appropriate arrangements for the continuation of treatment, when necessary, during interruptions such as vacations, and following termination."
2. American Medical Association Council on Ethical and Judicial Affairs' (2000) Code of Medical Ethics, 2000–2001 Edition. 7.03: Records of Physicians Upon Retirement or Departure from a Group. "A patient's records may be necessary to the patient in the future not only for medical care but also for employment, insurance, litigation, or other reasons. When a physician retires or dies, patients should be notified and urged to find a new physician and should be informed that upon authorization, records will be sent to the new physician. Records which may be of value to a patient and which are not forwarded to a new physician should be retained, either by the treating physician, another physician, or such other person lawfully permitted to act as a custodian of the records."

3. American Psychological Association (1992) Ethical Principles of Psychologists and Code of Conduct: 4.08 Interruption of Services. a) "Psychologists make reasonable efforts to plan for facilitating care in the event that psychological services are interrupted by factors such as the psychologists's illness, death, unavailability, or relocation or by the client's relocation or financial limitations." b) "When entering into employment or contractual relationships, psychologists provide for orderly and appropriate resolution of responsibility for patient or client care in the event that the employment or contractual relationship ends, with paramount consideration given to the welfare of the patient or client." 5.09. Preserving Records and Data. "A psychologist makes plans in advance so that confidentiality of records and data is protected in the event of the psychologist's death, incapacity, or withdrawal from the position or practice."
4. National Association of Social Workers (1996) Code of Ethics: Section I. Social Workers' Ethical Responsibilities to Clients. 1.15. Interruption of Services. "Social workers should make reasonable efforts to ensure continuity of services in the event that services are interrupted by factors such as unavailability, relocation, illness, disability or death." 1.16. Termination of Services. (e) "Social workers who anticipate the termination or interruption of services to clients should notify clients promptly and seek the transfer, referral, or continuation of services in relation to the clients' needs and preferences." (f) "Social workers who are leaving an employment setting should inform clients of appropriate options for the continuation of services and of the benefits and risks of the options."

Legal or Administrative Guidelines

When practices close for any reason, patients or their legally authorized representatives continue to have rights under state and federal privacy rules and laws for access to their records within the time frame that the records must be maintained. Some regulatory boards, such as in Minnesota, have recognized the need for contingency plans and require practitioners to have plans for continuity of care, including access to records. See, for example, the American State Psychology Boards' requirements in appendix P.

PROCEDURES THAT PROMOTE CONTINUITY OF CARE

The following are descriptions of some of the more common ways to prevent problems in suspending or closing practices.

Communicating With Clients About Changes in Practice

Practitioners should openly discuss the issue of continuity of care with new clients and make sure all clients know and understand their policies and procedures for interruptions in practice. Ideally, clinicians should do this verbally and in writing, using brochures or information sheets that include other information about therapists' practices, such as fees for missed appointments, which clients can sign and therapists can place in their records. The more clients are involved in and have some amount of control over their treatment, the less likely they are to feel anxiety or abandonment when changes arise during the course of treatment.

During treatment, therapists should share with clients, and document in the records, the specific arrangements they have discussed with their clients in anticipation of interruptions of practice. Discussions about serious and irrevocable events, such as the unexpected incapacitation or death of the therapist, should be reserved until a strong therapeutic alliance has been established and the client is stable and has sufficient ego strength to sustain the notion of losing the therapist permanently. Still, therapists should address this topic and options candidly and thoroughly. However painful an issue may be, the client–therapist relationship always benefits from direct and realistic communication.

Information about therapists' contingency plans for unlikely or unexpected events often arises naturally in the context of preparing for practitioners' vacations or other temporary leaves. The following case example illustrates the emergence of such information in the context of anticipating a therapist's vacation.

A 35-year-old female client, whose mother had died of a heart attack when the client was only 4 years old, had been in out-patient psychotherapy for 1 year to treat her delayed-onset posttraumatic stress disorder and major depressive disorder. Five years earlier, she had been physically assaulted in her workplace when she was on night duty. In her therapy, the client had benefitted from opportunities to discuss her feelings about the traumatic events related to the assault, her fears of being alone, her intense dependence upon her husband, and her fears of losing her therapist. Her anxiety decreased after she completed and discussed a narrative of her traumatic events with her therapist, and as she gained new awareness that her intense fears were related to the traumatic sudden death of her mother when she was a young child. She began learning how to anchor herself in the present when her fears surfaced so she could clarify her feelings and options; she gradually began practicing being on her own.

As the therapist prepared her client for the therapist's 2-week vacation, the therapist was mindful of the client's childhood history of early maternal loss, her current clinical status, and the importance of using the therapeutic relationship to support her client's emerging autonomy:

Therapist: Before we begin today, I want to look ahead with you to the next 3 weeks. As I mentioned last week, I'll be out of the office for 2 weeks starting next week, so our next appointment will be 3 weeks from today.

Client: Yes, I remember.

Therapist: Mary Jones will again be taking emergency calls for me while I am away. Do you have her number?

Client: I think I still do, but would you write it down for me again on a card?

Therapist: Sure. It will also be on my voice mail message while I am away. I don't expect you will be having any emergencies at this point, but it's good to have her number anyway.

Client: I don't expect to either. I am feeling much better now than I was before.

Therapist: [Writes the number down and hands card to client.] Yes. I know you have been feeling better, more secure now. I feel lucky that Mary is available to my clients just in case. She and I have very similar approaches to our work and I trust her completely. As I mentioned a few weeks ago, I am in good health and don't plan to retire for another 15 years, but she is the colleague who has agreed to take responsibility for talking with my clients in the unlikely event I would die or become disabled.

Client: Yes, I remember we talked about that. I had been worried about that and it is good to know there is a plan.

Therapist: [After talking with the client about the worries and questions she had been having.] Shall we turn now to what you want to be sure to cover in our appointment today?

Collaborating With Other Professionals

Practitioners need to develop relationships with other practitioners and construct detailed plans for a range of possibilities, including emergencies during vacations or other leaves of absence, illnesses or disabilities, closure of practice, and death. Practitioners must be sure another trusted practitioner can gain access to important information and documents, such as client files and the names, phone numbers, and addresses of clients and their designated contact persons. Prior to planned interruptions, therapists should record a brief synopsis of each client's problems and diagnoses, physician's name, and whether and to what extent the client may be at risk to themselves or others. For unexpected interruptions of service, it is much easier for trusted colleagues to assess clients' current status, potential needs for further care, and what referrals and plans are indicated when therapists have maintained legible, contemporaneous records. Practitioners should consider using an attorney to document and make legal the parameters of the colleague's responsibilities.

Notifying Current Clients When Practices Close Permanently

When practices close permanently, the primary practitioners or other professionals need to communicate with current clients their current status, need for further services, if any, and what referrals or other plans have already been made or should be made.

In the event of a practitioner's sudden, unexpected incapacitation or death, notification tasks are easier in institutions. This is because records belong to the institution, not just to the solo practitioner, and support staff or professional staff are always on site anyway and can locate the practitioner's calendar in order to cancel appointments and make arrangements for continuity of care. In private practices, designated professionals need to be contacted in order to assume notification and assessment tasks with patients.

Notifying Former Clients

Practitioners should consider whether to notify former patients (whose records are still being retained) of their practice's closing to advise them how they may obtain access to their records. (The Code of Ethics for the American Medical Association requires that physicians do so.) Patients whose records are no longer being retained but who have experienced significant help from psychotherapists often find security in knowing they can return to their former practitioners at a later date, should they need further help. When they intend to retire or close their practices, practitioners may therefore wish to consider sending these patients announcements. Routinely asking patients at the time their therapy is ending whether they would like to be notified whenever the practice closes can help practitioners identify in advance which patients wish to be notified.

Storing Records Securely

When practices are suspended or closed, it is mandatory under state and federal laws that client records continue to be stored in a locked room or similar facility. Access to confidential client-identifiable information should continue to be limited to expressly authorized individuals. In most instances, records are obtained and reviewed for one of three reasons:

- to review and respond to requests from clients or their legal representatives for clients' records;
- to provide information in the event of a post-mortem audit of the therapist's billings to third party payers (usually the maximum is 3 years, but under some contracts it may be 5);
- to provide information to protect the therapist's estate in the event of a lawsuit

In the United States, for example, practitioners cannot be tried after their death; however, their estates can be sued. In Minnesota, two patients sued the estate of their former psychiatrist 2 years after he died from suicide. The estate required the psychiatrist's records in order to defend the estate's assets (Schoener, 2001a).

Defining the Role of Designated Agents

All practitioners need to have a designated agent, that is, a person who is legally authorized to assume the tasks of their practices in the event of temporary or permanent cessation. Designated agents should have the clinical, ethical, and legal knowledge and experience to manage all aspects of the clinician's practice or know how to gain competent assistance if necessary.

In addition to communicating with clients about their needs and making appropriate plans, one of the most important tasks of a designated agent is managing requests for client records. The designated agent must be able to accurately assess the legitimacy of requests for client records by clients, client guardians, or legal agents of clients and to know how to legally and ethically respond to requests for records.

Besides protecting the confidentiality of and making decisions about requests for client records, designated agents must be able to adequately attend to other tasks, including:

- financial and clerical matters, such as sorting and responding to important correspondence;
- monitoring client billing and ensuring up-to-date payment;
- communicating with professional organizations and regulatory boards;
- negotiating contracts (or securing an attorney to do so);
- canceling subscriptions;

- working with the practitioner's attorney to dissolve the professional estate (in the event of the practitioner's death).

Designated agents can perform their roles much more efficiently if practitioners prepare a detailed list of the specific tasks that need to be completed and the information needed to complete these tasks. A list includes the following: (a) Names and phone numbers of people who have agreed to handle certain matters, and the specific outcome to be accomplished by each person; and (b) specific directions necessary to accomplish each task, such as:

- how to change voice mail greeting;
- location of keys to files, mailbox, locked rooms, and so on;
- location of list of current and former client names, addresses, phone numbers;
- location of billing and banking information for deposits;
- location of managed care and other contracts;
- names, addresses, phone numbers of landlords or tenants;
- location of professional liability insurance information: name, address, phone number of agent;
- names of professional regulatory boards by whom practitioner was licensed (and contact person if applicable);
- location of office insurance contract and name, address, and phone number of agent;
- names, addresses, phone numbers of important professional contacts and colleagues;
- list of professional memberships;
- list of dues and subscriptions and records of previous payments;
- description of how designated agents (and others, if applicable) are to be paid for their time and expenses for managing the practice after it closes;
- list of who, besides the designated agent, is authorized to open and handle mail;
- name, address, phone number of executor of estate (if other than designated agent);
- name, address, phone number of attorney (if any).

Where to Store "Professional Wills" or Advance Directives

Practitioners often erroneously assume that provisions made ahead of time for patients should be included in their personal wills. However, personal wills are not the appropriate places for such information for several reasons. Wills are usually in the possession of the practitioner's attorney and many attorneys recommend against disseminating copies of wills to prevent legal problems after death. Wills are rarely obtained immediately after death; they must be approved in probate court before they can be completely operational. Finally, wills are not easily altered; therefore, changing designated agents is extremely costly and time consuming.

Practitioners should leave their "professional wills" with (a) persons such as family members who would be the first to know of a sudden incapacitation or death who could notify the designated colleagues; (b) colleagues who routinely provide coverage for them during anticipated temporary leaves; and (c) colleagues who have agreed to assume responsibility for them after their practices close permanently. To facilitate information getting to former clients who are searching for practitioners who have retired or died, professional associations could also maintain a list of "designated colleagues" in their annual membership renewal information. Clients would thus be able to get the necessary information by contacting the professional associations.

SUMMARY

Proactive procedures for management of tasks involved in suspensions or closures of practices can protect everyone who is associated with the clinician's practice. This chapter discussed the clinical, ethical, and legal reasons why practitioners should prepare in advance for disposition of records in the event of temporary suspension or closing of their practices. It recommended specific procedures psychotherapists in any setting could use to adequately protect the confidentiality of client records or provide access to client records to appropriate agents after their retirement, incapacitation, or death.

Epilogue

Lest I end as abruptly as did the unlucky therapist on the ski slope in the last chapter, I would like to close by reflecting on experiences while creating this book and on the comments of colleagues who have read it.

I learned a great deal from the writing itself. As I read the final proofs, I found myself wishing I had had such a book when I was in graduate school or at the time I received my first subpoena for the records of a client. I gained insight into how to conduct my practice, including how to plan for unexpected interruptions, and for retirement. My hope is that this book will also be useful to others.

The book was harder to write than I expected. First, I thought it would be shorter. But it expanded along the way. I found it difficult to focus only on record keeping without addressing all aspects of practice. More and more case prototypes kept emerging in my mind, but to include them meant I must discuss their clinical and ethical contexts. Meanwhile, the U.S. Department of Health and Human Services promulgated the federal privacy rule and then, just before the book was ready to go to print, modified it. I needed time to study the rule and its changes. Writing chapter 11, which focuses on the closing of a practice, was the most difficult because it meant facing my own mortality and the inevitability of eventually leaving the work I love.

I was delighted to find broader applications for the book than I originally planned. For example, though discussion of clinical research is beyond the scope of this book, a University of Minnesota professor nevertheless used the information on confidentiality in chapters 4 and 5 for his lecture to nurses and physicians in the clinical research training program. Another colleague suggested that the chapter on supervision and sample supervision contract, in appendix K, could serve as a model for other academic fields. He noted that most graduate programs fail to impart knowledge or practical strategies for assessing learning needs, for establishing clear contracts with advisees, or for documenting supervision.

Colleagues also shared their concerns with me. For example, one joked that "all the forms and consents and contracts here, laid end-to-end, might wrap several practitioners alive." Or, that "all the detailed verbal explanations about privacy, security, etc., presented at the very outset of treatment, might cause more than glazed eyes in a client."

My response is that readers will find in the book what they can use. They must stay true to their own style. They can extract from, condense, and modify this material to fit their needs. With experience, incorporation of good and sufficient record keeping into daily practice becomes routine.

Finally, we are dealing with rapid change in government policies and rules on records and privacy in health practice. The information herein should help us navigate through the disturbing waters of uncertain regulations.

In the end, writing this book has been both very difficult and marvelously rewarding. It has broadened and constructively strengthened my concepts and feelings about our field. I hope the same for you, the reader.

ELLEN T. LUEPKER
St. Paul, Minnesota

References

American Association for Marriage and Family Therapy. (2001). *Code of ethics*. Washington, DC: Author.

American Association of Pastoral Counselors. (1994). *Code of ethics*. Fairfax, VA: Author.

American Association of State Psychology Boards. (1991). *AASPB code of conduct*. Montgomery, AL: Author.

American Counseling Association. (1996). *Code of ethics and standards of practice*. Alexandria, VA: Author.

American Group Psychotherapy Association and National Registry of Certified Group Psychotherapists. (2002). *Guidelines for ethics*. New York, NY: Author.

American Medical Association Council on Ethical and Judicial Affairs. (2000). *Code of medical ethics: Current opinions with annotations*. Washington, DC: Author.

American Nurses' Association. (1984). *A statement on psychiatric–mental health nursing practice and standards of psychiatric mental health clinical nursing practice*. Washington DC: American Nurses' Publishing.

American Psychiatric Association. (2001a). *Principles of medical ethics with annotations especially applicable to psychiatry*. Washington, DC: Author.

American Psychiatric Association. (2001b, March 12). Technical amendment to the final rule standards for confidentiality of individually identifiable health information: Letter to Secretary Thompson at the U.S. Department of Health and Human Services. (*Federal Register,* February 28, 2001, pp. 12738–12739). Washington, DC: Author.

American Psychological Association. (1992). Ethical principles of psychologists and code of conduct. *American Psychologist, 47,* 1597–1611.

American Psychological Association. (1981). *Specialty guidelines for the delivery of services*. Washington, DC: Author.

Appelbaum, P. S. (2000). Threats to confidentiality of medical records: No place to hide. *Journal of the American Medical Association, 283*(6), 795–797.

Associated Press. (1997, October 6). McGovern rethinks Eagleton. *Washington Post,* p. A8.

Association for Specialists in Group Work. (1998). *Best practice guidelines*. Arlington, VA: Author.

Association of State and Provincial Psychology Boards. (1998). *Disciplinary data system, August 1983–January 1998*. Montgomery, AL: Author.

Bridge, P. J., & Bascue, L. O. (1988). A record form for psychotherapy supervisors. In P. Keller and S. Heyman (Eds.), *Innovations in clinical practice* (pp. 331–336). Sarasota, FL: Professional Resource Exchange.

Brooke, P. S. (1994). Legal and ethical aspects of mental health care. In E. M. Varcarolis (Ed.), *Foundations of psychiatric mental health nursing* (pp. 6–66). Philadelphia, PA: W.B. Saunders Company.

Carter, P. I. (1999). Health information privacy: Can Congress protect confidential medical information in the "Information Age"? *William Mitchell Law Review*, 25(1), 223–286.

Clinical Social Work Federation. (1997). *Code of ethics*. Arlington, VA: Author.

Clinical Social Work Federation. (1991). *Standards of practice for clinical social work practice*. Arlington, VA: Author.

Clough, J. D., Rowan, D. W., & Nickelson, D. E. (1999, October). Keeping our patients' secrets. *Cleveland Clinic Journal of Medicine*, 66(9), 554–558.

Court of Appeals of Maryland. (1999, September Term). #134. *In re: adoption/guardianship #CCJ14746 in the Circuit Court for Washington County*.

Currier, M., & Sotto, L. (2001). New privacy requirements for health information. *The Practical Lawyer*, 47(6), 47–50.

Dwyer, J., & Shih, A. (1998). The ethics of tailoring the patient's chart. *Psychiatric Services*, 49(10), 1309–1312.

Federal Register. (2002, August). Volume 67, #157: Rules and regulations. (53181-53273).

Federal Register. (2000, December 28). Volume 65, Number 25: Rules and regulations, standards for the privacy of individually identifiable health information. *Final rule*. 45CFR. Parts 160 through 164.

Freed, A. O. (1978, October). Clients' rights and casework records. *Social Casework*, 59(8), 458–464.

Furlong, A. (1998). Should we or shouldn't we? Some aspects of the confidentiality of clinical reporting and dossier access. *International Journal of Psychoanalysis*, 79, 727–739.

Gabbard, G. O., & Wilkinson, S. M. (1994). *Management of countertransference with borderline patients*. Washington, D.C.: American Psychiatric Press.

Gartrell, N. (1992). Boundaries in lesbian therapy relationships. *Women and Therapy*, 12(3), 29–50.

Goldman, J. (1998). Protecting privacy to improve health care. *Health Affairs*, 17(6), 47–61.

Grady, D. (1997, March 12). Hospital computer files as an open book. *New York Times*, p. C8.

Grange, A., Renvoize, E., & Pinder, J. (1998). Patients' rights to access their healthcare records. *Nursing Standard*, 13(6), 41–42.

Griffith, E. E. H., Zonana, H., Pinsince, A. J., & Adams, A. K. (1988). Institutional response to inpatients' threats against the President. *Hospital and Community Psychiatry*, 39, 11.

Herman, J. L. (1992). *Trauma and recovery*. New York: Basic Books.

Hasman, A., Hanson, N. R., Lassen, A., Rabol, R., & Holm, S. (1997). What do people talk about on Danish elevators? *Ugeskr. Laeger, 159,* 6819–6821.

Health Care Privacy Project (2001). *Sumary of HIPAA Privacy Regulations*. Washington, DC: Georgetown University.

Hughes, G. (2001). *Confidentiality and security of ambulatory health records. Documentation for ambulatory care* (pp. 43–69). Chicago: American Health Information and Management Association.

Jaffee v. Redmond. (1996). 116 Supreme Court 1923, 135, L.Ed.2d 337.

Joint Commision on Accredidation of Health Care Organizations (2001). *2001 BHC clinical record review tool for open and closed records for behavioral health care.* Author.

Kagle, J. D. (1991). *Social work records*. Belmont, CA: Wadsworth.

Kaiser, T. L. (1997). *Supervisory relationships: Exploring the human wlement*. Pacific Grove, CA: Brooks/Cole.

Kern, S. I. (1996). Responding to subpoenas and other demands for records and testimony. *New Jersey Medicine, 93*(2), 85–88.

Kramer, D. (1996). Physicians who keep lax records put careers in danger, college course warns. *Canadian Medical Association Journal, 155*(10), 1469–1472.

Krasner, R. F., Howard, K. I., & Brown, A. S. (1998, November). Acquisition of psychotherapeutic skill: An empirical study. *Journal of Clinical Psychology, 54*(7), 895–903.

Lerner, M. (2001, November 8). Web posting has health and university officials scrambling; mental health records of children from twenty families were mistakenly put onto the internet. *Star Tribune Newspaper of the Twin Cities*, p. 1B.

Luepker, E. T. (1999). Effects of practitioners' sexual misconduct: A follow-up study. *Journal of the American Academy of Psychiatry and the Law, 27*(1), 51–63.

Luepker, E. T. (1989). Clinical assessment of clients who have been sexually exploited by their therapists and development of differential treatment plans. In G. R. Schoener, J. Gonsiorek, J. H. Milgrom, E. T. Luepker, & R. Conroe (Eds), *Psychotherapists' sexual involvement with clients: Intervention and prevention* (pp. 159–176). Minneapolis, MN: Walk-In Counseling Center.

Markoff, J. (1997, April 4). Patient files turn up in used computer. *New York Times*, p. A9.

McLeod, P., & Polowy, C. I. (2000). *Social workers and child abuse reporting: A review of state mandatory reporting requirements: Office of the General Council law note*. Washington DC: National Association of Social Workers.

Milgrom, J. H. (1989). Advocacy: Assisting sexually exploited clients through the complaint process. In G. R. Schoener, J. Gonsiorek, J. H. Milgrom, E. T. Luepker, & R. Conroe (Eds), *Psychotherapists' sexual involvement with clients: Intervention and prevention* (pp. 305–312). Minneapolis, MN: Walk-In Counseling Center.

Mishler, E. G. (1979). Meaning in context: Is there any other kind? *Harvard Educational Review, 49*(1), 1–19.

Mitchell, R. (2001). *Documentation in Counseling Records*. Alexandria, VA: American Counseling Association.

Monahan, J. (1993). Limiting therapist exposure to Tarsoff liability: Guidelines for risk containment. *American Psychologist, 48*(3), 242–250.

Moline, M. E., Williams, G. T., & Austin, K. M. (1998). *Documenting psychotherapy: Essentials for mental health practitioners.* Beverly Hills, CA: Sage.

National Association of Social Workers. (1996). *Code of ethics.* Washington, DC: Author.

National Association of Social Workers. (1991). *NASW guidelines on the private practice of clinical social work.* Washington, DC: Author.

North Carolina Society for Clinical Social Work. (2001). *A suggested model for the sudden termination of a clinical social work practice.* Durham, NC: Author.

Office for Civil Rights. (2001, October 18). *Standards for privacy of individually identifiable health information.* Washington, DC: Author. Retrieved from http://www.hhs.gov

Piper, A. (1994). Truce on the battlefield. *Journal of Law, Medicine, & Ethics, 22*(4), 301–313.

Privacy Act of 1974. 5 United States Code 552A.

Reamer, F. G. (1995). Malpractice claims against social workers: First facts. *Social Work, 40*(5), 595–601.

Salomon, F., Marshal, M., Key, T., & Weller, J. (1997, December). Ethics beyond the grave: Dealing with the impact of one's death. *The Arizona Psychologist, 17*(6), 1–6.

Sanford, S. M., Hartnett, T., & Jolly, B. T. (1999, Summer). Lessons from the past: The roots of the informed consent process. *The Monitor.*

Schoener, G. R. (2001a, October 12). Advanced ethical/legal and practice issues for therapists and supervisors. Paper presented at a workshop sponsored by the Kenwood Therapy Center, Minneapolis, MN.

Schoener, G. R. (2001b, August 24) Searching for Mercy Street: Protecting clients after death. *American Psychological Association Symposium on Psychotherapists' Duties after Death—Some Clinical, Ethical, and Legal Guidance.* Paper presented at the American Psychological Association Annual Convention, San Francisco, CA.

Schoener, G. R. (2001c, October 12). Duty to warn or protect in Minnesota in 2001. Paper presented at a workshop sponsored by the Kenwood Therapy Center, Minneapolis, MN.

Schoener, G. R., & Conroe, R. M. (1989). The role of supervision and case consultation in primary prevention. In G. R. Schoener, J. Gonsiorek, J. H. Milgrom, E. T. Luepker, & R. Conroe (Eds.), *Psychotherapists' sexual involvement with clients: Intervention and prevention* (pp. 477–493). Minneapolis, MN: Walk-In Counseling Center.

Social Security Act. (1997). 18 United States Code, 1852.

Stanberry, B. (1998). The legal and ethical aspects of telemedicine. 2: Data protection, security and European law. *Journal of Telemedicine and Telecare, 4,* 18–24.

Tarasoff v. Regents of the University of California. (1974). 529 P 2d 553, 118 Cal. Rptr. 129.

Tarasoff v. Regents of the University of California. (1976). 551 P 2d 334, 131 Cal. Reptr. 14.

Time magazine, (1996, September 2), *Where are they now*, p. 17.

Townes, B. L., Wagner, N. N., & Christ, A. (1967). Therapeutic use of psychological reports. *Journal of American Academy of Child Psychiatry, 6,* 698.

Townsend, M. C. (1999). Legal issues in psychiatric/mental health nursing. *Essentials of Psychiatric/Mental Health Nursing* (pp. 145–149). Philadelphia: F.A. Davis Company.

Tyler, J. D., Sloan, L. L., & King, A. R. (2000). Psychotherapy supervision practices of academic faculty: A national survey. *Psychotherapy, 37.*

United States Department of Health and Human Services. (2001a). *Final privacy rule—regulation text.* Retrieved from http://www.aspe.hhs.gov/admnsimp/final/PvcTxt01.htm

United States Department of Health and Human Services. (2001b, May 9). *Protecting the privacy of patients' health information.* Retrieved from http://www.aspe.hhs.gov/admnsimp/final/pvcfact2.htm

United States Department of Health and Human Services. (2001c, July 6). *Standards for privacy of individually identifiable health information.* Retrieved from http://www.hhs.gov/ocr/hipaa/finalmaster.html

United States Department of Health and Human Services. (2000, December 28). Standards for privacy of individually identifiable health information. *Federal Register, 65*(250), 82461–82510.

United States v. Patillo. (1971). 438 F2d 13. 4th Circuit.

Wahlberg, D. (1999, February 10). Patient records exposed on web. *Ann Arbor News,* p. 1A.

Webster's New Dictionary and Thesaurus. (1996). New York: Simon and Schuster, Inc.

Weintraub, M. I. (1999, May). Documentation and informed consent. *Neurologic Clinics, 17*(2), 371–381.

Welch, B. L. (2001a). Caution: State licensing board ahead. *Insight: Safeguarding Psychologists Against Liability Risks.* Edition 1, 2001. Amityville: The American Professional Agency.

Welch, B. L. (2001b). Keeping up: The need for continuing education. *Insight: Safeguarding Psychologists Against Liability Risks.* Edition 2, 2001. Amityville: The American Professional Agency.

Welch, B. L. (2000). Reducing your suicide liability. *Insight: Safeguarding Psychologists Against Liability Risks.* Edition 1, 2000. Amityville: The American Professional Agency.

Whitman, S. M., & Jacobs, E. G. (1998). Responsibilities of the psychotherapy supervisor. *American Journal of Psychotherapy, 52*(2).

Zinsser, W. (1988). *Writing to learn.* New York: Harper and Row.

Zuckerman, E. L. (1997). *The paper office: Forms, guidelines, and resources.* New York: The Guilford Press.

Excerpts From Mental Health Professions' Codes of Ethics on Informed Consent

1. American Association for Marriage and Family Therapy (2001) Code of Ethics. Principle I, Responsibility to Clients, Section 1.2: "Marriage and family therapists obtain appropriate informed consent to therapy or related procedures as early as feasible in the therapeutic relationship, and use language that is reasonably understandable to clients. The content of informed consent may vary depending upon the client and treatment plan; however, informed consent generally necessitates that the client: a) has the capacity to consent; b) has been adequately informed of significant information concerning treatment processes and procedures; c) has been adequately informed of potential risks and benefits of treatments for which generally recognized standards do not yet exist; d) has freely and without undue influence expressed consent; and e) has provided consent that is appropriately documented. When persons, due to age or mental status, are legally incapable of giving informed consent, marriage and family therapists obtain informed permission from a legally authorized person, if such substitute consent is legally permissible."
2. American Association of Pastoral Counselors Code of Ethics (1994), Principle II, Professional Practices, C: "Fees and financial arrangements, as with all contractual matters, are always discussed without hesitation or equivocation at the onset and are established in a straight-forward, professional manner."
3. American Counseling Association (1996) Code of Ethics and Standards of Practice. Section A, "The Counseling Relationship." A.3. "Client Rights. a. Disclosure to Clients. When counseling is initiated, and throughout

the counseling process as necessary, counselors inform clients of the purposes, goals, techniques, procedures, limitations, potential risks, and benefits of services to be performed, and other pertinent information. Counselors take steps to ensure that clients understand the implications of diagnosis, the intended use of tests and reports, fees, and billing arrangements. Clients have the right to expect confidentiality and to be provided with an explanation of its limitations, including supervision and/or treatment team professionals; to obtain clear information about their case records; to participate in the ongoing counseling plans: and to refuse any recommended services and be advised of the consequences of such refusal. b. Freedom of Choice. Counselors offer clients the freedom to choose whether to enter into a counseling relationship and to determine which professional(s) will provide counseling. Restrictions that limit choices of clients are fully explained. c. Inability to Give Consent. When counseling minors or persons unable to give voluntary informed consent, counselors act in these clients' best interests."

4. American Group Psychotherapy Association Guidelines for Ethics. Section on Responsibility to Patient/Client, #1.1: "The group psychotherapist shall provide the potential group patient/client with information about the nature of group psychotherapy and apprise them of their risks, rights and obligations as members of a therapy group."

5. American Medical Association Code of Medical Ethics, Council on Ethical and Judicial Affairs, (2000–2001). Section 8.08. Informed Consent. "The patient's right of self-decision can be effectively exercised only if the patient possesses enough information to enable an intelligent choice. The patient should make his or her own determination on treatment. The physician's obligation is to present the medical facts accurately to the patient or to the individual responsible for the patient's care and to make recommendations for management in accordance with good medical practice. The physician has an ethical obligation to help the patient make choices from among the therapeutic alternatives consistent with good medical practice. Informed consent is a basic social policy for which exceptions are permitted: 1) where the patient is unconscious or otherwise incapable of consenting and harm from failure to treat is imminent; or 2) when risk-disclosure poses such a serious psychological threat of detriment to the patient as to be medically contraindicated. Social policy does not accept the paternalistic view that the physician may remain silent because divulgence might prompt the patient to forego needed therapy. Rational, informed patients should not be expected to act uniformly, even under similar circumstances, in agreeing to or refusing treatment."

6. American Psychiatric Association (2001). The Principles of Medical Ethics, with Annotations Especially Applicable to Psychiatry:

7. American Psychological Association (1992), section 4.02, "Informed Consent to Therapy": a) "Psychologists obtain appropriate informed consent to therapy or related procedures, using language that is reasonably understandable to participants. The content of informed consent will vary depending on many circumstances; however, informed consent generally implies that the person 1) has the capacity to consent, 2) has been informed of significant information concerning the procedure, 3) has freely and without undue influence expressed consent, and 4) consent has been appropriately documented." b) "When persons are legally incapable of giving informed consent, psychologists obtain informed permission from a legally authorized person, if such substitute consent is permitted by law." c) "In addition, psychologists 1) inform those persons who are legally incapable of giving informed consent about the proposed interventions in a manner commensurate with the persons' psychological capacities, 2) see their assent to those interventions, and 3) consider such persons' preferences and best interests."

8. Clinical Social Work Federation Code of Ethics (1997), Principle II, Responsibility to Clients, Section 1. Informed consent to Treatments, a): "Clinical social work treatment takes place within a context of informed consent. This requires that the client(s) be informed of the extent and nature of the services being offered as well as the mutual limits, rights, opportunities, and obligations associated with the provision of and payment for those services. In order for the consent to be valid, the client(s) must be informed in a manner which is clear to them, must choose freely and without undue influence, and must have the capacity to make an informed choice. In instances where clients are not of legal age or competent to give a meaningful consent, they will be informed in a manner which is consistent with their level of understanding in such situations, authorization for treatment will be obtained from an appropriate third party, such as a parent or other legal guardian." b) "Clinical social workers have a duty to understand the potential impact on all aspects of treatment resulting from participation in various third party payment mechanisms, and to disclose fully their knowledge of these features to the client. Such features might include, but are not limited to: limitations of confidentiality; payment limitations related to provide choice; a summary of the treatment review process required by the plan; the comparative treatment orientations of the plan and of the clinical social worker; the possibility that benefits may be limited under the plan; the clinical social worker's relationship to the plan and any incentives to limit or deny care; and the availability of alternative treatment options."

9. National Association of Social Workers (1996) Code of Ethics, Section 1.03, Informed Consent: "a) Social workers should provide services to

clients only in the context of a professional relationship based, when appropriate, on valid informed consent. Social workers should use clear and understandable language to inform clients of the purpose of the services, risks related to the services, limits to services because of the requirements of a third-party payer, relevant costs, reasonable alternatives, clients' rights to refuse or withdraw consent, and the time frame covered the consent. Social workers should provide clients with an opportunity to ask questions. b) In instances when clients are not literate or have difficulty understanding the primary language used in the practice setting, social workers should take steps to ensure clients' comprehension. This may include providing clients with a detailed verbal explanation or arranging for a qualified interpreter or translator whenever possible. c) In instances when clients lack the capacity to provide informed consent, social workers should protect clients' interests by seeking permission from an appropriate third party, informing clients consistent with the clients' level of understanding. In such instances social workers should seek to ensure that the third party acts in a manner consistent with clients' wishes and interests. Social workers should take reasonable steps to enhance such clients' ability to give informed consent. d) In instances when clients are receiving services involuntarily, social workers should provide information about the nature and extent of services and about the extent of clients' right to refuse service. e) Social workers who provide services via electronic media (such as computer, telephone, radio, and television) should inform recipients of the limitations and risks associated with such services. f) Social workers should obtain clients' informed consent before audio taping or video taping clients or permitting observation of services to clients by a third party."

Sample Client
Information Form

(Note: The following provides psychotherapy clients with information about policies and procedures. It is consistent with ethical standards and with the federal privacy rule, which requires practitioners covered by the rule to provide patients with a clear written notice of privacy practices. This statement is not legal or clinical advice. Practitioners should consult their attorneys to clarify how to implement state and federal laws and rules in their own practices.)

(Therapist Letterhead)

CLIENT INFORMATION

Welcome to my practice. I will be continually working to provide you with appropriate, high-quality services. I believe that a client who understands and participates in his/her care can achieve better results. I have the responsibility to give you the best care possible, to respect your rights, and to recognize your responsibilities as a client. I have prepared this information handout to help you identify these rights and responsibilities.

YOUR RIGHTS AS A CLIENT

Your Right to Privacy and Confidentiality

I follow the privacy provisions of state and federal laws and rules. You have the right to know the policies, practices, and limitations of the privacy of the information that you will share with me.

Your treatment record will be stored in a locked cabinet or computer which is protected from unauthorized access. It is accessible only to me and to personnel whom I have authorized to help me provide treatment to you. Your treatment record includes your diagnosis, treatment plan, progress notes, psychological test report, psychiatric and other medical reports, and closing summary.

Your billing record will be stored separately in a locked cabinet or computer protected from unauthorized access. It is accessible only to me or my billing office staff whom I have authorized to perform billing services. If you request that your insurance company pay for my services, I will share only the minimum information necessary for your insurance company to process claims. I provide the following billing information to my billing staff for submission of claims to your insurance company: a) name and address of your insurance company; b) your subscriber and group plan numbers; c) your name, birth date, social security number, diagnosis, dates of service, type of service. If your insurance company requires further information in order to process your claim (such as date of onset of your problems, history of your problems, symptoms that meet criteria for your diagnosis, your progress in treatment to date, and your goals and objectives for treatment), I will first consult you about your insurance company's request and give you the option to decide what, if anything, may be released. It is your choice whether or not to use your insurance coverage for payment of my services.

All personnel (clinical, support, or billing) authorized to have access to your information in this office will limit their access and use of your health care information to only what is necessary. They have agreed to carefully abide by the privacy practices of this office.

If you are receiving clinical services from other health care professionals, I will need to routinely confer with them about your diagnosis, treatment plan, and progress for the purpose of coordinating your treatment.

At times, I may also seek out professional consultation about some aspect of my work with you. Usually it will not be necessary to share your identifying information with the consultant(s). The consulting professional(s) also must abide by applicable laws and ethics and protect your confidentiality in all cases.

Other than the routine disclosures noted above which are necessary to perform treatment and billing services on your behalf, no information will be released to any other persons or agencies outside of this office without your written authorization except by court order. If anyone outside of this office requests information from me or from your records, your permission in writing on a special "authorization for release of information" form is necessary. Before giving permission, satisfy yourself that the information is really needed, that you understand the information being sent out, and that giving the information will help you. You have the right to approve or refuse the release of information to anyone, except as provided by law.

Exceptions to the Above Information Release Procedures

1. When I have knowledge of, or reasonable cause to believe, that a child is being neglected or physically or sexually abused, in which case state law requires that such information be reported.
2. Reporting of maltreatment of vulnerable adults as specified in state law.
3. Reporting of alleged practitioner sexual misconduct as specified in state law.
4. Reporting of instances of threatened homicide or physical violence against another. I must report such threats to the appropriate police agency as well as to the intended victim.
5. In cases of threatened suicide, at least one concerned person and/or the appropriate police agency may be contacted to intervene and the client will be referred for evaluation.
6. In cases in which a client, with a history of sexual and/or physical abuse of others, terminates therapy against my advice, I will notify those past victims of the abuse that the client has terminated therapy against my advice so that proper precautions can be taken.
7. It is my policy to employ the use of a collection agency or to file in small claims court on all accounts which are overdue by 90 days. Information necessary to pursue such payment due to me will be shared with the agency or court.

Right Not to Be Discriminated Against

You have the right not to be discriminated against in the provision of professional services on the basis of race, age, gender, ethnic origin, disabilities, creed, or sexual orientation.

Right to Know Your Therapist's Qualifications

You are entitled to ask me what my training is, where I received it, if I am licensed or certified, my professional competencies, experience, education, biases or attitudes, and any other relevant information that may be important to you in the provision of services. You have the right to expect that I have met the minimum qualifications of training and experience required by state law and to examine public records maintained by the licensure boards that regulate my practice at (address) _____ and (phone) _____.

My professional competencies include the following: child, adolescent, and adult psychotherapy; couples and family therapy; group psychotherapy; clinical research; consultation; teaching; supervision; and forensic evaluation.

Right to Be Informed

You have the right to be informed of my assessment of your problem in language you understand and to know available treatment alternatives. You also have the right to understand the purpose of the professional services, including an estimate of the number of therapy or consultation sessions, the length of time involved, the cost of the services, the method of treatment, and the expected outcomes of therapy. In addition, you have the right and responsibility to help develop your own treatment plan. If medication is being considered for you, you have the right to be informed by your physician of treatment alternatives, action of the medication, and possible side effects.

Right to Read Your Own Records

You have the right to read your own records. I will assist you in understanding your written records by being available to answer questions and to explain the meaning of test scores and technical terminology. You may inform me of any inaccuracies of information in your file and give me a written amendment, which I will place in your file. In addition, you have the right to be told why the information I am requesting is needed and be told how the information will be used. You should also be informed of the consequences, if any, of refusing to supply requested information. The information collected will be used by me for evaluation and treatment purposes. If you choose to not supply such information, I cannot determine which services are most appropriate for you and that will make it more difficult for me to carry out an effective treatment plan for you.

My records retention policy is as follows: The complete record will be retained for seven years. At the end of seven years, the record will be entirely destroyed, leaving only the name of the client and date of record destruction. The time period begins from the date of the last visit. (Or for minors, from the date they reach 18.) Should there be any further direct client contacts, the counting period will begin again at the date of the new service.

Right to Refuse Treatment

You have the right to consent to or refuse recommended treatment. You can be treated without consent only if there is an emergency and in my opinion failure to act immediately would jeopardize your health. In such emergency cases, I will make reasonable efforts to involve a close relative or friend prior to providing emergency services. No audio or video recording of a treatment session can be made without your written permission.

Right to Voice Grievances

You have the right to voice grievances and request changes in your treatment without restraint, interference, coercion, discrimination, or reprisal. I encourage you to share your concerns directly with me. You also have the right to report a complaint about my services to the state licensure board that regulates my practice at (address) _____ (phone)_____. You have the right to report violations of my privacy practices to the Secretary of Health and Human Services at _____.

Right Not to Be Subjected to Harrassment

You have the right to not be subjected to sexual, physical, or verbal harrassment.

Minors' Right to Privacy

All non-emancipated minor clients under the age of 18 must have the consent of their parents or guardians following an initial intake session to receive further treatment services. State law provides that minors have the right to request that their records be withheld from their parents or guardians. If a minor client requests that records be withheld, and I concur that the denial of parental access is in the best interests of the child, information in the minor's file will not be disclosed to the parents. I may deny a parent's or legal guardian's request for access to his or her child's treatment record when, in my professional judgment, parental or guardian access to the record would result in harm to the child.

Rights of Adults Judged Unable to Give Informed Consent

For adults judged not able to give informed consent, the same policy as that for minors (see above) applies regarding permission for services and requests that records be withheld.

Referral Rights

You have the right not to be referred or terminated without explanation and notice. You have the right to active assistance from me in referring you to other appropriate services.

YOUR RESPONSIBILITIES

As a client, you have responsibilities as well as rights. You can help yourself by being responsible in the following ways:

To Be Honest

You are responsible for being honest and direct about everything that relates to you as a client. Please tell me exactly how you feel about the things that are happening to you in your life.

To Understand Your Treatment Plan

You are responsible for understanding your treatment plan to your own satisfaction. If you do not understand, ask me. Be sure you do understand since this is important for the success of the treatment plan.

To Follow the Treatment Plan

It is your responsibility to discuss with me whether or not you think you can and/or want to follow a certain treatment plan.

To Keep Appointments

You are responsible for keeping appointments. If you cannot keep an appointment, notify me as soon as possible so that another client can be seen. In any case, you will be charged for appointments when canceled with less than 24 hours' notice.

To Know Your Fee

I am willing to discuss my fees with you and to provide a clear understanding for you of the costs of all associated services.

To Keep Me Informed

So that I may contact you whenever necessary, I will rely upon you to notify me of any changes in your name, address, home or work phone numbers.

YOUR THERAPIST'S RIGHTS AND RESPONSIBILITIES

I have the responsibility to provide care appropriate to your situation, as determined by prevailing community standards. To accomplish this goal, I also have certain rights, including:

1. The right to information needed to provide appropriate care.
2. The right to be reimbursed, as agreed, for services provided.
3. The right to provide services in an atmosphere free of verbal, physical, or sexual harassment.
4. The right and ethical obligation to refuse to provide services that are not clinically indicated.

EMERGENCY PROCEDURES

Should you feel that your situation requires immediate attention, I am available to return your phone calls from 9:00 a.m. to 5:00 p.m., Monday through Friday. You may leave a message on my voice messaging service. I check my messages throughout the day, but not in the evenings or on weekends.

If you feel that you are in a crisis and need to talk to me immediately at night, during the weekend or a holiday, and I am not immediately available, you may call your local crisis intervention center at _____. If you do speak with me, you may be billed at my current hourly rate for individual therapy for the time I spend with you on the phone. You should be advised that your insurance company may not reimburse you for the telephone consultation charge.

FEE INFORMATION

My fee for direct clinical services (e.g., psychotherapy) is $ _____ per 50-minute session. The fee for consultation and supervision of mental health professionals is also $____ per 50-minute session. Under most circumstances, it is inappropriate for a psychotherapist to become involved in a treatment client's legal case. However, should this become necessary, the fee for any time utilized in a forensic situation is $____ per 1-hour unit.

Every client receiving services shall be responsible for the full payment of those services. I expect clients to make a payment at each session, or upon receipt of a bill which is mailed on a monthly basis. Payment for your session should be made directly to me. If at any time you find there are any problems regarding fee payment, or you need to make arrangements for a payment plan, I will be glad to speak to you regarding your concern.

A finance charge of one and one-half percent (1.5%) per month (annual percentage rate of 18%) will be imposed on all past-due accounts. Payments will be applied to the oldest balance first. No finance charge will be assessed against any billing for services until the charge for such services remains unpaid for 60 days.

There may be circumstances under which you may be billed for time outside your actual therapy sessions, such as consultation time between me and other therapists, telephone consultations, special reports and court evaluations, or communication with your insurance company for prior authorizations for further therapy sessions.

THANK YOU

I am committed to providing you with high-quality services, and I appreciate your decision to work with me. If you have any questions or concerns at any time during the course of your therapy, please feel free to speak to me.

Sample Treatment Plan Form

TREATMENT PLAN

Client Name _____ Diagnosis _____ *Reasons* (specific
Date of Birth _____ DSM IV or ICD Code _____ diagnostic criteria)
Date of Initial Evaluation _____

Problems	Goals	Treatment Procedures	Estimated Time	Progress

Therapist Signature: _____ Date: _____

Client Signature: _____

Sample Revised Treatment Plan Form

REVISED TREATMENT PLAN

Client Name _____   Current Diagnosis _____   *Reasons for current diagnosis*

Date of Birth _____   Date of DX Change (If Any) _____   (specific diagnostic criteria)

Date of Initial Evaluation _____   DSM IV or ICD Code _____

Initial Diagnosis _____

DSM IV or ICD Code _____

Problems	Goals	Treatment Procedures	Estimated Time for RX	Progress

Therapist Signature: _____   Date: _____   Client Signature: _____

Sample Closing Summary Form

CLOSING SUMMARY

Client Name _____

Date of Birth _____

Dates of Services _____ To _____

Frequency of Sessions _____

Diagnosis _____

At Initial Evaluation _____

At Termination _____

Reasons (specific diagnostic criteria) _____

Problems and Goals	Description of Treatment	Progress	Outcome and Status at Termination

Date: _____

Therapist Signature: _____

Sample Face Sheet and Statement of Understanding and Consent for Treatment and Billing Form

(Therapist letterhead, including name, degree, title, office address, telephone, and fax number)

Date of Initial Appointment:_____

Name of Client:_____ Gender: M_____ F_____

Address:_____ Birthdate: ___ /____ /____

Telephone: Home:_____ Work:_____

Best time to call: _____(Home) _____(Work)

Occupation: _____Place of work or school:_____

Referred by:_____

Name of Parent or Guardian (if applicable)_____

Address_____

Telephone: Home:_____Work: _____

Name and address of person responsible for payment: _____

_____

If applicable, third party payer name and address:

_____

Insurance ID# _____

Insurance Group # _____

Name of Policy Holder (if other than above)_____

Relationship: _____

I have read the "Client Information" form, which includes a description of this office's privacy practices. I have discussed its contents with (therapist's name). I understand and agree that the policies stated in the "Client Information Form" of which I retain a copy, apply to me.

Client signature_____ Date: _____

I understand and agree that I am responsible to pay all charges for services incurred by me.

Client signature_____ Date: _____

I hereby request that (name of third party payer) reimburse (name of practitioner) directly for services covered by (third party payer).

Client signature_____ Date: _____

I hereby authorize (name of practitioner) to release information about diagnosis, dates of treatment, and services provided, acquired in the course of my evaluation and/or treatment as may be necessary to process claims for insurance reimbursement. This release will expire one year from the date below. I understand that my therapist will have discussed my diagnosis and treatment plan with me prior to releasing this information to the insurance company. Should the insurance company require more detailed information, I understand that my therapist will consult me prior to the releasing of such information and that I will at that time have the right to either authorize or deny release of any further information.

I agree to promptly pay for charges incurred if for any reason my insurance carrier does not pay any portion of it.

Client signature_____ Date: _____

Sample Consent
for Treatment of Minor Child
Form

(Therapist letterhead, including name, degree, title, office address, telephone, and fax number)

Consent for Treatment of My Minor Child

I agree to therapeutic services provided to my minor child at this office.

Client's name_____

Address_____

Parent/Guardian signature_____

Address (if different than client's address)_____

Date _____

As a parent, I understand that I have the right to information concerning my minor child in therapy, except where otherwise stated by law. I also understand that this therapist believes in providing a minor child with a private environment in which to disclose himself/herself to facilitate therapy. I therefore give permission to this therapist to use his/her discretion, in accordance with professional ethics and state and federal laws and rules, in deciding what information revealed by my child is to be shared with me.

Parent/Guardian signature_____
Date_____

Sample Record of Nonroutine Disclosures Form

Date and time of disclosure:

Purpose of disclosure:

What information was provided and to whom (name, organization, telephone):

Response of receiving party:

Date and time of disclosure:

Purpose of disclosure:

What information was provided and to whom (name, organization, telephone):

Response of receiving party:

Date and time of disclosure:

Purpose of disclosure:

What information was provided and to whom (name, organization, telephone):

Response of receiving party:

Sample Authorization for Release of Information Form

(Note: This sample form is not legal or clinical advice. Practitioners must consult their professional associations and attorneys to assure compliance with applicable regulations.)

(Therapist letterhead, including name, degree, title, office address, phone, and fax)

Authorization for Release of Information

Client's name_____

Address_____

Client's date of birth:_____

This will authorize: _____

to release to_____
the following:

_____ Information from the medical/case record maintained while I am/was a patient at the above-stated facility during the period of _____ through _____.

_____ Information from my medical/case record at any time during the next six months, or until such time as I revoke such consent, including the following:

____ Discharge Summary
____ Social/Court Service Summary(ies)
____ Consultations
____ Psychological Testing
____ Intake Interview
____ Other

This information is needed, and will be used, only for the following purpose(s):

_____

_____

This information may not be re-disclosed to anyone else, except for the above intended purpose(s).

I understand that I may revoke this consent at any time, except to the extent action has been taken in reliance upon it. I understand that this consent will automatically expire without my express revocation upon fulfillment of the above-stated purpose, or one year from this date, whichever is sooner.

Signature of Client _____ Date _____

Signature of Guardian/Relationship_____ Date _____

Signature of Witness _____ Date _____

Excerpts of Ethical Statements on Confidentiality From Mental Health Professional Organizations

1. American Association for Marriage and Family Therapy (2001) Code of Ethics, section 2.2: "Marriage and family therapists do not disclose client confidences except by written authorization or waiver, or where mandated or permitted by law. Verbal authorization will not be sufficient except in emergency situations, unless prohibited by law. When providing couple, family, or group treatment, the therapist does not disclose information outside the treatment context without a written authorization from each individual competent to execute a waiver. In the context of couple, family or group treatment, the therapist may not reveal any individual's confidences to others without the prior written permission of that individual." In section 2.4: "Marriage and family therapists store or dispose of client records in ways that maintain confidentiality."

2. American Counseling Association (1996) Code of Ethics and Standards of Practice, section B.1.a: "Counselors respect their clients' right to privacy and avoid illegal and unwarranted disclosures of confidential information." In section B.1.c: "The general requirement that counselors keep information confidential does not apply when disclosure is required to prevent clear and imminent danger to the client or others or when legal requirements demand that confidential information be revealed. Coun-

selors consult with other professionals when in doubt as to the validity of an exception." In section 1. G: "When counseling is initiated and throughout the counseling process as necessary, counselors inform clients of the limitations of confidentiality and identify foreseeable situations in which confidentiality must be breached." B.4.b: "Counselors are responsible for securing the safety and confidentiality of any records they create, maintain, transfer, or destroy whether the records are written, taped, computerized, or stored in any other medium." In section B.4.d, this code also addresses situations involving multiple clients, stating that "in situations involving multiple clients, access to records is limited to those parts of records that do not include confidential information related to another client." Also, in section B.4.c, the ACA code requires counselors to obtain "written permission from clients to disclose or transfer records to legitimate third parties unless exceptions to confidentiality exist as listed in section B.1. Steps are taken to ensure that receivers of counseling records are sensitive to their confidential nature."

3. American Association of Pastoral Counselors (1994) Code of Ethics, Principle IV, Confidentiality: "As members of AAPC we respect the integrity and protect the welfare of all persons with whom we are working and have an obligation to safguard information about them that has been obtained in the course of the counseling process. A. All records kept on a client are stored or disposed of in a manner that assures security and confidentiality. B. We treat all communications from clients with professional confidence. C. Except in those situations where the identity of the client is necessary to the understanding of the case, we use only the first names of our clients when engaged in supervision or consultation. It is our responsibility to convey the importance of confidentiality to the supervisor/consultant; this is particularly important when the supervision is shared by other professionals, as in a supervisory group. D. We do not disclose client confidences to anyone, except: as mandated by law; to prevent a clear and immediate danger to someone; in the course of a civil, criminal or disciplinary action arising from the counseling where the pastoral counselor is a defendant; for purposes of supervision or consultation; or by previously obtained written permission. In cases involving more than one person (as client) written permission must be obtained from all legally accountable persons who have been present during the counseling before any disclosure can be made. E. We obtain informed written consent of clients before audio and/or video tape recording or permitting third party observation of their sessions. F. We do not use these standards of confidentiality to avoid intervention when it is necessary, e.g., when there is evidence of abuse of minors, the elderly, the disabled, the physically or mentally incompetent. G. When current or

former clients are referred to in a publication, while teaching or in a public presentation, their identity is thoroughly disguised."

4. American Group Psychotherapy Association (2001) Guidelines for Ethics. "Responsibility to Patient/Client. 2. The group psychotherapist safeguards the patient/client's right to privacy by judiciously protecting information of a confidential nature. 2.1. The group shall agree that the patient/client as well as the psychotherapist shall protect the identity of its members. 2.2. The group psychotherapist shall not use identifiable information about the group or its members for teaching purposes, publication or professional presentations unless permission has been obtained and all measures have been taken to preserve patient/client anonymity. 2.3. Except where required by law, the group psychotherapist shall share information about the group members with others only after obtaining appropriate patient/client consent. Specific permission must be requested to permit conferring with the referring therapist or with the individual therapist where the patient/client is in conjoint therapy. 2.4. When clinical examination suggests that a patient/client may be dangerous to himself/herself or others, it is the group psychotherapist's ethical and legal obligation to take appropriate steps in order to be responsible to society in general, as well as the patient/client."

5. American Nurses' Association (1994) Standards of Psychiatric–Mental Health Clinical Nursing Practice. Standard V.I: "The psychiatric–mental health nurse maintains client confidentiality and appropriate professional boundaries."

6. American Psychiatric Association (2001) The Principles of Medical Ethics, with Annotations Especially Applicable to Psychiatry, section 4: "A physician shall respect the rights of patients, of colleagues, and of other health professionals, and shall safeguard patient confidences within the constraints of the law." An excerpt from section 4.1: "Psychiatric records, including even the identification of a person as a patient, must be protected with extreme care. Confidentiality is essential to psychiatric treatment. Growing concern regarding the civil rights of patients and the possible adverse effects of computerization, duplication equipment, and data banks makes the dissemination of confidential information an increasing hazard. Because of the sensitive and private nature of the information with which the psychiatrist deals, he/she must be circumspect in the information that he/she chooses to disclose to others about a patient. The welfare of the patient must be a continuing consideration." In section 4 2: "A psychiatrist may release confidential information only with the authorization of the patient or under proper legal compulsion." In section 4.3: "Clinical and other materials used in teaching and writing must be adequately disguised in order to preserve the anonymity of the

individuals involved." In section 4.4: "The ethical responsibility of maintaining confidentiality holds equally for the consultations in which the patient may not have been present and in which the consultee was not a physician. In such instances, the physician consultant should alert the consultee to his/her duty of confidentiality." In section 4.5: "Ethically, the psychiatrist may disclose only that information which is relevant to a given situation. He/she should avoid offering speculation as fact. Sensitive information such as an individual's sexual orientation or fantasy material is usually considered unnecessary." In section 4.6: "Psychiatrists are often asked to examine individuals for security purposes, to determine suitability for various jobs, and to determine legal competence. The psychiatrist must fully describe the nature and purpose and lack of confidentiality of the examination to the examinee at the beginning of the examination." In section 4.7: "Careful judgment must be exercised by the psychiatrist in order to include, when appropriate, the parents or guardian in the treatment of a minor, At the same time, the psychiatrist must assure the minor proper confidentiality." In section 4.8: "Psychiatrists at times may find it necessary, in order to protect the patient or the community from imminent danger, to reveal confidential information disclosed by the patient." In section 4.10: "With regard for the person's dignity and privacy and with truly informed consent, it is ethical to present a patient to a scientific gathering if the confidentiality of the presentation is understood and accepted by the audience." In section 4.11: "It is ethical to present a patient or former patient to a public gathering or to the news media only if the patient is fully informed of enduring loss of confidentiality, is competent, and consents in writing without coercion."

7. American Psychological Association (1992) Ethical Principles of Psychologists and Code of Conduct, section 5.04: "Psychologists maintain appropriate confidentiality in creating, storing, accessing, transferring, and disposing of records under their control, whether these are written, automated, or in any other medium. Psychologists maintain and dispose of records in accordance with law and in a manner that permits compliance with the requirements of this Ethics Code." In section 5.05a: "Psychologists disclose confidential information without the consent of the individual only as mandated by law, or where permitted by law for a valid purpose, such as 1) to provide needed professional services to the patient or the individual or organizational client, 2) to obtain appropriate professional consultations, 3) to protect the patient or client or others from harm, or 4) to obtain payment for services, in which instance disclosure is limited to the minimum that is necessary to achieve the purpose."

8. Association for Specialists in Group Work (1989) Ethical Guidelines for Group Counselors. In section 3e: "Group counselors video or audiotape a group session only with prior consent, and the members' knowledge of how the tape will be used." Also, in section 3h: "Group counselors store or dispose of group member records (written, audio, video, etc.) in ways that maintain confidentiality."

9. Clinical Social Work Federation (1997) Code of Ethics, Principle III.a: "Clinical social workers have a primary obligation to maintain the privacy of both current and former clients, whether living or deceased, and to maintain the confidentiality of material that has been transmitted to them in any of their professional roles. Exceptions to this responsibility will occur only when there are overriding legal or professional reasons and, whenever possible, with the written informed consent of the client(s)." Principle III.b sets forth the requirement that clinical social workers "know and observe both legal and professional standards for maintaining privacy of records, and mandatory reporting obligations." This section also notes that "when confidential information is released to a third party, the clinical social worker will ensure that the information divulged is limited to the minimum amount required to accomplish the purpose for which the release is being made." Principle III.c addresses issues and limitations in safeguarding confidentiality of individuals when clinical social workers are treating couples, families, and groups. Principle III.e also cautions that "the development of new technologies for the storage and transmission of data poses a great danger to the privacy of individuals. Clinical social workers take special precautions to protect the confidentiality of material stored or transmitted through computers, electronic mail, facsimile machines, telephones, telephone answering machines, and all other electronic or computer technology. When using these technologies, disclosure of identifying information regarding the clients(s) should be avoided whenever possible."

10. National Association of Social Workers (1996) Code of Ethics, section 1.07, a–r, "Privacy and Confidentiality," lists extensive requirements for protecting patients' privacy and confidential communications and for discerning specific conditions under which practitioners may give other parties access to records. "Social workers should protect the confidentiality of all information obtained in the course of professional service, except for compelling professional reasons. The general expectation that social workers will keep information confidential does not apply when disclosure is necessary to prevent serious, foreseeable, and imminent harm to a client or other identifiable person. In all instances, social workers should disclose the least amount of confidential information neces-

sary to achieve the desired purpose; only information that is directly relevant to the purpose for which the disclosure is made should be revealed (section 1.07 c)." Section 1.07 includes detailed requirements for maintaining security of records in all forms (including electronic) and obtaining consent for disclosure of confidential information from the patient or person legally authorized to consent.

Sample Clinical Supervision Contract

GENERAL INFORMATION

- Name of clinical supervisor
- Name of supervisee, address, telephone
- Name of graduate school supervisee has attended or is attending
- Professional degree or status of current professional training
- Name of regulatory board if supervisee is meeting licensure requirements
- Name of place of employment and employer if supervision is being conducted outside of place of employment
- Purpose of supervision (e.g., to fulfill graduate school, licensure, or employment requirements)
- Number of supervision hours required
- Frequency of supervision sessions necessary to meet requirements
- Types of cases required to meet requirements
- Date formal supervision evaluation(s) must be conducted
- Criteria that will be used in formal evaluations
- Individuals to whom supervisory evaluations will be sent

LIST OF INFORMATION TO INCLUDE IN CLINICAL SUPERVISION LEARNING NEEDS ASSESSMENT

- Transcripts of supervisee's academic courses
- Resume or list of prior professional experiences, responsibilities, and duties

- Prior professional experience that is relevant to the current patient population
- Knowledge and skills supervisee acquired from previous professional training and experience, including but not limited to: evaluation and treatment, ethics, state and federal laws and rules, record keeping, and methods for establishing an appropriate treatment relationship with clients and patients
- Professional strengths supervisee and his or her teachers and former supervisors have identified
- Professional weaknesses or concerns about supervisee's practice that the supervisee, previous supervisors, or teachers have identified
- Supervisee's greatest sources of professional concerns and anxiety
- Supervisee's specific learning needs, including skills supervisee needs to develop
- How supervisee learns best

SUPERVISEE'S RIGHTS

- The right to have weekly (or other predictable-frequency) supervisory sessions that will focus on my learning needs and my clients' treatment needs
- The right to understand and to participate in the development of my learning objectives, activities to meet learning objectives, and standards for mastery of learning objectives
- The right to know my supervisor's professional qualifications (training, licensure, competencies, experience, education, treatment approach, biases)
- The right to have regularly scheduled performance evaluations and to have my performance evaluations sent in a timely manner to the appropriate institution (for example, graduate school, regulatory board, employer)
- The right not to be discriminated against in the provision of supervisory services on the basis of my race, gender, ethnic origin, disability, creed, or sexual orientation
- The right not to be harrassed or exploited in other ways to meet my supervisor's personal needs

SUPERVISEE'S RESPONSIBILITIES

- To bring all of my clinical cases, including records, to my clinical supervisor for honest and direct discussion and review
- To provide my clinical supervisor with access at any time to my patients' records for review

- To thoroughly present each of my clients' cases verbally and in writing, including all factors relevant to diagnosis and treatment, such as: presenting problems, history of problems, significant childhood, family relationship, work, and other life history, medical treatment, medications, past treatment, mental status observations, diagnoses and treatment plans, my clinical interventions, including referrals, means of evaluating progress, record keeping, and other professional issues, including transference and countertransference feelings
- To inform my clients of exceptions to confidentiality, including that my clinical supervisor will be discussing my sessions and reviewing and signing all of my case notes
- To read, understand, and adhere to this office's security and privacy policies and procedures
- To follow state and federal laws and rules and professional ethics code requirements and to discuss ethical and legal questions or problems as they arise in each of my cases

SUPERVISOR'S RESPONSIBILITIES

- To provide supervision that is appropriate to my supervisee's professional needs and that meets the requirements of professional ethics and state and federal laws and rules
- To schedule regular supervisory conferences with my supervisee and be available for emergencies
- To conduct a learning needs assessment, establish clear learning objectives, activities for mastery of learning objectives, and criteria for mastery of learning objectives
- To teach practical clinical skills, including the characteristics and contents of good clinical records, and help my supervisee integrate theoretical knowledge with clinical skills in order to develop professional competence
- To regularly assess my supervisee's progress, including identification of errors, weaknesses, and strengths, provide appropriate feedback to the supervisee, and work with my supervisee to develop plans for improvement
- To help my supervisee identify when a patient may have special problems that require another professional's consultation
- To help my supervisee appropriately manage transference, countertransference, and professional boundary issues as indicated
- To conduct formal performance evaluations at 6-month intervals (or other pre-determined interval)
- To honestly communicate my supervisee's performance evaluation results,

including professional strengths as well as any unresolved practice errors and ethical concerns, to those persons who require supervisee's performance evaluation

SUPERVISOR'S RIGHTS

- The right to information needed to provide appropriate clinical supervision
- To right be compensated promptly for supervision services as agreed upon and when payment arrangement is applicable
- The right to provide supervision in an atmosphere free of verbal, physical, or sexual harassment

Signatures of All Concerned Parties

- Supervisee's and supervisor's signature
- Other relevant signatures depending on contractual purpose of supervision (e.g., to meet graduate school, internship, pre-licensure, or employment requirements). Relevant parties could include representatives from graduate school, employer, or regulatory board.

Sample Informed Consent Statement for Mental Health Evaluation in a Personal Injury Case

(Note: The informed consent statement below illustrates how an evaluation witness implements the ethical duty to inform the evaluee of the purpose of the mental health evaluation in the legal case and the limits of confidentiality, and to obtain written consent prior to conducting the evaluation. Practitioners should consult their professional ethics codes and their attorneys when developing informed consent statements.)

I, (name and date of birth of evaluee), plaintiff in a civil suit, agree to undergo an evaluation by (name, degree, and licensure of evaluator), for the purpose of evaluating me for possible psychological damages. I understand this is an evaluation requested by my attorney (name of attorney and law firm), and that (name of evaluator) may, or may not, arrive at findings adverse to my litigation. I also understand that my evaluation report is likely to be made available to both plaintiff and defense attorneys, and other legitimate parties to this legal action.

I understand and willingly agree to the above, and agree to hold (name of evaluator) harmless in the proper exercise of this evaluation. I give permission for (name of evaluator and evaluator's consulting colleagues) to exchange information as necessary for (name of evaluator) to arrive at her professional opinions and to develop her report.

_____   _____ _____

Name of Evaluee   Date   Name of Evaluator   Date

Sample Letter From a Therapist to a Judge in a Child Custody Case

(Therapist's letterhead)

(Date)
Judge Smith
County Family Court
Re: *Jones v. Jones*

Your honor:

I am a clinical psychologist in private practice at (office address) providing psychotherapy to (name of child) age 4, whose parents are disputing custody and visitation rights in your courtroom. I received a subpoena from (name of child) mother's attorney, asking me to appear in your courtroom next week, at 9:00 a.m., February 2nd. I am writing to respectfully request that the court dismiss me from the obligation of appearing for the following ethical and clinical reasons:

First, Mr. and Mrs. Jones hired me to provide psychotherapy to their son, (name of child). They and their son understood from the beginning of his treatment that what he disclosed to me in his therapy was to be held in confidence. They understand that I am professionally obligated to maintain the confidentiality of all parties involved in the therapy.

Second, I am professionally obligated to "do no harm." The cornerstone of the therapy relationship is trust. In my professional opinion, it would be detrimental to my therapeutic relationship with my patient, (name of child), and his family were I to engage in a dual role. If I were to testify in your courtroom, I would be departing from my primary role of assisting my patient with his psychological and family problems. I would be assuming a different role of judging and evaluating. It is important that I remain in my neutral, supportive professional role with my patient and his parents in order to prevent harm to the child.

Third, in my role as therapist, I have not evaluated either parent regarding their "fitness to parent," because that is not my professional role. Such an evaluation would be most appropriately conducted by an independent, neutral examiner who is not, nor will be, in the role of a therapist to the family and/or child.

Finally, I have informed both parents of my position in this matter and they have agreed with me that it is not in their son's best interest for me to testify.

My intention is to be cooperative with the court. I therefore wish to inform the court of potential problems that will arise should I be required to testify in this case. I hope that the court will understand the ethical problems I would face should I be called to tesify in this legal situation. If the court requires mental health information regarding this child and his parents, I respectfully request that the court appoint an independent examiner to conduct an evaluation.

Thank you for your time and consideration.

Respectfully submitted,
(Name, degree, and license of therapist)

Organizations to Contact for Further Information About Forensics

Academy of Forensic Psychology
   http://www.abfp.com

American Academy of Psychiatry and the Law
   One Regency Drive
   P.O. Box 30
   Bloomfield, CT 06002
   (800) 331-1389
   www.emory.edu/AAPL

Clinical Social Work Federation
Committee on Clinical Social Work and the Law
   P.O. Box 3740
   Arlington, VA 22203
   (800) 270-9739

National Organization of Forensic Social Work
   http://www.nofsw.org

Excerpts of Ethical Statements on Record Retention and Destruction From Mental Health Organizations

1. American Association for Marriage and Family Therapy (2001) Code of Ethics. Principle II. Confidentiality. Section 2.4: "Marriage and family therapists store, safeguard, and dispose of client records in ways that maintain confidentiality and in accord with applicable laws and professional standards."
2. American Association of Pastoral Counselors (1994) Code of Ethics, Section IV A: "All records kept on a client are stored or disposed of in a manner that assures security and confidentiality."
3. American Counseling Association (1996) Code of Ethics and Standards of Practice, Section B.4a: "Requirement of Records. Counselors maintain records necessary for rendering professional services to their clients and as required by laws, regulations, or agency or institution procedures."
4. American Medical Association Council on Ethical and Judicial Affairs (2000) Code of Medical Ethics, 2000–2001 Edition. 7.05. Retention of Medical Records: "Physicians have an obligation to retain patient records which may reasonably be of value to a patient . . . Medical considerations are the primary basis for deciding how long to retain medical records . . . In deciding whether to keep certain parts of the record, an

appropriate criterion is whether a physician would want the information if he or she were seeing the patient for the first time." 2) "If a particular record no longer needs to be kept for medical reasons, the physician should check state laws to see if there is a requirement that records be kept for a minimum length of time . . . " 3) "In all cases, medical records should be kept for at least as long as the length of time of the statute of limitations for medical malpractice claims . . . "4) "Whatever the statute of limitations, a physician should measure time from the last professional contact with the patient." 5) "If a patient is a minor, the statute of limitations for medical malpractice claims may not apply until the patient reaches the age of majority."

5. American Psychological Association (1992) Ethical Principles of Psychologists and Code of Conduct, Section 5.04: Maintenance of Records: "Psychologists maintain and dispose of records in accordance with law and in a manner that permits compliance with the requirements of this Ethics Code."

6. American Psychological Association (1981) Specialty Guidelines for Clinical Psychological Services, Section 2.3.4: "Each clinical psychological service unit follows an established record retention and disposition policy," that "conforms to federal or state statutes or administrative regulations where such are applicable." These guidelines recommend in the absence of legal and administrative regulations "a) that the full record be retained intact for three years after the completion of planned services or after the date of last contact with the user, whichever is later; b) that a full record or summary of the record be maintained for an additional 12 years; and c) that the record may be disposed of no sooner than 15 years after the completion of planned services or after the date of the last contact, whichever is later."

7. American Psychological Association Specialty Guidelines for Counseling Psychology (1981): Section 2.3.4: "Each counseling psychological service unit follows an established record retention and disposition policy." These guidelines recommend that the policy on record retention and disposition conform to state statutes or federal regulations where applicable. When there are no legal regulations, the guidelines recommend: 1) keeping the entire record for four years after completion of the planned services or after the date of the last contact, whichever is later; 2) retaining a summary of the record for an additional three years (if the entire record is not retained); 3) that the record be disposed of no sooner than seven years after the completion of planned services or after the date of last contact.

8. Clinical Social Work Federation (1997) Code of Ethics, Principle II, Section 2e: "All requirements regarding the establishment, maintenance,

and disposal of records relate equally to written and to electronic records. Clinical social workers establish a policy on record retention and disposal, or are aware of agency policies regarding these issues, and communicate it to the client."

9. National Association of Social Workers (1996) Code of Ethics, Section 107.n: "Social workers should transfer or dispose of clients' records in a manner that protects clients' confidentiality and is consistent with state statutes governing records and social work licensure." In Section 3.04.d: "Social workers should store records following the termination of services to ensure reasonable future access. Records should be maintained for the number of years required by state statutes or relevant contracts."

10. National Association of Social Workers Guidelines (1991) on the Private Practice of Clinical Social Work: "The social worker should consult with an attorney before disposing of or transferring client records. State or federal guidelines may be applicable, and there may be liability issues to consider."

Additional Excerpts of Ethical Statements on Continuity of Care From Mental Health Organizations

1. American Association for Marriage and Family Therapy (2001) Code of Ethics, Section 1, Responsibility to Clients, 1.6: "Marriage and family therapists assist persons in obtaining other therapeutic services if the therapist is unable or unwilling, for appropriate reasons, to provide professional help." 1.7: "Marriage and family therapists do not abandon or neglect clients in treatment without making reasonable arrangements for the continuation of such treatment."

2. American Association of State Psychology Boards (1991) Code of Conduct, Section III, Rules of Conduct. A. Competence. 7. Continuity of care. "The psychologist shall make arrangements for another appropriate professional or professionals to deal with emergency needs of his/her clients, as appropriate, during periods of his/her foreseeable absences from professional availability." C. Client Welfare. 2. Termination of services. "Whenever professional services are terminated, the psychologist shall offer to help locate alternative sources of professional services or assistance if indicated."

3. American Medical Association Council on Ethical and Judicial Affairs (2000) Code of Medical Ethics, 2000–2001 Edition. "The patients of a physician who leaves a group practice should be notified that the physi-

cian is leaving the group. Patients of the physician should also be notified of the physician's new address and offered the opportunity to have their medical records forwarded to the departing physician at his or her new practice. It is unethical to withhold such information upon request of a patient. If the responsibility for notifying patients falls to the departing physician rather than to the group, the group should not interfere with the discharge of these duties by withholding patient lists or other necessary information."

7.04 Sale of a Medical Practice. "A physician or the estate of a deceased physician may sell to another physician the elements which comprise his or her practice, such as furniture, fixtures, equipment, office leasehold, and goodwill. In the sale of a medical practice, the purchaser is buying not only furniture and fixtures, but also goodwill, i.e., the opportunity to take over the patients of the seller.

"The transfer of records of patients is subject, however, to the following: 1) All active patients should be notified that the physician (or the estate) is transferring the practice to another physician who will retain custody of their records and that at their written request, within a reasonable time as specified in the notice, the records or copies will be sent to any other physician of their choice. Rather than destroy the records of a deceased physician, it is better that they be transferred to a practicing physician who will retain them subject to requests from patients that they be sent to another physician." 2) "A reasonable charge may be made for the cost of duplicating records."

4. Clinical Social Work Federation (1997) Code of Ethics, Principle II, Responsibility to Clients, #2, Practice Management and Termination, a) . . . "Clinical social workers do not abandon clients by withdrawing services precipitously, except under extraordinary circumstances. . . . When interruption or termination of service is anticipated, the clinical social worker gives reasonable notification and provides for transfer, referral, or continuation of service in a manner as consistent as possible with the client needs and preferences." Also, see Clinical Social Work Federation (1991) Standards of Practice for Clinical Social Work Practice, Section XVI, part C: "The clinical social worker shall be obligated to keep appropriate records to protect the client in the event of the social worker's absence, illness, or death . . . "; see also part G: "Arrangements for record keeping in the event of death of the clinical social worker shall be made with a colleague who can assume responsibility for the cases."

Index